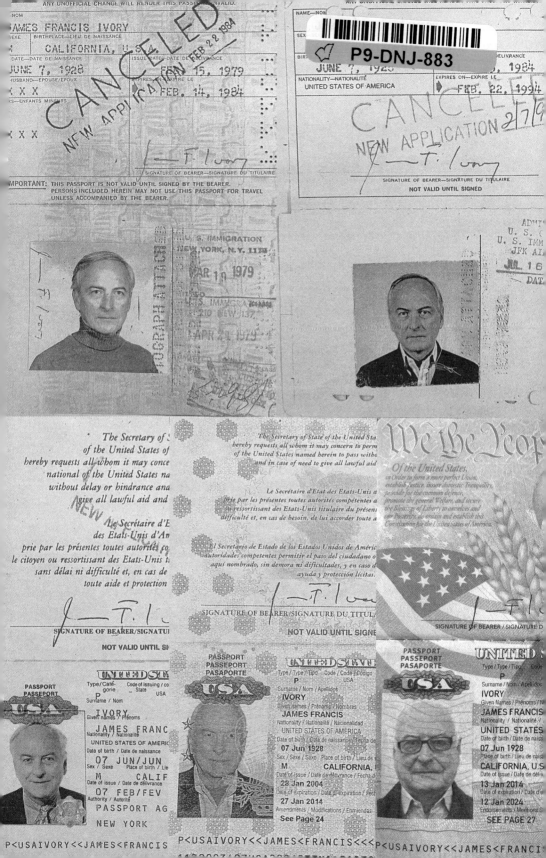

For

Melissa Chung

Jeremiah Rusconi

Peter Cameron

SOLID IVORY

SOLID IVORY

~ *memoirs* ~

JAMES IVORY

EDITED BY PETER CAMERON

Farrar, Straus and Giroux *New York*

Farrar, Straus and Giroux
120 Broadway, New York 10271

Printed in the United States of America
First edition, 2021

Adapted from James Ivory's memoirs originally published
by Shrinking Violet Press.

Illustration credits can be found on pages 391–399.

Library of Congress Cataloging-in-Publication Data
Names: Ivory, James, author. | Cameron, Peter, 1959– editor.
Title: Solid Ivory : memoirs / James Ivory ; edited by Peter Cameron.
Description: First edition. | New York : Farrar, Straus and Giroux, 2021.
Identifiers: LCCN 2021026128 | ISBN 9780374601591 (hardcover)
Subjects: LCSH: Ivory, James. | Motion picture producers and directors—
    United States—Biography. | Gay motion picture producers and
    directors—United States—Biography.
Classification: LCC PN1998.3.I89 A3 2021 | DDC 791.4302/33092 [B]—dc23
LC record available at https://lccn.loc.gov/2021026128

Our books may be purchased in bulk for promotional, educational, or business
use. Please contact your local bookseller or the Macmillan Corporate and
Premium Sales Department at 1-800-221-7945, extension 5442, or by email at
MacmillanSpecialMarkets@macmillan.com.

www.fsgbooks.com
www.twitter.com/fsgbooks • www.facebook.com/fsgbooks

1   3   5   7   9   10   8   6   4   2

Ismail Merchant, Ruth Prawer Jhabvala, James Ivory

Contents

~

VI. ETCETERA

I

GROWING UP

James Ivory, age five

Klamath Falls

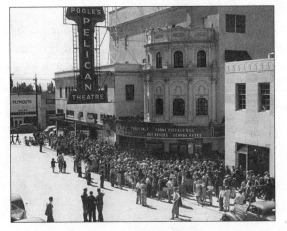

The Pelican Theatre, Klamath Falls, Oregon*

My First Movie, Age Five

I grew up in Klamath Falls, Oregon, a very western lumber and cattle-ranching town. In 1933, when I was five, there were two theaters

---

* The Pelican Theatre was the town's combination of Carnegie Hall, where the Community Concerts regularly took place, and Grauman's Chinese Theatre of Hollywood, where the biggest movies were sure to play. The audience was stunned once at a Community Concert piano recital, when José Iturbi abruptly stopped playing and faced them, saying, "I will go on when there is complete silence and everyone has taken his seat." He glared fiercely at one of the town's mightiest barons, Nelson Reed, and his wife, who were noisily settling into their seats. Everybody talked about this public denunciation for years: they had no idea who José Iturbi was, but they certainly knew in Klamath Falls who Nelson Reed was. The Pelican Theatre is where I saw *Gone with the Wind*, after my sixth-grade teacher, a nun, had told the class that if any of us went to see it, we must cover our ears when Rhett Butler said "Damn."

showing first-run films, the Pelican and the Pine Tree, and two more playing second-runs, the Rainbow and the Vox. The Vox showed cowboy films exclusively and stood at the far end of Main Street, which the nice people avoided if they could. At the other end, next to the town's biggest bank, stood the new resplendent Pelican, an ornate motion picture palace in the Spanish Renaissance style with, as I remember, a gilded and carved proscenium arch around the screen, as if enclosing a high altar. This was the theater which played the biggest Hollywood hits, and this was where my parents took me one spring Sunday afternoon, to see my first movie.

It happened like this: we had been to someone's house on top of the hill that lay between our neighborhood and the downtown section of Klamath Falls for the midday meal. Roast beef with mashed potatoes and gravy must have been served, because I had spotted my fresh white shirt with gravy, right on the front, and I was very conscious of this brown stain as we were riding back home in our car. Then I heard my parents debating:

Father: What do you think?
Mother: I think he's big enough. What's playing?

We abruptly changed course and headed back to Main Street and the Pelican Theatre. Once there, I would have been too excited to worry much about the gravy spot.

I remember nothing whatsoever of the main feature I saw that afternoon. Years later my parents told me it had starred Janet Gaynor. I remember sitting in the dark, thrilled, amid silent spectators, on a plush seat my father had to push down, enveloped in a constantly shifting light above my head, while huge white faces on the screen spoke to one another. What they were saying I have no memory of. What I do have the clearest, sharpest memory of is the newsreel. There was an arresting shot in it that I can see to this day: civil war was raging somewhere in what must have been a Latin city. There were rioters in the street amid a lot of smoke. The year 1933 was too early for the Spanish Civil War, so perhaps the newsreel showed a South American city under some sort of siege. The newsreel camera had been placed high up in a window and was aimed out onto an avenue lined with imposing buildings. Immediately, to camera left, looters or demonstrators were smashing up an office or apartment. They were tossing things over the railing of a balcony right in front of the camera. Two men brought out a large bronze statue that resembled the Oscar statuette and stood it on the railing, where it tottered for a moment before being tipped over into the street, into which it dropped headfirst. Was this the figure of a deposed king or dictator, or just an ornament? Were patriotic citizens toppling it down onto the mob? I got the impression, even at that early age, of a house being looted, and that seems to go along with the pleasure I took as a child in seeing burned-down houses and wrecked cars, making my father drive out of his way so I could view them: anar-

chic upheaval in which domestic things got smashed to bits. Watching the heavy statue of the dictator—if that's what he was—being tipped over onto the heads of a mob was the first action sequence I can recall seeing on any screen, and I wonder if I acquired my love of disaster movies, with all their disorder, physical destruction, and mass annihilation, from this long-ago newsreel image.

Do I remember my first movie mainly because of the spot on my shirt? Because they are linked events in my memory suggesting

Janet Gaynor in *Tess of the Storm Country* (1932)

each other? Tumultuous rioting in a foreign city in which houses got looted, and the inherent disorder of an eye-catching food stain on my fresh Sunday shirt?

Assembling Ancestors

When I was ten, my maternal grandmother De Loney told me about a relative named Mrs. Clarke. She told me two stories about Mrs. Clarke, which didn't—or couldn't—jibe: either she had succumbed in a New Orleans cholera epidemic in the 1850s, or she had cut up her fabulous ball gowns to make bandages for injured Confederate soldiers during our Civil War ten years later. My grandmother had a daguerreotype of Mrs. Clarke, which she gave to me. It had lost its case, and there was only the plate itself surrounded by an oval of pressed and gilt metal. The image is of a plain woman, her dark hair flat on her head and parted in the middle, wearing a black silk full-skirted gown. At her neck there is a dab of gold to represent her brooch, which the photographer had added.

Because I was adopted by my parents when I was a baby, I have never known who my true antecedents were. And so I became interested in my adopted ancestors, and began collecting cased images like that of Mrs. Clarke, later buying them from a dealer in Savannah, assembling a group of virtual ancestors. I preferred family groups of well-dressed people—pretty girls with lively, intelligent faces (these were often English; American girls in the 1850s too often looked blank and repressed, almost unknowable); and handsome, waistcoated young gentlemen in stiff collars. I have to admit I was also on the lookout for a spirited "Mammy," like the large-hearted Hattie McDaniel in the film *Gone with the Wind*. My cousin Mary De Loney in Austin inherited a daguerreotype of a family slave of our great-grandfather John Hailey. She wore a white headcloth like Hattie McDaniel's. But I never found an image resembling the Oscar-winning McDaniel.

My grandmother De Loney told me these and other stories as she lay in bed in my uncle Randolph's house in Port Arthur, Texas. She could provide five generations of family names: her married name, De Loney; her maiden name, Hailey (she was Hallie Hailey); and Hammett, Locke, and Randolph, taking me right back to

Albert De Loney, 1918

the eighteenth century. But she never spoke once of her husband, Isaac Fox De Loney, my grandfather, or of his family, who were descended from the Brodnax family of the early Virginia colony at Jamestown.

In that house in Port Arthur he was persona non grata. In time, as I grew older, I learned about him from his children—first from my mother, another Hallie, who couldn't speak of her father, whom she adored, without weeping; from mother's tougher sister, Evelyn; and from their other brother, Albert, or "Ab." Both daughters claimed their father had looks and charm. His sons, however, had other memories, and the elder, Randolph, grew to hate him. His father would drop out every so often, leaving his growing family to cope somehow in Bogalusa, Louisiana. Months later, he would reappear. At each of these reappearances my grandmother became pregnant. When she died in 1942—she had been born in 1863—my uncle Randolph wouldn't put her married name on her tombstone and inscribed her maiden name instead: Hailey.

I thought of this interesting-sounding grandfather as a kind of riverboat gambler, with glossy black hair and a dashing mustache, who somehow lived by his wits, and I wanted to know more about him. My uncle Ab must have been the one who told me that my De Loney grandfather had been murdered by a gang of Black workers manning a levee on the Mississippi River during a flood, and that his body had been thrown into the water. He had been an exceptionally cruel taskmaster, Uncle Ab said. But there is an alternative version of how Isaac De

Loney died. The year is certain—1933—and it took place in "where-abouts unknown." His was a watery grave in both versions, but, according to another set of De Loney descendants in Texas, their grandfather had been an insatiable gambler, and he was thrown overboard from a riverboat by other disgruntled gamblers. As he was born in 1858, he was seventy-five in 1933—rather too old, I think, to have been bossing a gang of Black people during a flood. The riverboat version of his dramatic end was described with humor by my Texas cousins, and is the more likely one. In either case he died, as he had mostly lived, and was punished, because of his bad behavior.

Hallie De Loney, my mother, at age seventeen, Bogalusa, Louisiana

Perhaps later on, his two sons each preferred one version of how he died for different reasons. The elder, Randolph, stern and unforgiving, may have thought being tossed overboard by his fellow gamblers was the more appropriate death for his father, who was his enemy. And Albert—Uncle Ab—not very much liking all indiscreet talk of out-of-control gambling, preferred to blame the gang of Black workers.

These stories—or all of the stories that I've heard—fed my imagination; at one time I thought of making a film about him and my other grandfather, John—my Ivory grandfather—who, in upstate New York in the 1880s, not long after emigrating from Ireland, became a labor organizer in the hammer factory where he worked. He incited the other men to strike. Their strike was broken, of course, and so was he. He could never get another job in the town of Norwich, being considered a dangerous rabble-rouser. I wanted to call my film something like "My Romantic Grandfathers."

Grandmother De Loney, circa 1925

I was seven when my grandmother De Loney came all the way from Texas to visit us in Klamath Falls. She descended from her train with the complaint that her berth had been right over a pair of wheels of the sleeping car. "Darlin', I was almost rattled to death," she told my father. In Oregon she always felt cold, even sitting out in the sun wrapped up in a blanket. She had brought a little cruet with her—or my mother supplied it—containing tiny hot green chilies in vinegar, which she doused her food with at the table. My memories of her then stand out because of another, stronger memory of her stay: I had been caught by my mother with another little boy named Eddy, who lived across the street from us, during one of those exploratory sexual acts children so like. My father had made me a playhouse from the big wooden case in which our Victorian square piano had been shipped. Standing it on its side, he cut a little door through which Eddy and I could enter, and a little window. One day Eddy and I were in there, trying out putting our penises into each other's mouths. I don't know whose idea that was, but I made clear that Eddy's dick must not touch my lips or tongue, nor the inside of my mouth. I had learned all about germs at school by then. Eddy went first, and I can still exactly see him doing it. I can also remember his acrid odor as he carried out my instructions and I took charge, guiding his little white wormlike penis myself. Then it was my turn, and he opened his mouth wide. I could make a drawing to this day of where we sat, and stood, as we performed. Just then my mother opened the door of the playhouse. She dragged me away from Eddy and pulled me out. He was sent home, and, taking me by the hand, she walked with me to our house. All my mother said to me then was how upset and disappointed Grandmother would be if she knew what Eddy and I had been doing in my playhouse.

I doubt my mother said anything about it to my father (he never spoke of it to me), because I know that for her it would have been unthinkable. If she had told him about Eddy, he would have been relieved to know that I wasn't just interested in other boys: when I was seven, I also loved exploring with Jeanne Marie, my best friend. We would play doctor down in her basement whenever her parents were away, the details of which are just as vivid today in my memory as those of my one session with Eddy.

Someone from North Carolina told me once that family surnames were often given to Southern boys as middle names at their christening in order to establish some grander family connection. To show where the money was, or the political power. Uncle Ab's middle name was Fox. Albert Fox De Loney. I never asked who the Foxes were, but that name came into the family with Margaret Bonner Fox, a Virginian, born in 1793. She married Edward Brodnax Walker De Loney— two ringing surnames bestowed as given names—who was my uncle Ab's great-grandfather. Fox can be a Jewish name, and I thought of the Twentieth Century–Fox Studios in Hollywood. But if the Foxes being memorialized by my Louisiana grandparents had been Jewish, my grandfather De Loney might have nixed that name at once.

When Uncle Ab was about twenty-three, and World War I began, he volunteered to join the Lafayette Escadrille, hoping to become a fighter pilot. The Lafayette Escadrille was an American military unit that had been formed to fight against the Germans in France.

Its recruits were generally "boys of good family." Many were from the South, with fiery temperaments. But my fiery grandfather De Loney was adamant: his younger boy was not to go to that slaughterhouse. He had already lost one son, Bruce, who died from diphtheria in his youth. My uncle Ab disobeyed his father, and went off to France, where he reconnected with my father, a lieutenant in a cavalry regiment whom he had met before the war in Louisiana. Both Uncle Ab and my father were posted far from the front. Uncle Ab never learned to fly, and my father never rode into battle on horseback. Cavalry charges had become a thing of the past, something from the Civil War.

John Hailey, my maternal
great-grandfather, circa 1850s

And what about our Civil War? My great-grandfather John Hailey broke his leg in a battle, when his horse was shot out from under him. I know very little about him, what he did, who he was. He was a slave owner, but apparently not a slave driver out of *Uncle Tom's Cabin*, like his son-in-law, Isaac, whose body was maybe tossed into the Mississippi River. John's daughter, Hallie, my grandmother, grew up during Reconstruction. She told me the Hailey family lived on a ruinous plantation, and she had a terrible story about a trusted family employee who killed his old parents by driving nails into their skulls. And she spoke to me, lying in bed in Port Arthur half a century later, of a big house making ghostly sounds as winds blew through closed-off, empty rooms. As much Southern gothic as anyone could want. From that house—or maybe another one down there—I have two large silver soupspoons (the kind that butlers all over the South hid in their masters' tree trunks, so that Yankee soldiers wouldn't get them), and a pressed-glass saltcellar that we use every day in my house in Claverack, New York.

Both my great-grandfather—John Hailey—and his wife, Sarah (Sallie) Hailey (née Hammett), my great-grandmother, lived on until the early 1900s. Their granddaughter Evelyn, my aunt, remembered seeing them on a wide porch in Louisiana. Because of the pain from his war injury, John Hailey, seeking comfort, would turn a straight-backed chair upside down and lean it against the wall, and then rest himself against it, while stretching his legs out on the porch floor. When his wife died, he "turned his face to the wall," refusing food, as described in so many lovelorn, romantic tales, and died, inconsolable. He is a middle-aged man in the daguerreotype on the previous page, most likely made in the 1850s, so he would have been born in the early 1820s.

My father, Edward Patrick Ivory, 1917

The strike at the hammer factory in Norwich, New York, that my paternal grandfather led was such an affront to the town, home of Norwich Pharmaceuticals, the maker of Unguentine. It had been a brave thing for him to do: a young man from Cork—of the "Irish Need Not Apply" variety—who had walked off the boat from Ireland and turned one of the town's main industries on its head after having been given a much-coveted job there.

One of his sons—I think not my father—described his disillusioned state afterward, and how he sat in the back of a relative's shop, useless, for years. But he helped raise his six sons and a daughter, saw them educated and some of them married, before he died in 1912. They all did well—three of them, including my father, very well, founding flourishing businesses and becoming leaders in their communities. But when my father became a mill owner himself, he never let his workers unionize, perhaps seeing in that the seeds of future disruption.

The Ivory boys—Jim, John, Will, Dave, Pat (my father), and Tom—had a large carriage block of stone, suitable for a mansion, with

The De Loney house, Bogalusa, Louisiana

the name Ivory carved on it, placed in front of their modest house on Adelaide Street, where they grew up. Adelaide Street, I discovered when my father took me to Norwich once when I was in my thirties, was definitely on the wrong side of the tracks. We drove up to his old family home, to which Dad had arranged to gain entrance, and he invited me to go inside with him. But in one of those loutish moments sons everywhere seem to have sooner or later with sentimental parents, I refused, and sat in the car looking at the huge carriage block.

Years after he was gone, when I was installed in my own big house in Claverack, built by a Van Rensselaer no less, with plenty of rooms through which other winds blow, I tried to buy that carriage block. But there were distant cousins in Norwich, whose surname wasn't even Ivory, who wanted to keep the stone for their annual family reunions, of the kind we had in Port Arthur when I was a child, so that members attending could sit, or stand, on it, and be photographed.

My father had little interest in his Irish roots. He never visited Ireland; he could easily have done so twice in his life—after his time in the army, when he chose to stay in Europe for a year, and again toward the end of his life, when he met me and Ismail Merchant in Rome in 1963. He traveled to Vienna then, and afterward returned to France, where he looked up the old friends he'd corresponded with since the Armistice of 1918. Ireland did not excite his imagination as Italy and France did. When he was growing up, he and his brothers and sister must have been acutely aware of the dislike and social disdain for Irish immigrants. Surely he'd heard of, and maybe as a boy had seen, HELP WANTED signs in Yankee businesses that added NO IRISH NEED APPLY. He had a distant and garrulous cousin named Dennis O'Sullivan who

My father and Ismail in Rome, 1963

used to visit us when we lived in California. Dennis would talk end-lessly of the delights of "the Old Sod," as he called Ireland. My father was too polite ever to let himself seem bored by Dennis, and made sure I was equally polite to him as he went on and on about the glories of Ireland and the Irish. Dennis was my introduction to life's boring adult conver-sations. Whenever my mother heard Dennis was coming, she hid herself in the bedroom un-til Dad made her come out and greet him.

Who then were the Ivorys of Ireland? According to *Com-mon Irish Names*, a little book I picked up in Dublin, Ivory is not an Irish name. It is a Scottish name that had once been French: *Ivry*—the same as the Paris métro line. The only distinguished Irishman named Ivory was the great architect Thomas Ivory, who

My parents in New York City, circa 1920

embellished the center of Dublin at the end of the eighteenth cen-tury. I once found an old bank in Edinburgh in a soot-blackened, very fine classic building of the sort Thomas Ivory had designed for Dublin, called Ivory and Simes.

Of my paternal grandmother I know next to nothing. She died many years before I was born. Her name was Mary Condon, and she and my grandfather—John Ivory—had been childhood sweethearts. He emigrated first, and when he had established himself in Norwich, where there were relatives, she followed. This was in the days before Ellis Island. I have a photograph of her: she stands in front of the house on Adelaide Street, a buxom middle-aged woman wearing a long skirt and apron. I don't easily identify with her, as I do with my maternal, Southern grandmother, who was something of a free spirit—and a forgiving spirit as well, taking in her irresponsible, if charming, gambling husband again and again.

And how did the Ivorys first meet the De Loneys? At a swimming party in the summer of 1916 in Bogalusa, where my father had a job with the Great Southern Lumber Company after graduating from college. My mother was sixteen, my father twenty-four. He wrote in his diary after their first meeting that she came from a fine old Southern family, although he presumed there were "pecuniary difficulties."

What happened next? The United States went to war. My father, who had enrolled in the Army Reserve Officers Training Corps when he was in college in Syracuse, reported to Camp Pike in Arkansas and was commissioned a second lieutenant in the cavalry. He was deployed to France in 1917.

Before he left, he made my mother promise she would enroll in college, and she began studying at Rice Institute (now University) in Houston. They considered themselves to be in love, and corresponded regularly. I have their hundreds of letters to each other— hers to him in Montsûrs, France, and his to her in Texas, then later at Louisiana State University in Baton Rouge, where she joined the Delta Zeta sorority. She went for her final year to Barnard College in New York, where my father was living while he worked in New Jersey for Thomas Edison. At Barnard she majored in home economics and took a part-time job at Gimbel's department store selling lingerie. She boarded on East Sixty-Second Street between Lexington and Third Avenues—only a few doors east on the same block where I myself would live forty-five years later, after I had moved permanently to New York City. At one point in 1918 my father stopped writing to my mother. Just ceased, without explanation. She became frantic. Where was he, why was he no longer writing, was he in danger (he was far, far from the front), was he sick? The silence went on for several months. He offered no explanation when he resumed writing. I think he was unwilling to commit to her, got cold feet, or—unthinkable!—had found someone else. There may have been a "someone else." Among his letters there were a few from a young

Frenchwoman. My French was not up to discovering hidden or disguised familiarity when I read her letters to my father in the 1970s. They seemed to me to be straightforward expressions of friendship and nothing more. It is impossible for me to imagine my father having any sort of full-fledged *affaire* with any young Frenchwoman. He was not a sensual man, and if I got that wrong and he secretly was, it was very well hidden. Perhaps he was not yet committed to the idea of marriage; while always an optimist, economically (and jobless), he might not have felt ready to marry. Or was he not emotionally ready? To me that is more likely, even though my mother was beautiful, fun-loving, and lively, plus intelligent. So my father's long silence will remain a mystery.

In 1919 he returned to the United States and began living in New York City, from where he could easily commute to New Jersey and also visit his family in Norwich. My mother joined him there and in 1921 they went to Dallas where my grandmother De Loney lived, and got married.

Bill Wilson

Bill was my first friend. We started grade school together at the Sacred Heart Academy; though I was a year younger than Bill—I was five—he was my closest friend. He was a Protestant and it was strange that his parents enrolled him in a parochial school, particularly since the public school was across the street from the

Sister Rose de Lima

Academy. Convenience must not have had much to do with it; perhaps the Wilsons thought the education was better. It was hard to see him on the weekends, because he lived on one side of the town and I lived on the other, but I have memories of our playing together outside of school, so our parents must have managed it. He was as outgoing as I was shy—or perhaps "standoffish" is a better description of the way I tended to appear—and big for his age, the sort of rugged little boy who is easy and popular with the other boys. I naturally looked up to him and it seems strange that he should have chosen me for a while to be his best friend.

One of the reasons is that our sweet second-grade teacher, Sister Rose de Lima, felt she saw evidence of artistic talent in our drawings. She sent a note to our parents suggesting private art lessons, and these were duly arranged for Friday afternoons. We felt distinctly privileged when we left the other kids every week, and could look down from our second-story studio to the playground during recess at the untalented pursuing their noisy games in the muck. Meanwhile, we had been selected to fill in little rectangles with different washes of color, from the palest tints across the spectrum to the brightest at the opposite end. These lessons cost a dollar each and I would continue to take them as long as I stayed at the Academy, long after Bill deserted me to go to the Fremont School. In the fourth grade, I would gradually pass from watercolors to oil, and from copying pictures chosen for me by my teacher, Sister Paschalis, to painting my own from nature.

And it was in Bill Wilson's company that I was exposed to things other than the disciplines of the artist's craft: he first caused me to focus on the difference between some boys' bodies and others, including mine. At recess we used to all stand in a line at the long common urinoir. Some of us small boys were so short we could just barely reach up to get ourselves over the cold, smooth enameled lip of the trough, and in this position of maximum exposure, we were the subject of a good deal of scrutiny and comment from the taller Bill. There was no such thing as the kind of furtive glance one tries to hide in the men's rooms of adult life. We openly looked at one another and compared, but there was no touching. By that age—five or six—we all knew that if you touched someone's penis, you did it in private. Some of the boys had not been circumcised; Bill pointed this out to me, speaking of it in a way that made them seem like the Unclean. There was a financial angle to it, too, for he told us that the operation cost money and that some boys' parents were too poor to have it done.

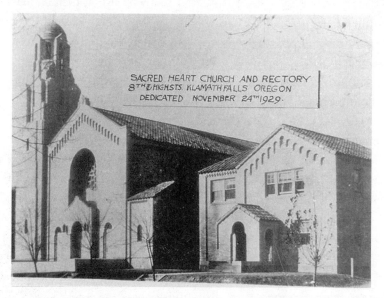

The Sacred Heart Church, Klamath Falls, Oregon

One can imagine the uncut little boys looking down at themselves and starting to cry. This is what went on in the parochial school's boys' lavatory, as Bill and I looked with curiosity and some distaste at our less fortunate classmate's foreskins—a curiosity about that vestigial membrane that, for me if not for Bill, would not be fully satisfied until I had grown up and sailed off to the continents of the poor and benighted.

From the first grade, as I learned to observe the Catholic holy days of obligation (always looked forward to, when they fell on a weekday, because school would be let out at the Academy), we could expect to celebrate the Feast of the Circumcision on New Year's Day: that is, the circumcision of Jesus. It must very soon have sunk in that if it was necessary for the Son of God to have had the costly operation just like

Bill Wilson and me, it was a very important matter, and that those of my schoolmates who were uncircumcised not only had poor parents but were somehow not among the elect. Circumcised men, we had learned in Sister Rose de Lima's Bible history class, being Jews, were Gods and Masters. Even their oppressors, the ancient Egyptians, who early on excited my interest, had had the operation. I don't know how I found all this out. Sister Rose de Lima would not, I think, have informed her class about what was always done to Jewish and Egyptian boys. Probably Bill, the authority on all such things, had told us as we peed together at the urinal. With Bill's hierarchy of the cut and the uncut firmly fixed in my mind, I confidently faced the world, knowing who my equals were, as I set out from the Sacred Heart Academy.

However, I'm afraid the feeling that uncircumcised men are in some way socially inferior has stayed with me all of my life—as regards my own country, where baby boys are often routinely taken away after ten days, in order to be made more "clean" and "healthy." Or once were. Enlightened middle-class American mothers today find circumcision barbaric. When I got to high school in 1942 and we all undressed together in gym class, I would sometimes have to square the exception to Bill's rule with the known facts of a schoolmate's financial background, as with my friend Milton, inexplicably intact, whose father was the bank president.

"Not Free from Blemish"

Such puzzling questions, if I had wanted to ask them, would not be cleared up for me by my own father, who was emotionally unable to speak about any aspect of sex, and who had left everything about human reproduction to my mother. As I was packing my things to leave for army basic training in 1953, my father came into my bedroom and sat on the edge of the bed without speaking, but clearly moved by something. After an uncomfortable pause he brought himself to say that I would soon be mixing closely with a great many other young men, and that on seeing some of them I was not to conclude that I was Jewish because I had been circumcised. I stifled a laugh—he was tearing up—and I was twenty-five by then and sexually experienced.

Hugh Grant and Anthony Hopkins in *The Remains of the Day* (1993)

This was a bit like the scene in my film *The Remains of the Day* when Stevens, the butler (played by Anthony Hopkins), is ordered to inform Lord Darlington's godson, who has just gotten engaged, of the "birds and the bees." That sophisticated young man (played by Hugh Grant) stares at Stevens incredulously when his godfather's butler attempts to carry out the assignment.

Smoothly, making it sound unimportant, I told my father that I had had many friends in high school and college who were circumcised like myself. I was certain that most of them were not Jewish; when they were, I knew. He took this in, appeared satisfied, then got up abruptly and left the room on the verge of weeping. I might have asked him, and blamed myself later for not having done so, "Would it be so very terrible if I *were* Jewish?" And to that I might have added: "You're also circumcised I've noticed, and I never imagined for one second that *you* were Jewish." I made neither retort, however, and was glad I hadn't; it was obvious our little talk had already put him through far too much.

But what my father could not bring himself to mention in any way was the central fact that I had been adopted, and that therefore my origins were obscure. Or, to put it in a more elegant way, quoting the illegitimate Alexander Hamilton, my birth was "not free from blemish." The most interesting and important of all the facts of my early life he and I never discussed, or even alluded to, not once. He lived on to be seventy-five, serene, clearheaded, and right up to the end, reading his ancient Roman history—the three volumes of Edward Gibbon—and his newspaper, the *Fresno Bee*, every morning, until one day he fell over dead, the newspaper in his hand.

The overwhelming and unwanted task of breaking the news to me of my having been adopted had (along with the "birds and the bees") been left to my brave and articulate mother, who came out with it one afternoon when she was driving me home from school, aged ten. It's not that my father was inarticulate. Hardly. He spoke quite brilliantly on many subjects—but not sex and the related emotions. That he blocked off. Like many men of that period, he felt that talking about personal emotions of any kind was "unmanly." The undreamed-of issue (for me) of my being adopted came up because of a gossiping nun who, on seeing my birth certificate, spread the news among my classmates. They, in turn, lost no time in informing me of this in the schoolyard. The nun had read, too, that I was originally named Richard Jerome Hazen (as I found out later), and then renamed James Francis Ivory by my adoptive parents at my christening.

I had a great many questions to ask my mother. Some remain unanswered to this day, like "Who are the Hazens?" She pulled the car over and stopped in front of a large, ugly house under construction. (I cannot pass it when I go back to Klamath Falls every summer without remembering that tense day; the house where we parked is still ugly and misshapen, as well as unpainted; someone, I suppose, must live in it—some uncircumcised person?) It slowly dawned on me, as I sat tearfully in the car in the dusk with my mother, that my adoption must be a big thing if everybody at school was talking about it. I realized, too, that somehow I must have lost caste in my schoolmates' eyes, even if I had been "chosen," as my mother now delicately tried to put it, by her and Dad. Had I been a foundling then, left in a box outside the front door of the Sacred Heart Academy?

I'd read about such unfortunate children. The sisters could be counted on to tell us all about them with relish, gazing down benignly at any parentless kids they knew of through their rimless eyeglasses.

But their stories could never include me, I knew, no matter how romantic the idea of being a foundling might seem to some. I had many pre–Sacred Heart memories of an earlier life in St. Paul: for instance, of living in a big white house by a Minnesota lake, on which my adoptive father, holding me all bundled up in his arms, took me iceboating. I can still squint at the sun's glare, hear the swooshing racket of the boat's keel gliding over the ice, the wind banging on the sails, feel the speed, and I remember the sense of safety I felt in my father's arms. I was four.

On "the K"

Not everything you might want to know about sex could be learned in the Sacred Heart boys' lavatory. More down-to-earth information was passed on to me by Bill Wilson and Earl Kruger on the side of the high hill called "the K" overlooking the town. ("The K" was a huge letter "K," for Klamath, formed of big rocks painted white and laid out on the hillside—it's still there, repainted every so often.) My schoolmate Earl was a beautiful and cherubic-looking boy with golden curls. He stands beside me in our First Communion picture, with folded hands and angelic expression.

One day Bill, Earl, and I were sitting under one of the scrubby

My First Communion (first row, second from right),
with the angelic Earl beside me

pines that managed to take root on a bleak and windy hillside outside of Klamath Falls, where Earl proceeded to demonstrate what happens between men and women in bed. He scratched a little line in the earth, digging it out with his finger, and lay down over it, but first opening his pants in order to place his cherubic (and uncircumcised) member in the hole he had dug.

"That's what they do," he told us, and Bill said, "Yes, that's right." I see now that some vast and primitive sexual drama was being enacted by a little boy and Mother Earth, in front of a solemn chorus of approving onlookers, but I remember thinking, if that's what men and women do together in bed, it must be dirty and senseless.* A year or two later my mother enlightened me further, telling me about the Father, who places a Seed in the Mother, which grows into a Child nine months later. When I was a teenager, all the parts fell

---

* A scene almost exactly like this, but with slightly older boys, appeared in the first part of Bernardo Bertolucci's film *1900* (1976).

into place, you might say, rather accidentally, when I learned that the missing ingredients of pleasure and excitement, which both Earl and my mother had omitted mentioning, far outweigh any senselessness and dirt.

Opposite Palettes

Bill and I continued to play together after he changed schools, but we drifted apart, and his interest in painting and drawing didn't last very long, though his Friday afternoon lessons with me continued for a while. It seemed he looked forward with less and less enthusiasm to my visits, sometimes not bothering to be at home, and gradually they came to an end, but not before another grotesque incident. He owned a real human skull, which he kept in his garage, and which was supposed to have been the head of an Indian. One day we took it and crept up behind a woman who was lying in a hammock reading a book. Slowly, we lowered it into view so that the two were face-to-face. She screamed wildly and leapt out of the hammock and we ran away with the skull, laughing.

Bill and I were reunited in high school. My father took me out of the Academy because there were no athletics, and he wanted me to have the benefit of the public high school sports program. A vain hope! I remember going with him to see Father Casey, the parish priest, whose permission was needed for this, and Father Casey gave his murmured, gentle assent. By this time Bill and I had hopelessly diverged as types. He was on every athletic team, was big and burly, with a handsome, but quickly maturing face, and had strings of girl-friends, while I was the skinny boy with underdeveloped biceps who always hung back when a baseball happened to come in my direction. When teams were chosen, I was drawn by lot, not for what I was likely to do to help win, but because I was a handicap, the loser in the draw getting me. As for girlfriends, mine were in quite a different relation to me than Bill's. However, he recognized our old friendship, we were always cordial with each other, and sometimes he became protective. The school lettermen patrolled the halls at breaks, on the lookout for sassy types like myself who broke rules and talked back, and when I was sometimes "arrested," Bill wouldn't allow the others to paddle me with the huge wooden paddle that, in some college fraternity hazings, had killed people.

We went to our respective colleges in Oregon, he was pledged by Beta Theta Pi, married his high school sweetheart, and disappeared. We would not meet again for forty years, when we had gone quite gray and discovered we were both avid readers, sometimes of the same books. And later we exchanged color photographs of our first oil paintings. These were of small birds perched in a landscape, and we found that our palettes had been opposites: Bill had chosen cooler colors, blues and purples and chilly shades of green—or had he?—while I'd opted for warmer tones, yellow, red, and orange. Had these been our natural inclinations, as observed by Sister Paschalis, as she dealt these palettes to us? Just as she saw, for certain, that she must inevitably touch up our little robins and

sparrows with a master's flick of her brush, adding a delicate claw here, or the glint of a tiny eye there. In later life I turned to chillier colors myself, and told my cameramen and art directors that I wanted certain films of mine to be predominantly cool in color, as for instance *Maurice*.

A Bit Apart

The Sacred Heart Academy gave a Christmas party for all of its students in the parish hall my first year there, which would have been in

1933, when I was five, though I can't be sure that it was not in the second year, when I was six. In any case, one of the features of the program was that all the youngest children, the ones likely to still believe in Santa Claus, were asked what gift they would like him to bring down the chimney. When it was my turn, I spoke up loudly, "A doll's house." The hall broke into shouts of laughter—the older boys, of course, but also our teachers, who were nuns and who must have smiled in their special way, with a hand over their mouths. I didn't know why I was being laughed at by everybody. I didn't like the feeling. But from that day on, as I reckon it, I began to regard myself as being a bit apart from all the others—apart, different, but not lesser in any way I think: maybe starting then, I began to think of myself as something *more*, in

Me playing with assorted Christmas gifts, including a tank, a train,
a clothes washer and ironing board, and "Doll Boy"

the sense of being distinct and perhaps also higher in value. This was confirmed when Bill Wilson and I—he had not laughed at me when I said I wanted Santa Claus to bring me a doll's house—were singled out for our private Friday afternoon drawing and painting class. Thus began my lifetime's work—my life "in art"—but one linked very early in the public view with sexual identity.

A Significant Memory?

During my junior year in high school, sometime in the winter months, I went with my parents to have dinner at the Officers' Club

at the Marine base near Klamath Falls. I don't know whose guests we were—possibly the man I'm going to write about. I wore slacks and a tweed sport jacket, and to complete my ensemble, a pink satin bow tie. It was the sort of trashy thing, like plaid shoelaces, that teenage boys wore in the early 1940s and that must have seemed, to a Marine officer who might have had his own memories of other teenage boys, slightly older than I, in battle fatigues in the Far East or North Africa, particularly silly and effeminate. We had already had our dinner, I think, and were sitting around afterward in the lounge, the grown-ups enjoying a drink or brandy perhaps.

Suddenly a middle-aged officer with a short graying bristling mustache (our host, or someone who passed by?) came up to me and confronted me on the subject of the pink satin necktie. He did not like it; it was stupid and girlish. A silence fell. Was he drunk? I expected my father, or at least my mother, or even my sister, who was very pugnacious and quick to take offense, to come to my rescue. But no one spoke. I could feel my parents' embarrassment, particularly my father's, yet he said nothing. The officer went on, standing over me, and began to criticize more than merely my tie. He did not like my appearance generally, nor my manner. I was slim—too slim—and rather too pretty a boy, with my hair worked up into a kind of pompadour, with delicate frowning eyebrows that to the Marine must have looked almost plucked, and no doubt I was lolling back with my knees crossed, a large loafer swinging negligently on an out-of-scale teenage foot. Could there have been a "lucky penny" inserted in the cross strap of those loafers? That, too, was in style. But the Marine ran out of steam somehow. Perhaps because we all remained silent. Perhaps because, though the unwilling center of attention, I didn't go to pieces. Perhaps because he began to reproach himself, or saw that he was being rude and overbearing, or just plain drunk. And then he said a fatal thing, and I'm surprised I had the cheek to take it up, except that for me it seemed to be a sink-or-swim kind of situation. He said, "What do you think of me?" And I replied, "I think you're pompous." There must have been an intake of breath on the part of my parents, perhaps one of them even said, "Jim!" in warning. And then it was over. The bullying stopped, the man went off, we left for home. I felt cross in the car with myself because I had mispronounced "pompous," inserting an extra syllable, so it came out "pom-poo-ous." I had only just learned that word and no doubt was waiting for the right occasion to use it. I never wore that tie again; I kept it in my drawer for a while and then threw it away.

Now that I am older and have reached that officer's age and more than likely surpassed it, I see that the key sentence in all this must be "What do you think of me?" Was this fellow one of the thousands of repressed, latent homosexuals who were in the services, officers and noncommissioned officers alike who, upon meeting an effeminate-seeming boy, felt irresistibly that he must be bullied or harassed, whether in or out of the barracks? I'll never know, and there must be several valid reasons that he might have chosen to pick on me that night. The other thing I will never know is why my father kept silent. It did not diminish him in my eyes, but I wondered about it then, as I do now. Was he pursuing some deal with the Marine Corps? They would have needed a lot of lumber to build their base. Was this officer someone who requisitioned lumber and who might, if peeved, have gone off to one of the other big lumber companies in Klamath Falls? We never spoke of this episode, not once. It was as if it had never happened. It was too embarrassing to mention. But my mother must have said something that night as they lay there with the lights out. She probably accused my father, said he should have come to my rescue. And he, so quick to justify himself in all things, probably said that I didn't need being rescued, that I could obviously take care of myself and the whole affair boded well for my future in the world of men, for, as he always kept reminding her, and telling me, "We live in a world of men."

Gus and Petite

Gus Luellewitz, my father's business partner, was a son of a bitch, no doubt about that. Petite was his second wife. Gus brought the capital to Ivory Pine Company, and the sort of business acumen and experience the senior partner is expected to contribute, but in later years he became more and more dictatorial and secretive until finally, when my father was sixty-eight and Gus well over ninety, they split up.

Gus and Petite

Gus had gone through bankruptcy proceedings several times but had always sprung back stronger and richer than ever. He seems always to have been a lumberman. In appearance he was a bit like William Randolph Hearst and made the same kind of impression of ancient, fleshy power and inscrutability, with little, hooded, almost reptilian eyes seen in a mass of discolored pouches. He seemed to lie in wait and watch people; I know he often watched *me*. I felt his gaze to be not unkind, yet he must have wondered what sort of strange bird his partner had sired, could I be useful to him or would I be harmful? His own son was certainly no use. This was Mac, an alcoholic. Mac was married to Elsie, and in the early years of the partnership he was involved in the company in some way. He and Elsie used to come all the way up from Los Angeles to Klamath Falls (a distance of nearly a thousand miles) in their chauffeur-driven black limousine; it was the first time I had seen a car like that. Mac was

It was these big logs that sent me to college, to France, to Venice, and just about everywhere else I wanted to go when I was a young man

supposed to do something or other for his father, but once out of the old man's sight and as soon as he could ditch Elsie with my mother, he would be off on some roaring drunk. Then he would disappear and finally be brought back after several days by my father, who had been obliged to comb all the taverns for miles around. Elsie would sober her husband up, he would apologize profusely to my mother for being a cad, and the couple would climb into their car and start the trip back.

My father was supposed to have "loved" Mac and this is why he tried to help him out. They were about the same age, and there was something of the movie star in Mac's dark looks and glossy hair and devil-may-care attitude, which was such a contrast to the cold control of Gus. Elsie also projected something of a glamorous image; she wore her hair pulled back in a bun, like Dorothy Lamour, and large gold earrings, and had a leopard-skin coat.

Gus was always disinheriting his son, always threatening him, and eventually Mac really did drink himself to death. My father, to some extent, became a surrogate for Mac. But very little human warmth came from Gus. It all had to come from my father. I never heard my father criticize Gus, no matter how dreadful and impossible he became; he kept his anger well reined and just put his head down and pushed forward.

My mother told me when she was middle-aged that in the early days, when they had gone riding in my father's car, he and Gus sat up front and she sat on the seat behind, alone; Gus would then let his hand slip lower and lower until he could put it on my mother's knee. She would be terrified. I asked her, "Did Daddy know about that?" She said she didn't know, but there was nothing he could do, which in a way seems perfectly true.*

Gus was first married to a woman not much younger than himself, and I met her once or twice. She was motherly and shapeless, featureless. She died mysteriously from drinking the water in one of the American grand hotels, some place like the Palmer House in Chicago or the Davenport in Spokane, or the Fairmont in San Francisco; some sort of plague water came out of the tap, she drank it, and hours later she was dead. Then Gus married Petite, who was perhaps twenty years his junior. She must have been beautiful when she was young and she wasn't bad-looking at the end of the 1930s, when Gus married her. To me, she seemed a sophisticated woman of the world. She had a particularly agreeable speaking voice, low and somehow cultivated, like women in films then, women like Joan Crawford and Rosalind Russell, both of whom were types like herself. Petite was said to have been involved in the movies in some vague way, perhaps as a bit player. She wore expensive,

---

* It is possible my mother never told my father of this, if one is ready to believe that in the close, confined space of a prewar Oldsmobile sedan, he didn't see what his boss was doing. But my father was very good at not seeing things he chose not to see.

dressy clothes that looked like something out of a film, and she had a diamond bracelet that she wore most of the time—a long slinky row of lozenge-shaped diamonds set in platinum, which slid up and down her wrist. Her hands were always perfectly manicured, the nails long and red. Later on, we learned from one of her loquacious relatives that she protected her hands at night when she was in bed with a pair of white gloves. Certainly her hands did make a rich, elegant impression.

Petite often made the long drive from Los Angeles along with Gus, and sometimes their limousine would call for my sister and me at the Academy and wait until school was out, when we would emerge and find my mother sitting in the car with Petite while the chauffeur was holding the door open for us.

Petite and Gus always gave us very expensive Christmas presents, the kind of baubles that boutiques in Magnin's and Bullock's Westwood carried; they never had much intrinsic value. I looked forward to receiving these, as did my sister. So much so that other and much better presents from our parents, things we had asked for, ended up on Christmas morning seeming to be less than the unexpected, glittery things in the fancy wrappings of those Californian stores. Once they gave me a music box in the shape of a colonial secretary desk. Petite would have picked it out, never Gus.

Petite had a number of poor relatives that she cared for and liked to have around. One was her sister Vera Beale, who had the hard face of a Saks saleswoman, and was just as worn. Another was a niece named Rose Hogan who was almost Petite's age. She had never married but certainly had not given up. She had very large breasts and a large, pleasant, plain face, which she liked to frame in wraparound turbans. She always had to be invited places, and my sister and I must have picked up on the note of pity and occasional scorn in our elders' references to her. Her difficult spinster's position was not enhanced by having no apparent fixed work, although she was supposed to do a bit of designing, and she ended up as a kind of companion to my mother, and babysitter, when we moved to Palm Springs in 1941 to escape the Klamath Falls winter. Her charges were ages thirteen (me) and ten (my sister), old enough to tease her about her boy-

The Jonathan Club, Los Angeles

friend, Walter. We were always demanding, "When is Walter going to pop the question, Rose?" She had been encouraging Walter for a long time, maybe years; they had grown old together talking about it, but Walter never did get up the nerve to ask Rose to marry him. I remember a dry, spare man in his forties, with a kind face drained of any interest or energy. The feature I most recall was a very large tuft of black pubic hair which I saw when I climbed up on the sundeck of our house where he was taking a sunbath in the nude. Perhaps I was planning to ask him "When are you going to pop the question, Walter?" but when I saw him lying there, I turned around and crept back down the stairs, embarrassed for him. Now that I think about it, perhaps it was a little strange for a conventional-appearing man like Walter to be sunbathing in the nude in 1941 on a housetop, where insolent teenagers could accost him.

All these people liked to be together playing bridge or attending the races: Gus and Petite; Vera Beale and her husband, Charlie; Rose; Fred, Gus's dull nephew who looked like him, but without the authority, and who had been a bookkeeper at Dad's mill, and Renée, his wife. Sometimes they were joined by Barney Oldfield, the early race-car driver. By that time Oldfield was a little old wizened man.

Gus loved horse racing and owned racehorses, but at the very end of his life he was implicated in a race-fixing scandal.

A horse of his was supposed to have been given an amphetamine. Nothing was ever proved and the charges were withdrawn, but it was as if some stain was on his honor, and Gus never recovered. It was about that time that things went wrong with my father, who, under pressure, had a massive heart attack. When he recovered, he broke away from Gus and sold him his share in the company. Gus was so terrible then that he would not even let my father have the desk that he had sat at for nearly thirty years; it was "company property."

The last time I saw Gus was with my father at their club in Los Angeles, the Jonathan. They did not meet, but Gus was surrounded by the corps of lawyers he needed to, in effect, disinherit his other "son," my father. He was an ancient huddled presence, scarcely alive, animated only by revenge and an old man's spite, sitting in a sort of heap on a huge sofa, the baleful eyes looking at me in a dim way as I saluted him from afar.

I never saw Petite again, but she outlived Gus by several years, staying on in their house in Brentwood, playing cards with Vera and Charlie and Barney Oldfield, until she too died and the house was put up for sale. I met a man somewhere who had gone to school with Petite long, long ago, in some little town in Utah (I think), and he replied when I wondered how old she might be, "She pretends to be young, but I know for a fact she's in her seventies—she'd have to be. Haw! Haw!"

She declined, in her movie-star house, with its peach-colored heavy silk curtains that kept out the light, no doubt embalmed before her death with the expensive unguents she wore, in her diamond bracelet and white gloves, like a sort of Duchess of Windsor— declined slowly and just flickered out. Gus's grandson (Mac's son) ran the mill by that time; it took two families three generations, apparently, to produce a capable young businessman with a feeling for lumber. It was much easier to produce alcoholics and film directors.

Eating in the Depression

My Gastronomical Roots

I have friends whose tastes in food are highly refined, friends who have had every advantage of expensive education and good example in matters culinary, who know all about vintages and what to do when the hollandaise sauce curdles, yet who douse their hamburgers with quantities of ketchup and bite into the oozing horror with a look of being transported—which is what is happening to them: they are going right back to when they were young and happy and well looked after, back to their fraternity house dining table, or to their boarding school lunches. If you ask, What about all that ketchup? they look sheepish. In this period of self-conscious gastronomy, even your closest friends don't like to say they crave ketchup and dream of mashed potatoes and gravy.

Now I see that food—or more properly, the tastes of certain foods—plays a huge part in our psychological makeup, so that how and where one's food habits were formed is no less revealing—or on a par with—discovering the origins of one's sexual orientation. In my own case, my eating tastes were definitely formed during the Depression years in Klamath Falls, to which my parents moved when my father lost all his savings in the stock market crash. Since that time, I have moved around a lot and lived for long stretches of time and eaten heartily in England, France, Italy, and India. But although I consider myself an advanced expert in the more sophisticated forms of cuisine of all these countries, my gastronomical roots remain dug deep in the impoverished soil of the American Depression.

Tramps

Tramps used to come to our back door for a handout in summer, perhaps in winter, too. My mother wouldn't let them in the house, but she would pass a plate out through the momentarily unlatched screen door. There were always stories going around of too softhearted housewives who had been raped or murdered by hungry bums. The tramps who came to our door would usually sit on the back steps, with the plate on the step above them, and quietly eat the meal Mother had given them, which was sometimes leftovers, or if there was enough, what we ourselves were eating. She also gave each of them a glass of water and a paper napkin. Sometimes the tramps would put what she gave them into the sack they carried and move up the street to the next house. Were they gathering provisions for some long trip in a railroad boxcar? Sometimes the more genteel ones ate my mother's food, and then fished dessert out of the sack and ate that, too—maybe

Me and my mother in the kitchen, Klamath Falls, 1934. She would see the tramps through the window on the right as they came up to our back door, which always had the screen door latched. She would tell them to sit on the steps they had just climbed. In a few minutes she passed down a plate, or plates, then latched the door again.

a somewhat soiled-looking piece of cake. One man I remember had a piece of blue cake, probably left over from a birthday party.

These men were always dirty and tired-looking. Perhaps they were genuinely out of work, men who had once had houses, wives, children, and jobs, but a good number must have been hoboes who rarely worked and who lived in hobo camps and had chosen that vagrant life and liked it; and now that armies of poor men tramped about asking for handouts, they joined their ranks for an easy meal.

Sometimes, if the tramp looked "nice," I was allowed to sit out on the back porch while he ate. But I don't think I did that very often, because most of them had a hangdog, shamed attitude and ate quickly, furtively, and left, careful to hand back the plate and utensils.

These men were ever present from the time we moved to Klamath Falls in 1933, until the Depression eased up a bit by Roosevelt's second term. We would see their shaggy heads and bent-over forms through the sunporch next to the kitchen, and Mother would nod to them to wait; perhaps some of them had been there more than once. Perhaps also there were "good" houses and "bad" houses, ones where you got a decent meal without being made to feel too bad, and others where you got nothing except a door slammed in your face. Once in a while a Black man would come through and this made my mother emotional; she would do more for him out of a sense of Southern noblesse oblige than she might have done for a white tramp, who might always have seemed a little menacing and a reminder of the very slippery path that everyone was on then—including my father. We had come to Oregon from Minnesota with a car and the clothes on our backs and some furniture, but with a rich man's promise. Luckily, that promise was made good.

The Cookhouse

Gus Luellewitz and my father started the Ivory Pine Company in Klamath Falls, reactivating the old Boy Scout Mill, as it was called, on Lower Klamath Lake. Gus put in all the money and stayed in Los

Angeles; my father managed the mill in Oregon and did all the work. He had a 49 percent ownership in the company, and Gus kept the controlling interest. Gus had been born in 1870, so he was over sixty and my father was forty-one. The mill prospered and the company moved to Bly, a small town fifty miles or so from where we lived. This was to be nearer to the supply of timber. A large, new mill was built, and all the other buildings, large and small, that a lumber company requires. The married workers had little houses near the stream that had been dammed up to form the millpond on which the cut logs floated; the single men lived in bunkhouses closer in, usually two to a bunkhouse. I went into some of those, even stayed in one once. When the door was open, the setting sun shone on the dusty plank floor. The logging trucks would roll to and fro, and a dense, white, powdery dust would be thrown up. From time to time the road would be

The cookhouse women, late 1930s or early 1940s

sprinkled, but these little huts must have been a pretty terrible place to live in. The men would fight and get roaring drunk and lash about on the metal cots. There was no indoor plumbing; the cabins had basins and pitchers for shaving, but the hot showers and toilets were somewhere else. There was a fetid atmosphere of perspiration and the vinegar smell of a sawmill, which is a combination of sap and a preservative put into the millpond to fight insects. One little window faced east, and under it there was a crude pine table, on which the men put their things, but there weren't many of those. Girlie magazines mostly, *True Detective*, and maybe a photograph of some girl in a distant town.

These unmarried men ate in the cookhouse, according to the shifts they worked, so the hours for the women who ran it must have been long ones. At Bly the cookhouse was run by Sarah McMillan and her teenage daughters. They were all of them as big as the men they fed, great strapping women with strong arms. They baked and roasted and cut all day long in their sweltering kitchen, which was dominated by a monstrous black stove into which they were forever shoving kindling. These women were hearty and popular, like their cooking. Ross McMillan worked at the mill as foreman of the logging operation, in charge of the trucks and felling. He was Sarah's husband, and there was a sister, or sister-in-law, present at all times. I remember these big women sitting during a lull in their day drinking coffee and gossiping and mopping their brows. They all lived in rooms on the back of the cookhouse and slept in big double beds of cast iron, the sort of beds the Joads loaded into their broken-down truck in John Ford's *The Grapes of Wrath*. I would look in on them sometimes and read comic books when I accompanied my father on one of his trips to the mill, from his office, which had stayed in town. I got on well with the teenage daughters, who were twice as big as I was, even when I myself reached my teens.

When my father came back from where we were logging, we would have one of the big dinners. Most days there were two kinds of meat, like roast beef and pork chops, or fried chicken and a big ham. Roast pork was very popular. This meat never ran out, and what was left was ground up into other things, but there was never any sense of stinginess, only of bounteous fare of the kind nineteenth-century European authors complained of in the American hotels they visited: heaped-up indiscriminate servings, falling over the edge of the coarse ironstone plates. There was every kind of fortifying thing, what the *New Yorker* writer Michael J. Arlen calls the "endangered species of starch," mostly potatoes in their many forms, macaroni and cheese, pumpkin pie, apple pie; green vegetables were in short supply, only canned peas and string beans; working-class men had little taste for fresh vegetables. But there were salads: lettuce and tomato, with a sort of diluted mayonnaise dressing, and gelatin salad, with grated carrots in it, or bits of canned fruit. There were Sarah's homemade biscuits, which, like most people's homemade biscuits, were tasteless doughy projectiles, with a hard crust; and lots of white bread, and butter. There were ketchup bottles on the plank tables (to which plank seats had been fixed, as on picnic trestles) and jars of Heinz mustard, and cucumber pickles. All this was washed down with coffee and water. The water was kept in aluminum pitchers. Sometimes there was Kool-Aid. The men did not stand in line to receive this food; they were served at their tables by the teenage McMillans, who carried out the platters, which then were passed from man to man.

Utter democracy was the rule in seating. The lowliest sat next to my father, according to empty seats becoming available. What was the décor of this establishment? Thin transparent cotton curtains strung on a wire, and a picture or two cut out of a magazine and tacked up on the pine walls, to make the place "homey." Sarah would go outside the cookhouse when she was ready to serve and, with a piece of metal pipe, bang on a suspended triangle of iron. You could hear that ringing for miles and I can hear it still across the decades. Then the men would troop in in their heavy work shoes, with their faces washed and their hair slicked down, if it was the evening meal, or with dusty hair and grimy necks if it was the midday one, and fall upon that food ravenously—much as film crews do, even in this age of affluence and dieting and food pickers. That was the lesson my father's cookhouse taught me, to feed hungry men as if they were stars and never skimp there.

Stomachache

The Sacred Heart Academy was run by the Sisters of St. Francis, a teaching order. If you were Catholic, the church required you to put your children into a Catholic school, if there was one, unless you received a dispensation from the parish priest in order to enroll them for some reason in the public schools. The Academy was private; tuition was three dollars a month per child. Nearly all the Catholic children attended, and a few Protestants for convenience, or because their parents were convinced the nuns provided better instruction, which they probably did. There were also a few Native American children there, who came down from their reservation at Chiloquin, and who boarded. As far as the nuns were concerned, these children were hardly human, with their flat, Asiatic faces and little black eyes, their straight black hair, and their feckless, often drunken parents. They formed a forlorn little group who never played with the other children and who sat in the back of the schoolroom, inert and, it was believed, uninstructible, with dirty noses. Their position was curious, for, outside the social system as they were, descendants of tribes who had harassed the town's founding fathers, they were individually extremely rich (for our town) due to their joint ownership, on the reservation, of the town's most valuable crop, timber. If they were full-blooded Native Americans, they later received, in the 1950s, a cash settlement each of $99,000. Very few of the town's leading citizens had $99,000—a lot of money even in the fifties. Most of the Native Americans' money was said to have been blown on alcohol, gambling, and new cars. But the nuns were very hard, actually, for the most part, and didn't spare much kindness even on their white charges. And where food was concerned, there were no frills. A child could bring a packed lunch tin, or eat in the Academy dining room. What a terrible odor that place had! It was the odor of the badly cooked, plain food of nuns, who are not supposed to have an interest in food, and who no doubt believed such an interest should be discouraged in children. But in fact, bad food only makes you want the tastiest of delicacies, so like so much else of their psychology, it backfired.

But at fifteen cents a head, you weren't likely to get much in the way of delicacies. It was like a boardinghouse, with the Sunday roast going through various incarnations lower and lower down the scale, except that, I suspect, the sisters ate the roast on Sunday when they entertained the priests to dinner, and served the scraps to the children all week long. The nuns boiled a lot of cabbage, and they made tasteless puddings out of stale bread, or stewed up the sourest of plums into a compote, and all these sour tastes and smells permeated their black habits and no doubt their very flesh, so that on a hot day in May you shrank from the approach of your teacher, who probably thought you were trying to hide something, and often smacked our hands with rulers. One knows how voluminously dressed lower-middle-class women in Victorian days must have smelled from these sisters. However, there was one good thing the nuns cooked: a red kidney bean, or chili, which was tasty perhaps because it hadn't been cooked too long (or soaked overnight); I always got sick from eating this, though not until safely home, when I would groan and hold my stomach and my mother would worry about appendicitis (this was

before sulfa drugs; any stomach cramp could mean a ready-to-burst appendix and peritonitis).

After a few months of this fare, I was given a lunch pail. But I did not like the smell of the inside of my lunch tin any better than the odor of the school dining room. No matter how much it was washed, the smell of the food combined with the smell of tin put me off. Lunch was some sort of sandwich, peanut butter or bologna; cocoa in a thermos; a cookie; and a banana or an apple. But I was always dropping my thermos; I could hear the shattering of glass inside, and when I took the cork out, shards of glass poured out with the wasted chocolate. This went on for years, but of course I went off in the morning having had a big breakfast, and came home to a big dinner at night, in which there were plenty of delicacies, so it didn't do me any harm, except, as I say, to make me interested in having nice things to eat on all occasions, not just morning and night.

By the sixth or seventh grade—I'm not sure when I started doing this—I was considered old enough to leave the school precincts and find my own lunch in town. I think I was given twenty-five cents a day for this purpose. I found a tasty lunch at the Woolworth's store counter, which I would vary: one day a hamburger with raw onion and dill pickle, the next day a bowl of chili. With this, hot chocolate if it was winter, and root beer the rest of the year. I remember hurrying down the two blocks to Main Street, where the five-and-tens stood almost side by side: Woolworth's and J. J. Newberry. I passed Beck's Bakery on the way and sometimes coming back I'd buy a fat doughnut, or a sort of custardy éclair with caramel frosting on it, or a thing with jelly inside and powdered sugar out. There were always birthday cakes in the window as a display, with roses and leaves and writing in green and pink on the white frosting. Everybody's birthday cakes came from Beck's. They all looked the same and tasted the same: too sweet. It would have been heresy to ask for a chocolate birthday cake, and only poor people had bright-colored cakes, baked at home, with food coloring added to the batter. So the tramp's blue cake would have been a poor person's cake passed on to another poor person. It always seemed to be winter on that street past Beck's, with a drizzly snow blowing in my face.

Woolworth's seemed bright and cheerfully aglow after the bleak streets, with the things you could order reproduced in color on a sheet of glass over the cook's range, and lit from behind: a ham sandwich on a plate, with an olive; a bowl of soup; a chocolate soda. My constant lunch companion was a girl named Patty Hooker. Sometimes some other girls came along with Patty, but usually it was just the two of us; so much so that we got talked about in time. It seems Patty did not have a good reputation. Various boys had made free with her in some way. I heard that I ought not to spend every noon hour with Patty. Probably some evil-tongued person, perhaps one of the sisters, who could always be counted on to pass on gossip, warned my mother, for Patty wasn't from a family that counted. I don't remember what happened. She wasn't in the school very long. But this was the first instance I know of in my life of an innocent relationship being darkened by that kind of rumor.

The Pelican Grill

The best restaurant in town we called the Pelican Grill, and it was in the same building in which my father had his office, and next door to the biggest bank. It was owned by a regal-looking woman named Avis McConnell. She combined something of the air of a turn-of-the-twentieth-century society lady, who always knew the right thing to say to her guests and how to make them feel at home, with that of a headmistress of a girls' boarding school, or the housemother of a sorority, who knew how to keep difficult people under her roof in line. She had a stately, gliding walk, and her large bosom stuck out in front and her seat was certainly meant to be covered by yards of rustling silk ending in a train, but this being the 1930s you had to imagine a bustle. She had white hair swept up from a handsome face, and a cultured voice. And she must have been a good deal better educated than most of her patrons. Certainly she had a highly developed aesthetic sense for the owner of a restaurant in Oregon, which she brought to bear on its decoration. There was a large dining room in front with booths on one side and a lunch counter opposite. Beyond that there was an even larger dining room. All the woodwork was dark stained, and there were little lamps in the booths which lit up prints of impressionist painters: it was in the Pelican Grill that I saw my first Renoir and Degas. The dark wainscot went up to the height of the division between the booths, and was finished off with a long running shelf, on which Avis had put pieces of copper and brass and pewter, or handsome pottery jars. Hung above the shelf were small prayer rugs from Persia. The whole subdued and even rich effect was very different from anything I had ever seen.

It was a pleasure to enter her restaurant. Avis always advanced to meet us and led us to our table, and she called my parents by their first names, and in every way she showed herself to be their equal. But, for a small town, she had an unconventional living arrangement. She shared her flat, which was above Beck's Bakery, with a rich rancher named Buck. She had been his mistress for years. This was accepted in the town and was not the subject of any particular gossip; that was the way it was. There was a flavor of the Old West in this, of gold-rush towns and ranches of fifty years earlier, and in fact, in those days she might have presided over one of the grander brothels in Colorado or Nevada, in a long rustling gown, with plumes in her hair and diamonds in her low-cut décolletage.

When I was old enough to understand some of these things, and to recognize that Avis was an unusual woman, I used to stand in the street and look up at her windows. An architect named Sheldon Brumbaugh, the first "modern" architect in Klamath Falls, had evidently transformed the top of the bakery into a very pleasant world for the two aging lovers. One could get a glimpse of the same taste that had been applied to her restaurant; she was one of the first to install painted reed blinds, and even when they were drawn I could see some objects on the windowsill that excited my curiosity. It must have been lonely out on Buck's ranch; perhaps he had an uncongenial wife there, or was a widower, so when he came to town he was met by a civilized and attractive woman who looked after him and provided the kind of home he wasn't able to have on his ranch. I tried to find out more about him a few years ago, but no one could tell me very much . . . except that he was supposed to have come from a prominent Philadelphia family.*

Avis died long ago; her custom-made rooms above the bakery have survived, though the bakery itself is long since gone. But the Pelican Grill is still the best restaurant in town for a quick lunch, which tends to be pizza these days, although all the carpets and pots and the Renoir ladies were swept away when the management changed about thirty years ago. My family moved to California in 1948, when my father and Gus built a new sawmill, but we kept our cabin at Lake of the Woods near Klamath Falls and went back there every summer. Once, when we had driven up from California, we went into the Pelican Grill to have lunch and Avis come up in her welcoming way and took my mother in her arms and was kissed by my father.

My mother had almost died of strangulation in that restaurant. She got a bone caught in her throat, and it lodged in her windpipe; the cook came out and thumped her sharply in the back and she was saved. This cook was as unlike Avis as anyone could be. In fact, she was supposed to be her partner. She looked like a man and had a man's red face and short-cropped hair. If *she* had been called Buck, you wouldn't have been surprised. She always wore white pants and a white short-sleeved shirt, and when she had had enough for the day, she just went home. Her specialty was chicken pot pie; it is not one of my favorite dishes by any means, but the crust was as light and flaky—the mark of a good chicken pot pie, or any pie for that

---

* Later on, I learned that he was some kind of Biddle, no less.

matter—as it was reputed to be in the Duncan Hines directory of good American restaurants, which listed the Pelican Grill.

The town's lumbermen all sat at lunch at a big round table in the corner of the back room and ate heartier things than the chicken pot pie, no doubt. There were no alcoholic beverages until late in the 1950s, Oregon being dry. Sometimes I joined my father at that table. I never knew any of the other businessmen; the table was like a club, and since I had no interest in joining that particular club, I never found out who any of the men were who talked so loudly and gestured so expansively. They must have thought me a bit odd, peering around as I always was to see the carpets and copper warming pans.

My father had an idea that I was not especially observant and one day Avis showed us to a table that some people had recently quit and that hadn't quite been tidied up. In the ashtray there were cigarette butts. To test my powers of observation my father asked me to tell him what I could about the people who had just been sitting there, judging from their cigarette butts. I stopped looking about the room long enough to give a glance to the butts, one of which had lipstick on it. He asked me what the sex was of the person who had been using the ashtray. I said, "A woman." He looked satisfied, congratulated me on my cleverness, and picked up the menu. I could have told him more but did not. The lipstick was a sort of rust that looks good on redheads and which they proverbially wear, or did then, with matching nail polish. Later on, I was cross with myself for not asking him, "Yes, and what was the color of the woman's hair? *You* tell *me*."

My Father's Table

I grew up in the Great Depression, but I was certainly never hungry and, apart from the tramps, scarcely knew that hunger existed. We were sheltered from all that, though no doubt, as with housewives in those days, my mother had a weekly budget to keep to and was expected to manage and do it with flair. She didn't really like to cook that much, but she knew how and did it without grumbling.

A wife was supposed to know how to cook, to set a nice table, to shop advantageously, and to appear at dinner fresh, combed, made up, and attractively dressed. This my mother always did, until the end of her days, although the shopping and cooking eventually passed into the hands of a series of Japanese servants whom she and my father had to instruct in Western methods. And somewhat into the hands of my father, who more and more, as he got older, took over the cooking of the meat, and particularly holiday birds. But in the thirties she did everything. She gave me a taste for certain things that I've never lost and am ready to eat in the most debased forms: for instance, mashed potatoes and gravy. I have never been able, in my own house, to attain the snowy whiteness and smooth consistency of her mashed potatoes, which were really a purée, and that before the days of food mills and blenders. Nor has anyone else I know, even though mashed potatoes are not a dish you normally find these days, except in diners, where it is one of the big attractions on their menus.

My mother fed me artichokes, and I'm surprised that, nearly fifty years later, there are many people in this country who have never tasted one or even know what it is. Perhaps this is because they were grown in California, at Salinas, and so were a West Coast specialty. My father must have first had them when he went to France in 1917. My mother made all kinds of Southern things she'd learned from her mother, or else gave a Southern twist to the usual things that everybody else cooked, though in time she did less and less of this. Perhaps my father, being from the north, didn't like those flavors, or didn't appreciate the effort she'd gone to. She made wonderful candied yams (her hateful brother-in-law, Henri de Coligny, told her one time that in Europe sweet potatoes were only fed to swine), and pineapple upside-down cake.

She regularly made us floating island pudding, or *île flottante*, as it's called in France, which I love to this day more than any other dessert. Did my grandmother De Loney teach her that, or was it learned in an advanced class in dessert cooking at Barnard? She first showed me how to put a little coffee in my milk to make a kind of café au lait that was more palatable than pure milk to drink, and she knew how

My sister, Charlotte, 1944

to make popovers, which we ate on Sunday mornings, after Mass, dripping with butter.

But sometimes she said, "What the hell," and if my father was away, we'd go to a tiny shack just big enough for a greasy black skillet, a greasy red counter, and four or five stools, to buy a paper bag full of hamburgers, which cost ten cents apiece. We would bring them home and she would serve them to us on the same china I still use. They were delicious, but of course the meat patties were the thinnest possible, and what went on them was in no way remarkable; however, that short-order cook must have had flair. He sliced the lettuce into the thinnest imaginable strips, also the onions, and he laid a very thin piece of dill pickle on the vegetable matting and sprinkled it all with coarse salt. It was junk food for the poorest of the poor, but all my life I've been searching for that exact combination in a hamburger. And there was a hard-up woman we knew who made chicken with noodles in broth, which she put up in jars and took round from house to house. There were always a couple of slices of white meat, some sections of hard-boiled egg, some bits of green pepper, and the broth, which was brownish. I loved this concoction, of which I am reminded a bit by wonton soup, and I looked forward very much to this woman's coming and would ask when we could expect to see her again. This was also Depression food. We had to give the woman back her quart jars. I think one of these, full, cost a dollar.

My father always served us, passing my mother her plate first, before the guests, in a chivalrous gesture which I've rarely seen in other American houses. I was served last, after my sister, who sat opposite me frowning and kicking the pedestal of the table until it was, by the end of her restless childhood, almost fibrous. My father sat with his back to the plate-glass window, which looked onto the street, tipping his slender-legged Hepplewhite chair backward; we always waited for it to go over, or to split, but it never did. My mother sat with her back to the kitchen door, through which she would disappear and reemerge as required, until the advent of the maids, about 1939. My sister sat with her back to the handsome mahogany and satinwood sideboard, at which I preferred to look rather than at her scowling face, pleased with its lines and mass and color, and with the classical drawer pulls with their urns and embossed ribbons. And she no doubt looked right past me, or through me, and out another window behind me, up the street toward the house of her greatest chums, Billy and Jeannie Selby, waiting for them to appear from their own supper, upon which she would leave unceremoniously, slamming the front door, and, perhaps in her haste, dashing up against the polished swelling front of the sideboard, whereupon I would rise furiously from my chair in protest. (That sideboard is now safely in my house in Claverack, where it has become the drinks table of my adult life. But as A. R. Gurney maintains in one of his plays, dining rooms of

The old sideboard, now my drinks table

the old-fashioned, genteel sort seem to have disappeared from American life.)

My mother had embroidered all the seats of the dining chairs in needlepoint; there were roses and other flowers upon a dark green ground that grew more and more frayed as we got older, but her hands became so arthritic she was never able to repair the damage. The chairs passed in time to the bishop of Fresno, who gave them in turn to the little colony of Spanish nuns who came to live in our house after my father's death.

I wonder where those chairs are now. And the kicked dining table, which was made of very beautiful mahogany and had two leaves and a foolproof extension apparatus that anybody could operate. When my father died and I came home from New York and found the family assembled (my mother had died four years earlier), and the evening meal was about to be served, I had the table set in style, and then, for the only time, I took my father's place at the head of the table, and as head of the household. My sister glowered at me. It was a kind of power play and she knew it, and it was possibly not very tactful, although I think my aunt and uncles approved of this symbolic gesture. It was the last real family dinner in that house and at that table.

The Giant Orange

GIANT ORANGE: that was what the sign said. From a segment of the rind that rose on hinges during the business day, cold orange juice, squeezed to order, was dispensed and served in tall glasses full

of shaved ice. These establishments were once all along the main roads in the Sacramento and San Joaquin Valleys, and when you arrived in their vicinity, on a baking summer day, but were still several miles off, big orange signboards with black letters announced GIANT ORANGE JUST AHEAD! The closer you got, panting with thirst and desire for cold orange juice, the more the signs would promise, such as fresh limeade, hot dogs, and burgers; if you passed the Giant Orange, there was another sign that said YOU PASSED IT! TURN AROUND. I now realize these would seem today to be the tackiest kind of roadside stand to most people, but they are for me somehow a holdover and reminder of the old California that has completely and utterly disappeared, the California of fabled orange groves and Spanish haciendas, of a wacky generosity (the glasses were big, not like those little Styrofoam cups of juice you buy on Fifth Avenue in New York) amid bizarre surroundings that recall the early days of films.

The flat landscape, the bright orange, like an object in a De Chirico painting, casting a long shadow, with a couple of countrywomen standing cheerfully inside ready to put the orange halves into their juicers for you, the tall palm trees off in the distance surrounding a ranch, the red glow of the sun that is just setting behind the mountains between these valleys and the Pacific, the big insects smacking against the screens, the smell of earth, the whir of the juicer, the sucking on straws when only the ice remains, the grinding of tires on gravel as other thirsty travelers pulled into the parking lot . . . There are still a few of these left along Route 99, but the freeways have stranded them for the most part.

In the Rose Room

By 1938 my father had prospered enough so that we could go on long trips and take vacations in San Francisco. He first rented a cabin at Lake of the Woods that summer, after the reunion of my mother's part of the family, which he couldn't attend, in Port Arthur, Texas. In 1940 we began the trips to the City over the Christmas holiday that became a family tradition. San Francisco was always, in Klamath Falls, referred to as "the City"—one went down to the City: but Portland, to the north, almost the same distance away, was simply Portland, for it had no glamour attached to it, and was something of a cow town, for all its famous roses. The Christmas trip to the City coincided with my mother's birthday, December 29, and her birthday celebration was always held in the Rose Room of the Palace Hotel. After the war started, we began staying in the Palace, too. Before that we always stayed at the El Cortez, which was less expensive. I hate to think of my father as a war profiteer, but, like so many businessmen at the end of the Depression, he was not only lifted out of the slump by the fighting in Europe, and later in the Far East, but made his fortune from it.

The Palace was San Francisco's and the West's most famous hotel. It was built in the 1870s and in its Victorian incarnation lasted until 1906, when the earthquake and fire wiped it out, whereupon it was rebuilt on the same site at Market and Montgomery Streets. Its second life lasted to the end of the 1950s, when the hotels on Nob Hill came into their own. The Palace was very much in the Grand Hotel tradition, with presidents and European royalty and movie stars and millionaires staying there (Caruso was asleep in it when the earthquake struck; President Harding died there after a state visit to Alaska; a set of solid gold plates made from the ore of a Nevada mine was reserved for such grandees). It must have been a bit like the old Ritz in New York, catering to a less flashy clientele than the Nob Hill hotels, and its restrained décor, very French, very classical, must have been a pleasant contrast to the riot of gilt and cast iron within which Los Angeles hotels like the Biltmore enveloped their visitors.

The focus of the Palace was its Garden Court dining room, and there the architects and designers concentrated their efforts to produce what must surely have been the most beautiful hotel dining room in the country. Anyway, I've never seen a more beautiful one. Spatially it took your breath away—rather as the best Hyatt extravaganzas do now, and by employing the same technique: unexpected soaring height in an interior court, from which filtered down a diffused and magical-seeming radiance. Over what had once been the courtyard, where the carriages and cabs drove up to let out guests, the new hotel had built a glass dome like those in the Grand and Petit Palais in Paris. This was held up by columns of colored marble, and there was every kind of crystal chandelier imaginable: large,

My mother's birthday dinner, probably 1947. Seated, left to right: me; Doris Ethridge, a high school friend; Can't-Remember-His-Name but a few years later he shot his wife's lover dead in a Cal classroom and was imprisoned for his "crime of passion" for five years (he had been invited on this night as my sister's escort); my sister, Charlotte; my uncle Richard Carter; Mother; Dad; and my aunt Evelyn Carter. When the Carters went to visit the prisoner, he came to meet them in the visitors' room from the prison's tennis courts wearing his white tennis shorts.

Standing, center: Adolph, the Rose Room's grand maître d'.

Dancing in the Rose Room

The Garden Court

bead-covered globes that had a rosy light inside, and others dripping with lusters that flashed.

At lunchtime the place was brightly lit from the daylight coming through the dome, and with all the potted trees and palms and flowering shrubs the place was a bit like a greenhouse. Outside of picture books showing the Hall of Mirrors at Versailles, I had never seen anything like this room, which was consecrated to French cuisine, and presided over by Adolph, the impressive maître d'hôtel. He did not call my father by his first name, certainly. But he recognized him as a regular and important customer, and this pleased my father and made him expansive.

But all this is taking me too far away from my mother's birthday party, which was always held in the Rose Room, the hotel ballroom, in which a dance band played. It was less beautiful than the Garden Court, but the food and service were very good, of the sort that have almost entirely disappeared from hotels in this country. My father liked to order the whole dinner in advance and he worked out the courses without much reference to the wishes of his dinner party guests, who for the most part were old friends, who never came to the Palace except with my father, and who were too polite to attempt to change anything; or my aunt and uncle from Berkeley,* whose likes and dislikes my father knew. Over the years the menu became traditional, too, so we always knew that old favorites would all appear in due course. The dinner began with vichyssoise—the subject of much conversation if the guest was a first-timer, sipping dubiously—and progressed to the entrée, which was a sautéed fowl under a glass bell; a Palace specialty called green goddess salad was served with this—a delicious concoction made of very bitter endive and a dressing of fresh tarragon and anchovy, but so subtle that even I would eat it, and I hate anchovies. For dessert there was a flaming cherries jubilee, which Adolph came to light himself, and if we carried on long enough, a tray of French pastries was brought around, from which I selected something full of marzipan.

Between courses my parents got up to dance, my father vigorously swooping about if it was a waltz, bearing my mother with him in her dark blue or black dress (she never wore bright colors at night; she didn't say so, but I know now that in those far-off days a lady wouldn't); or if it was a fox-trot, working his elbows in a way that looked old-fashioned to me, but was probably the way he learned back in the days when people did the two-step, before the First World War. When I was older, I would get up to dance, too, and would show off the new, "smooth" steps I'd learned at the Saturday night armory dances in Klamath Falls.

My mother was a very good dancer, very light in my arms, and my sister wasn't bad, either. The music was the Guy Lombardo type, not too noisy. When I was in college and driving across the American deserts at night, I would sometimes get this kind of hotel dance-band music on the car radio, coming from places like Salt Lake and Denver, and it conjured up the whole scene of those birthday dinners for me. The cost of one of these was one hundred dollars or so. The

---

* Evelyn and Richard Carter. I called Evelyn, my mother's sister, Aunt VV. It was she who had been married to the detestable Henri de Coligny, whom she divorced.

bar bill was never very excessive; the grown-ups would have at the most two highballs and there would be some wine and champagne with dessert. Where wine was concerned, my father never really got it right in the accepted way. He wanted a sweet wine with everything. He found such a sweet wine and ordered it in quantity—Wente Brothers sauternes, made from sémillon grapes, and even took it around the country with him to make sure he could get it. I never could wean him away from this wine, which is meant for dessert. He drank it with fish or with roast beef, he didn't care. I once gave him a fancy coffee-table book called *The Great Wines of France* in order to instruct him, and I don't think he even cracked it.

In 1956 I gave my own last party in the Garden Court, a wedding lunch for friends of mine from college. By then Adolph had retired. The green goddess salad was decidedly limp and there were other signs of the restaurants going downhill. I think this was the last time I ever ate there, but before then I used the place a lot while I was in college, getting tight in the bars and ordering tidbits under a glass bell all around for my friends and signing the check nonchalantly.

When I got out of army basic training at Fort Ord near Monterey, California, in December 1953, my mother came to collect me in the family limousine, which rolled up to the door of the barracks, and into which I climbed, having given my duffel bag to the chauffeur in front of all the other departing privates and my commanding officers. That should have made me cringe, but it felt sweet, sweet. We drove up to San Francisco and stayed at the Palace in a suite. It was my mother's present to me before I left for my assignment in Georgia, in the signal corps. When we went into the Garden Court for dinner, and were seated beneath the crystal chandeliers, I was reluctant to put my hands up on the table where anyone could see them—like Scarlett O'Hara, who didn't want Rhett Butler to see that she'd been picking cotton—because they were so blackened and callused from basic training.

A note about my father's preference for old, traditional hotels like the Palace in San Francisco. After I had moved to New York City to live, my father came there from time to time to see me. My apartment, which I shared with Ismail Merchant, was too small for him to be comfortable in. So when he came to town for the premiere of *Shakespeare Wallah*, I reserved a room for him at the Plaza Hotel—the "grand" old hotel of my first years in New York, the hotel of 1920s celebrities like F. Scott Fitzgerald. My father slept there one night and the next day moved to the St. Regis. When he met me in Rome in 1963, the very good hotel I had booked us into (the Massimo d'Azeglio) wasn't good enough for Dad, and the next day we moved to the Eden—the "traditional" hotel of upper-class English visitors to Rome. Similarly—now taking over the hotel reservations himself—before we left for Venice he booked us into the Gritti Palace on the Grand Canal. How had he known about the Gritti? For sure he would not have read Hemingway's *Across the River and into the Trees*. Where had my father—a working-class Irish boy who grew up in a small upstate New York town—acquired his taste for traditional, old-style luxury hotels? And then I found out. During the First World War, when he had been obliged to be in Paris for any reason, our army, which had requisitioned the Hôtel de Crillon on the Place de la Concorde to house its officers, put him in there.

Before Ismail and I had bought our apartment on rue Bonaparte, the Crillon became my hotel of choice in Paris, and I still return to it when I can. I imagine my uniformed father there, a mere second lieutenant, moving about in the Crillon's splendid lobbies and marble halls, and ordering dishes in the dining room that came to his table under a dome to be lifted for his inspection by someone like Adolph at the Palace Hotel. Being wartime, what was revealed might not have been up to the Crillon's usual standard. Not as bad as in the previous century when Paris was under siege and the grand hotels drew lots for the animals in the zoo. As the story goes, the Ritz Hotel in the Place Vendome was allotted the elephant's trunk.

The Palace Hotel has since been bought by the Sheraton chain and is just another Sheraton hotel now. Like the Pelican Grill, it has been cleared out and "brought up-to-date." For all I know, the solid gold service has been melted down since celebrities no longer go there. The Palace now gets the sort of convention and mass tourist trade the other San Francisco hotels attract. So it no longer exists to excite impressionable boys from small towns out west, who, in any case, in the present world, would have very different ideas about what is exciting, glamorous, or beautiful.

Dramatics: Blomie

"Expression is an important factor of acting!"
says Roberta Blomquist as she delivers a lecture
to her seventh period drama class.

Roberta Blomquist was the dramatics teacher in my high school.* She did not do this in a part-time, after-hours way when she was done teaching English. There was a scheduled class for each grade, and you took dramatics for credit, and in your four years, starting out as a stagehand or ticket taker, you might become the star of the annual big production. Her classes attracted all the oddballs, the school

---

* The photo and caption above are from *El Rodeo*, Klamath Union High School's yearbook.

weirdos, the types who did not quite fit in anywhere else—just as she herself was regarded by the townspeople as being different, unusual, artistic.

When I first knew her, she must have been in her late forties. She was small and energetic, with an actress's mobile face. She had dyed red hair and her makeup and nail polish were an ensemble of rusts and terra-cottas that set off her white skin. Her clothes were dramatic: they were different from what our mothers wore and seemed to have been devised with less regard for what was currently fashionable in San Francisco, than with an eye to making a statement. She loved modernistic jewelry, and when she no longer taught in the high school, she turned her little house into a studio where she made and sold her own jewelry.

Blomie was divorced and nobody knew anything about her husband, who had disappeared long ago. She had a son who was killed in a car wreck when he was starting college. There was a picture of him in her living room; he was handsome and blond and looked as if he were turning out well, though the children of "artistic" people so often take refuge in conformity, so who can tell? She never spoke of him. That part of her life was over. Her life now was molding the sons and daughters of lumbermen and ranchers, and of the townspeople, into actors, stage designers, producers, and directors. She had as good material to work with as anyone, anywhere, and our high school was large. Students who took her classes because they thought it might be a breeze not only quickly found out that they had to work very hard—to "produce," as she kept saying—but were soon caught up in a world of competing and jealousies and temperament that mirrored the professional theater on far-off Broadway, and that they had to please a sharp-eyed, sharp-tongued impresario who knew all the tricks and was not above playing one person against another for the common good, which was her theater.

There were two seasons of this company. The first culminated in a production just before Christmas, one that had a vaguely inspirational feeling to it, heavy on visions and miracles, where we learned all about the artifice of the stage, with its lights fading up or going down, and transparent scrims that slowly revealed the unseen—the kind of theater that is intended to send a shiver through you. The big spring production was more "commercial," was usually a comedy, and took place on the much larger stage of the school auditorium, where there was more scope for set building than the small stage of Blomie's domain. In my sophomore year she put on *Arsenic and Old Lace*, and I played the visiting clergyman the two dear old ladies didn't get around to murdering, though I was also much involved in working on their Victorian parlor in Brooklyn, finding bits of old furniture and oil lamps and so forth in Goodwill shops.

These productions were much appreciated by the townspeople. They were amateur of course, but were put on by someone who knew perfectly well what to aim for, and they must have had a gloss to them. However, photographs in my yearbook from *She Stoops to Conquer*, put on when I was a senior and after I had opted to leave Blomie, don't really bear this out. One sees overpainted childish faces and wigs made out of rolls of cotton. Still, for the people who had never seen a play in a big city (and that would have been most people in Klamath Falls), Blomie's productions must have had their entertainment value.

Me in 1946, the year I graduated
from high school

In this respect I was luckier than my friends, for one of the features of my family's annual trip to San Francisco at Christmas was going to the Geary or Curran Theatre to see road shows of Broadway hits. The actors on those stages always seemed to talk much louder than Blomie's student actors; you could hear every word clearly, and when the audience laughed, the actors waited before continuing, whereas, if we were lucky enough to get a laugh, we plunged right on so that the next line or two were lost. Later on, Blomie would shout at us for this kind of thing, and she could really shout when she wanted to. She had a low, worldly sort of way of speaking, all her words modulated properly, as if she were "on" as we say now, nothing sloppy, and she could go from a whisper to a roar in a second; could be standing next to you giving you some little instruction, and then let blast at somebody up in the flies who was doing something wrong. This, I now know, was called "projection" and you don't get very far without it in the theater.

When she thought your attitude was bad, she could freeze you out. Then you were no longer in the charmed circle of her favorites and could get back in only through hard work and acts of humility—that is, if you wanted to get back in. One might be glad to be out, which I'm getting to in a minute. For instance, it is well-known that actors do not get haircuts the day before they open in a play. On the stage a raw haircut makes you look pinheaded. But if you are beginning to feel that your social life will be improved by a more orderly appearance, you may choose to go to the barber anyway, which is what I did in my senior year, when I had to play another old man in a production that featured the school bad girl as the Angel of the Lord. (When the lights went up and the football team sitting in the audience saw her

Klamath Union High School

in diaphanous white and wearing what looked like the Virgin Mary's Assumption crown, there was an uproar.) I was shaky on my lines, not always supplying the right cues, and Blomie had stuck false hair to my naked scalp with heavy applications of spirit gum. I have not acted on the stage since, thank god.

I had started out as one of Blomie's favorite and most promising students, in whom she was fanning the divine spark, and I ended up disappointing her, letting her down, letting myself and my talent down. I lost interest in "all this."

Gradually I came to feel that to be so involved in Mrs. Blomquist's theater was not cool (which meant in 1945 just what it means now), and that I was in danger of cutting myself off from those I saw as my peers.

By one's senior year the spark that Blomie fanned in some was

The annual Elks Club dance, held in the spring. The nicest of the
high school dances, perhaps because—at least to me—it was held
in a beautiful building, and not in a gym. I am on the far right
in the white dinner jacket (the only one in town; it must have
cinched my being named Most Stylish in our high school annual).
I'm dancing with my date, Joanne O'Neill, then between
boyfriends. Baldy's Band was playing.

by now quite a blaze, and it made me uneasy to be too much with these other students, who walked and talked in a funny way, and who drew attention to themselves by everything they did. These classmates were not usually from quite the best families; they were never asked to the right parties, and when there was a big high school dance, they did not go, so that when the gym rocked to the swing music of Baldy's Band, and we traded dances, writing our partner's name down beforehand in a little tasseled book, Blomie's crew might be found on the other side of the school painting flats until late at night. These people seemed to be the unwanted, the unchosen, the unfashionable. The exception to this was Ted Reeves.

Ted and his brother Fred were identical twins; unless you knew them well, you could not tell them apart. Their father was the kindly manager of Safeway's; their mother was a sometimes malicious, small-minded woman who loved to gossip.* They did not have much money and lived in a small stucco house too close to the Southern Pacific Railroad track, but none of this in any way impaired their social success. Ted and Fred had always been popular, starting at Roosevelt grade school—*the* elementary school of the town, in the best neighborhood—and when they got to high school, they became more so. It was partly because they were twins, and partly because of their easy, outgoing personalities and physical energy. Almost at once they went on the cheerleading team, dressed in identical white sweaters and white pants, and in time became twin cheerleaders.

I can still see them stretched taut, leaping into the air at football games doing the yell called Locomotive K. They had neat, trim bodies and possessed great physical charm, but were not conventionally handsome, with their ski-slope noses (like Bob Hope's) and bad acne. It was always a pleasure to watch them at work; they made you feel good, and Klamath Union was envied by other high schools in the state because of the presence of Ted and Fred at football and basketball games.

---

* She once said to my mother, while they sat on a log by the water at Lake of the Woods, as her teenage sons, in their revealing, water-soaked bathing suits, horsed around in front of them, "My boys will make the girls they marry very happy someday."

My favorite at once was Ted. But it took me two years to become his inseparable friend. Even though I had known Fred since I was a child and we had played together, I never quite warmed to him. Fred was as conventional in his ideas and ambitions as Ted was unconventional. By our junior year a group of us had formed a clique of boys and girls; everyone worth knowing belonged to it, no one else counted. And at the center of that clique were Ted and me. We had similar interests. Both of us liked to draw and paint and design, and we joined the Art Club. We worked on the school newspaper, where I wrote a gossip column, and he provided cartoons.

The other thing we had in common was our immersion in Blomie's theater. Ted not only worked on the sets, he also became one of her main actors, and when we put on *Arsenic and Old Lace* he played the loony brother who thinks he's Teddy Roosevelt charging San Juan Hill. He did everything with a conviction and a sweet generosity, and somehow, because of that, Blomie never held it against him that he had so many interests, even though she warned him that he might ruin his vocal cords with all that cheering.

I knew quite soon that I loved and desired Ted, and since he seemed to prefer me to anybody else—except his girlfriend, Carmen—I

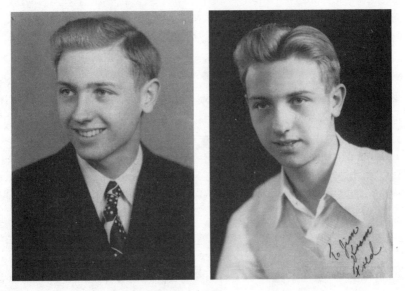

Ted (left) and Fred (right) Reeves, age seventeen

never got jealous. I had had crushes before, but they petered out. My feeling for Ted was more profound; I knew that it contained a very strong sexual attraction. I did not feel at all guilty about this, but I was determined not to let him suspect it, nor the intensity of my feelings for him, in case he then rejected me. We never took a gym class together, never swam nude in the big old school natatorium, so it was a long time before I ever saw him naked, and when I did, undressing and dressing in my bedroom where he had come to stay the night once, I stole a look at his heavy, charged-looking cock, of the sixteen-year-old, end-of-the-garden-hose variety, and felt my mouth go dry and my hands shake.

In the same term a bunch of us went on an overnight trip to attend a basketball game in nearby Ashland. Of course Ted and Fred had to go in order to lead the cheering, and their girlfriends came, too. I didn't have a regular girlfriend; when I needed to ask someone to one of the school proms, I invariably asked a girl from our clique who was momentarily at odds with her own boyfriend, or between boyfriends. That weekend, however, I did not have to bother about anything but sticking as close as possible to Ted, and when he walked Carmen back to where she was staying, I went along. There was a song made famous then by Bing Crosby called "Let's Take the Long Way Home," which we sang as we escorted her. The mood was a romantic one for me. I knew I would very shortly be the one to go to bed with Ted, not Carmen, despite the good-night kiss he would be giving her. Once she was safely inside we would go to our hotel, where we would get into the same double bed and fall asleep—if not in each other's arms, then side by side I knew, our bodies brushing together all night.

I woke early next morning very conscious of my need to take Ted in my arms, and conscious, too, of the danger of such an action. I lay next to him, listening to him breathe, and wondered if he was also awake. I imagined holding him and putting my hands all over his body. Then, without touching him or myself, I just flowed over, you might say, in a kind of waking wet dream. I was prone at sixteen to these outpourings, and if Ted ever noticed any of this that morning, he said nothing. I got up at once and washed myself off, and we went back to Klamath Falls on the bus, having let our moment pass.

We were together all the following summer of 1945, going to Lake of the Woods every weekend. During the week we did manual labor at the naval airfield, so we were always around each other. The Japanese surrendered and we celebrated the end of the war, and looked forward to our senior year knowing we wouldn't be called up.

But then things began to go wrong between Ted and me. It seemed he was avoiding me, and he was spending too much of his time with one of Blomie's stalwarts, a kid named Lou, who was definitely not our sort, as far as I could tell. We never argued, but we just weren't that close anymore. On another game trip, this one to Bend, I had wanted to ride on the bus with Ted, and instead he had asked Lou to sit up in front next to him. I couldn't imagine what was happening, and the more he seemed to keep me at arm's length, the more insistent I became, the more possessive, the more jealous.

ONE DAY BLOMIE called me into her little office to tell me something important. I wasn't getting along with her any better. It was about this time that she had stuck the spirit gum in my hair; things were definitely at a low point between us. So I waited apprehensively to hear what she had to say. And she told me that there was a bad, evil-tongued kind of person in this world, who would say irresponsible and damaging things about one out of spite and jealousy, and that our town had its share of persons like that—persons of a low class, who thought low, dirty things. And this person, or persons—she never told me who it was—had been spreading gossip about Ted and me, had been saying that our friendship was, well, of a nature that could only mean . . . and here she trailed off into silence to let it all sink in.

I had never heard any of the words which commonly are used in such situations: homosexual, fairy, pansy, queer, faggot, and of course not gay, which had only a limited currency then. And I did not hear them from Blomie, either, but that is what she meant. I thanked her and went home to think all this over. I felt no sense of shame or horror that I was being talked about in this way—if I was, for I wasn't sure I believed her. Instead I seized an opportunity to get out of her class, and out of her world of plays and dedicated souls in tacky clothes who had to paint scenery because they had nothing better to do. I did not tell my parents what she said, for fear of stirring them up, and for fear that they would forbid me to see Ted anymore. Instead I told them that I didn't think Blomie was a good person at all, and that I could no longer go on in her class and risk exposure to such a doubtful influence. I must have convinced them—perhaps I had even convinced myself of this—and I must have been a good enough actor to make them think I knew what was best for myself, without at the same time alarming them, either, probably just trailing off into silence when speaking of the unnameable just as I had seen her do.

Then I went to her and said that I was very sorry, but my parents thought it was best that I not go on in her classes anymore, that teachers who knew of and talked about such things as she had mentioned to me were themselves suspect . . . I think she must have been dreadfully hurt by the turn things had taken, and of course she could not risk taking it up with my parents. We parted, and I felt a great sense of relief that I had managed to talk myself out of her class so neatly. Now I was free to spend my time in more acceptable ways.

AND SOON AFTER I broke off with Ted, too. On the trip to Bend, when he had not let me sit with him on the bus (I got there on my own, I think, on another bus), I was sitting all by myself feeling rather forlorn in the town's best restaurant when I noticed two boys from the class below me at Klamath High,

Charlotte Carter and Bob Thompson

Dick Yates and his friend Larry Klahn. They seemed so happy with each other, so close, laughing about something, and I felt a pang that I didn't have a friendship like that with anyone now; and perhaps, too, I recognized that there was no trace of the sexual in it, that these were two "normal" young men that people wouldn't gossip about, except in relation to the girls they were taking out.

Not long after that, in one of those shifts that take place in high school, I stopped bothering about Ted, and managed to make friends with Dick Yates. Dick had a "best friend" named Milton Thompson, brother of the currently reigning senior star, Bob Thompson, a figure of glamour who had just moved to town from Salem, the state capitol. Their father ran the bank. Bob was a handsome, if sometimes wooden figure, like Gregory Peck; he was perfection, in his faded white corduroys and Arrow shirts, and played football, and his remoteness made him seem sophisticated—I think, in fact, he was voted "Most Sophisticated" in the school annual. He was like a god, and all the girls tried to "trap" him, as the expression went. My great intimate Charlotte Carter managed to do this, and our group rearranged itself. Ted Reeves was left to get on with his dramatics and what remained of his career as a cheerleader, and at that time, too, Carmen started going with our class president, Jimmy Howard, who, with his guns and duck hunting, and Rotary Club thoughts, was John Wayne to Bob Thompson's Gregory Peck. We were all, in a way, anticipating the new alliances that college brings.

All the rest of that year and through the summer, before I left for the University of Oregon, I stuck close to Dick and Milt. I came to appreciate the latter. He was a bundle of vagrant impulses that the family had stifled in the perfect Bob. He had a crooked smile and a wheezing laugh, he was deathly afraid of heights, nobody had told him about underarm odor, and he had eczema on his hands.

Every weekend we went skiing at Crater Lake, and from being *très artistique* I turned most improbably to being *très sportif.* The three of us went up the mountain in my parents' blue Oldsmobile, usually taking two or three girls along. There were no lifts to pull you up the slopes and no comfortable chalet where you could sit in front of a fire and drink cocoa. There was just snow, and pines, and great sweeping views of peaks and valleys, and silence, broken only by our huffing and puffing up, or gliding down as our skis broke the snow's crust.

Bob Thompson was there, too, with Charlotte, sailing down imperturbably like some damned Winged Victory from the Winter Olympics. And never, during any of this, did I think of Ted, whom I had buried away, and on graduation night when I took a party to Lake of the Woods, I did not ask Ted and Fred to join us.

Ted and Fred are an example of people whose lives peak in high school. In a larger world they would never have so much attention again, for college did not work out well for either. We all went up to the University of Oregon, but they both soon flunked out. That year, 1946, was the first one when returning veterans enrolled in great numbers and the competition was keen. Ted went into the School of Architecture and Allied Arts with me, but he couldn't study, or retain the lecture material, or pass the examinations; Fred took a premed course and didn't do any better. By spring semester they were both gone.

I had seen them from time to time, and had invited them to a Christmas party at which my father served drinks to everybody—unwisely perhaps, as two or three of the guests got drunk and were driven round and round until they sobered up. Mrs. Reeves complained the day after on the phone that Mr. Ivory was corrupting her sons by offering them alcohol, but everybody just laughed at her.

The next year Ted entered the Portland Museum Art School, and Fred continued at Southern Oregon State Normal School in Ashland. After that—for about fifteen years—I rarely saw them and heard about them only through mutual friends. They had slipped into the anonymity that awaits most small-town people. Both married and had children. Fred became a teacher and Ted took up window decorating for a men's store in San Francisco called Roos-Atkins.* When any of us did meet, however, we had only friendly feelings.

In 1966 we held our twentieth high school reunion. Before that I had heard some rumors about Ted. They passed from cabin to cabin at Lake of the Woods but lacked specifics, and had come from a doubtful and unpopular source: Charlotte Carter Fey's mother-in-law, who lived in San Francisco. It seemed that Ted had been asked to resign his job at Roos-Atkins because of a homosexual scandal of some kind involving one of the other employees, and the story had it that the two were actually caught in the act.

I could not help thinking of Ted and whoever the other poor wretch was being exposed in one of Ted's windows, the shade springing up on some lewd tableau, and Ted, discovered thus, smiling his big, ingratiating cheerleader's smile. He had separated from his wife as well, who (Mrs. Fey said) had gotten fed up with all the carryings-on, and they both now shared custody of their daughter.

---

* One of my certain destinations on my annual winter visits to San Francisco for my mother's birthday was the Roos-Atkins men's store, where I could find the kind of sharp clothes I wanted. It would be years before the men's stores in Klamath Falls stocked stuff like theirs. I had not discovered Brooks Brothers yet—that would come during my college years, when I began to read *The New Yorker*—though Brooks Brothers did have a fine outlet on San Francisco's Union Square, the best upscale shopping area in the city. Roos-Atkins had the most desirable sweaters—no one in my high school had anything like them. They were the 1940s fashion equivalent of today's wild T-shirts.

When our reunion took place, incredibly (to me) Ted brought a young man to it. Everyone else had wives, or like me came alone or with a woman. Little was made of this then. Gay lib hadn't really begun yet, and we were perhaps too innocent as a group to take in the significance of what Ted had done. Ten years later, the room would have been buzzing; and I feel that ten years from now no one would give a damn.

Everyone at a reunion takes up their old persona, goes back into the skulls of eighteen-year-olds. It doesn't matter that the boy voted Most Likely to Succeed has become an alcoholic pauper, or the person whose name and face you can't recall is now a millionaire. There were Ted and Fred, smiling, ebullient, laughing their loud laughs, horsing around; two decades of trouble and lack of distinction fell away. They were popular, the center of attention again. They still looked pretty good, though their hair was thinning. They had the same neat figures and their acne had cleared up. Ted still bit his fingernails. Fred still wore his hair swept up from his brow in a 1940s wave. They no longer dressed alike. At Ted's side was this tall, easygoing, good-looking youth, too old to be a son, and too young to be one of the husbands. So it is all true, I thought.

The reunion continued at Lake of the Woods in a series of smaller parties. Ted and I drove up alone together. I don't recall how this had been arranged, but it was in the air that we would have a talk. We were able to proceed from a point of unspoken mutual acknowledgment, and I was no more reticent than he.

Here I have a gap in my memory. Perhaps it is true: we remember events of long ago much better than things that have happened to us recently. Possibly I did not talk to Ted until three summers later, when he reappeared in Klamath Falls. That would have been 1969, when I was at the lake with my sister, for I remember her being there when Ted was. We must have—he and I—had an unspoken agreement then that we would get together, or a feeling that that was possible now, and was what we both wanted. We sat around the cabin for the few hours he was there and my sister never left us alone. I had the impression that she was watching us, that she suspected us. She, too, would have heard rumors by then, and she must long since have figured me out.

Probably it was on this occasion that Ted and I had our talk. We were in the car, he was driving, and he was so open about himself, said such leading things in order to draw me out, that I ended up confessing about the hotel room in Ashland where we slept together, and where just his presence next to me in bed was enough to make me come, and my feelings for him when we were in high school. Not a reluctant confession by any means. And then he told me, as we drove up the road we had so often gone up and down—now paved; twenty-five years earlier it had been a dusty rutted trail—that he had been in love with me then, and so much so that he was afraid I would find out and break off with him out of disgust; and that when I had broken off, without warning and without a word, in order to run around with Dick and Milt, he had felt terrible, abandoned by his best friend. And he told me about Lou, for I was curious about how he had "gotten started": Lou had seduced him our senior year. They used to go to Lou's house; his parents were never at home. Ted was afraid I might learn of this through somebody, but he didn't want to give Lou up because he liked their times together so much; these were his first experiences. Of course, how much better if they had been with me instead, I thought. Yes, how much better that would have been, remembering my own first experiences.

In talking with Ted about all these things as well as other matters, I came to feel that here was a person who deserved much better than he had managed to get out of life. He was far more sensitive and responsive than I had thought, and a good deal more intelligent than anybody gave him credit for. He had a naturally optimistic nature and a sense of humor, and his sweet generosity was intact, despite the things that had happened to him. He now knew that he would never make a name for himself, or ever do any of the things he had talked about with Blomie, but I had done them, and that was as thrilling as if they had happened to him: the films that got my name into *Time* magazine, my living in New York, the trips all over the world, the money that undoubtedly was a part of this worldly success. He had kept all the clippings of our films and when I went to see him once in Portland, he got them out, and played the LP record of *The Guru*.

In 1973 I was again at Lake of the Woods, and for a couple of days by myself. I called Ted up—he was living in Portland then—and asked him down. He came right away. We went to a tavern with Charlotte Carter Fey—now Abbey—and drank beer and talked about people we knew; Ted only wanted to talk about his new interest in Native American life. He had been initiated into a tribe and he showed us a photograph of himself as a brave, with a bonnet of eagle feathers on his head. He was learning all about Indian religions, about their crafts and social customs. It was hard to get him off this topic.

He and I went back to the cabin and sat in front of the fire and drank wine. The pauses in our conversation got longer and longer, the air more and more charged with thoughts of our past and with the possibilities of the moment: two adults who had had such strong feelings for each other and who were now sitting together intimately, and getting a little loose on wine. I suggested that we turn in and we went into the bedroom my parents had used, which I had taken over. We looked at each other a moment and then he touched me, ever so lightly and a bit humorously, on my fly. This made me assume an air of sulky coyness for a little while—my god, the things we do to people we know love us!—and I acted as if I needed to claim every advantage, however belatedly. I had to let him think that what we were doing was some kind of privilege—almost as if I were straight and out of an old affection and for old time's sake had consented to unusual intimacy with him.

I told him to undress and he stripped and stood in front of me presenting himself, unabashed, smiling the same somewhat goofy and endearing smile that had so beguiled me at seventeen. Well, about twenty-eight years had passed. Undoubtedly he was somewhat worn, somewhat stringy. He had never become the muscled, intimidating figure his father had urged him, for his own sake, to become.

But I didn't wait any longer. I stopped playing games, and pulled him down onto the bed beside me. I lay there, propped up on one elbow, as I looked at his naked body extended next to mine, and at his shapely, still attractive feet, moving my own up against them at last.

WHY DID MR. Reeves hope his sons would become muscled, intimidating figures for their own sakes? When Blomie warned me about low, jealous persons, she had been speaking about an element in school, and in the town, who hated our clique. I think she didn't imagine there were people who actually wanted to do physical harm to Ted and me—though what I'm about to describe had already happened to us, she knew of it, and it gave weight to what she said.

Earlier in the school year, Ted and I were coming out of a hamburger shack one night with a friend named Donald Eittreim when three unknown youths came up to us out of the darkness. One of them asked Ted: "Are you Ted or Fred?" When Ted identified himself, the kid punched him in the face and knocked him down between the parked cars. When I started to shout, I was hit in the mouth by another boy named (I found out later) Chili Mitchell. Donald Eittreim wasn't hit for some reason and our assailants jumped into their car and drove off fast. The whole thing must have lasted about a minute. We didn't know how badly we'd been cut up until we got home and could look in the mirror.

Strength and Health, September 1944

Our parents were amazed; our fathers could not understand why we hadn't fought back, but putting that aside, they proceeded to bring the boys to justice. Since we did not know who they were, they called the principal after talking to the police, and when Chili Mitchell, who had a bad record, bragged the next day in one of his classes of having beaten up some of the "400,"* an informant turned him in. The boys were arrested and formally accused of assault and battery and brought swiftly to trial, as an example. We had to take the witness stand and be asked whether the defendant's fists had actually connected with our faces. I pointed to my swollen lip as evidence.

Two of the boys were sentenced to six months in a juvenile detention home and the third was let off on probation. Each was sentenced separately, watched by his victim. When the third was being led out, he suddenly began to scream and shake his fist in our direction, vowing to get even. Judge Vandenberg (best known throughout the town for wearing bow ties) returned, we all rose again, he banged his gavel, and gave six months to the last boy as well. The parents of those three sat miserably through the proceedings: men and women who had humble jobs, who might even have been working in my father's mill or unloading the Safeway trucks for Mr. Reeves.

Our fathers decided that we had been taken advantage of because we looked like pushovers; we were thin and weak and an invitation to toughs like Chili Mitchell. Since I weighed 118 pounds, then I suppose that must have been true, but Ted and Fred were decently muscled. Still, it was decided that we would have to go to a private gym to work out, to lift weights, and all the rest of it. It was an early version of a health spa and catered to mostly older men who were getting out of shape. We went three nights a week, Fred, too.

Neither of my parents seemed to have Victorian attitudes about nudity. If I walked in on my mother in her bedroom, and she was naked, she calmly continued to dress. I knew I was not to stare. She had been brought up by her mother as an agnostic, if not an atheist. Grandmother De Loney bravely chose to take her brood on nature walks on Sundays rather than to the Presbyterian services in their little Louisiana town of Bogalusa, where she first met my father, a Catholic. When I was a child, he easily moved about naked in front of us upstairs, no doubt secure in his belief that generally males inhabited and had to make their way in a "world of men." This seemed to

---

* The old nickname, bestowed in the 1880s, to the top New York gentry, the group of "best" people, who could fit into Mrs. Astor's ballroom.

apply to women as well, though he must have donned a towel when my sister was around. But she and I were much more prudish as we grew older.

When Dad came into the steam room at the bodybuilders where I was made to work out after having been beaten up, I felt very uncomfortable, at sixteen, to be found by him sitting there exposed with my abundant crop of pubic hair and my new grown-up penis, both of which I had carefully kept hidden from my parents. He sized me up approvingly: in that department, at least, I seemed to him to have developed normally, even if my biceps were pitifully small.

I don't think I ever added a millimeter of muscle to my little biceps and I hated going, except that Ted was there with me and I liked the part unconnected to the exercises—the warm glow of the less public parts of the place: the rooms where massages were given, the showers and steam room, and the ultraviolet sunbathing booth, where you lay for two or three minutes in order to get one of those July-in-December tans.

I used to see Ted and Fred lying side by side under that eerie light, which turned their lips, their nails, and their cock-tips a deep purple. It always moved me to see them lying there like that—the Beloved and his double—but I did not desire Fred; it was only Ted I wanted. If ever proof was needed that physical desire is born out of the mixture of the spirit, or the intellect, and the accidents of upbringing that we call personality, for me it is that fact: I never considered Fred for an instant, and yet his body was the exact duplicate of Ted's. Or, to put it another way, his interest for me at such times lay merely in his being Ted's double. By staring at Fred I was satisfying my curiosity about Ted.

AFTER BEING TOGETHER at Lake of the Woods in 1973, I saw Ted two more times in Portland—once in 1975, and again in 1977. He was living in a house he bought in a pleasant neighborhood when he came to live permanently in Portland after the San Francisco upheaval and his divorce. He was working for a big department store again as a window decorator—he was the head of display, but he thought there

were factions in the store who were out to get him and he wasn't
sure how long he could hold out. He told me all this without rancor
or bitterness. He had a friend named Jim with whom he had been
living, an intelligent young man who was a great book collector, buying up remaindered books and first editions and art volumes with an
eye to opening up a mail-order bookstore in Portland. Ted's house
was packed with Jim's inventory. But Jim moved in with somebody
else, someone closer to his own age, who shared a house with his
mother. Ted and I went there to dinner once. Jim's friend had cooked
a provincial city gourmet meal and I was astonished to see him sit
afterward and fondle Jim in his mother's presence, running his hand
through his hair and so on as he sat on the arm of Jim's chair.

The 1977 visit with Ted happened when I went to Portland to
show *Roseland* to Michael Murphy, one of the film's financiers, and I
went out to Ted's house for a little while. He was hanging on to his
job somehow. He looked a little bent, but I felt that if he'd wanted to
he could have leapt up several feet in the air and given the school
yell: "With a K, with a K, with a K–L–A . . ."; as usual he was very
happy to see me, and presented two dark-skinned youths who sat
solemnly on the sofa. One was a Native American boy, the other

Ernest Vincz, Geraldine Chaplin, James Ivory, and Ismail
Merchant on the set of *Roseland* (1977)

was Mexican, both in their midteens. The Native American lived in the house with Ted and shared his bed. Both were woefully ignorant and I asked Ted where they were going. "Oh," he said, "they're going cruising. There's a toilet in a bar near here that everybody uses." He told me this in a perfectly matter-of-fact way; it seemed quite natural to him.

He drove me back to my hotel and on the way he told me that all his life he had been looking for someone like me. Not only had I been an inspiration to him, but he had always tried to find someone who was like me in personality and appearance, but never had. He described that idealized vision of myself, the friend he'd always wanted—someone with dark hair, someone slim, someone handsome, someone with class and style, and I wondered if he could see any of that in the white-haired person sitting next to him with the thickening waist and the liver-spotted hands any more than I could.*

I came back into Blomie's good graces in my forties. I always went to see her when I was in Klamath Falls. She was then about seventy, but still very active, making her jewelry and exhibiting it, sometimes selling it, and keeping up with her favorite students, most of whom failed to do anything with the talent she thought she saw in them, or who used it in a different way. Her hair was no longer red; she wore a blonde wig, but her face was the same, as were her theatrical voice and her memory. She could tell you what happened to anybody you wanted to remember, and as she was interested in character and the drama in people's lives you didn't get a flat account from her, but something she worked up a bit, which had an artistic shape and emphasis.

It was as if she had seen everything happen in our town, and knew that things would turn out, and people, too, in a predictable way, people being what they are. Sometimes she reminded me of a benign old witch—when she was younger. she used to entertain at children's parties as one; in fearful makeup and black clothes, roaring out spells

---

* The last time I saw Ted and Fred was at the final reunion of our high school class in 1996, fifty years after graduating. They were the life of the party and center of attention as always. Ted had gotten out of his immersion in Native American life and had turned to genealogy and the Scottish roots of the Reeves family. He was dressed in the tartan of his clan and wore the complete kit: kilt, tailored jacket which suited

and prophecies—hovering above the town and pulling strings on her marionette people.

She told me once that when she first arrived in Klamath Falls in the early 1930s from Walla Walla, Washington, she stood out in front of the high school, which was built on a hill, and saw in the distance—it was night—the burners from the big sawmills glowing red in the darkness, like a circle of volcanoes, and she had decided that this was the town for her.

---

him very well, sporran, and tam-o'-shanter. I think all our remaining class members were far more astonished and interested in his most recent transformation and new identity than they had been when at our twentieth reunion he brought that handsome young man as his date.

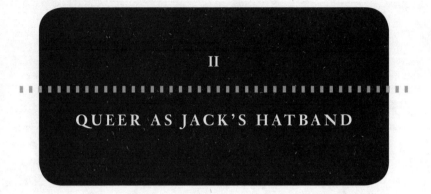

II

QUEER AS JACK'S HATBAND

The Boy Who Would Not Speak

Perhaps thy lot in life is higher
Than the fates assign to me
While they fulfil thy large desire
And bid my hopes as visions flee
But grant me still in joy or sorrow
In grief or hope to claim thy heart
And I will then defy the morrow
Whilst I fulfil a loyal part.

MEMORY SKETCH OF MARTIN GAY, BY EMERSON
In his Journal for 1821

I'm reading Caleb Crain's *American Sympathy*. In the section having to do with Emerson, there is a lot about another student at Harvard named Martin Gay, on whom Emerson had a crush. They never spoke—Gay was a couple of years younger—and never actually met, but Crain writes that each was aware of the other. At one point, as each rounded the corner of a building at Harvard at the same moment, they almost collided. Theirs was a romance—if you can call it that—of exchanged glances. Some were prolonged, Crain writes, others slight;

some suggested a possible recognition of a shared desire to know each other better. But this never happened. Through discreet inquiries Emerson learned that Gay at one point had led a student rebellion; he also found out that Gay was insufficiently studious. For a few years Emerson wrestled with his fascination with Gay, which was also disturbingly erotic. Emerson made a drawing of Gay, which he saved.

This sad story reminds me of myself when I was fifteen. There was a boy who moved into our neighborhood in Klamath Falls—I never learned which was his street or house—on whom I developed a similar crush. He was a stranger, and in the clique-dominated high school we both went to, that was not good. I myself belonged to no clique yet, though I viewed the different ones from afar and waited to be chosen. The boy—the stranger—was fine-looking. Handsome, light-haired, pleasingly light-framed, and I seem to remember that for his age, he was deep voiced. How I knew this I don't know, for we never spoke.

I often walked to school. So would he. The distance was about a mile and a half. We would join up at the corner of El Dorado and Manzanita Street, where my house was, without speaking, or even a salutation, when we would fall into step. It took about a half hour for us to walk to Klamath Union High if we took a shortcut across the football field. I wonder now how I timed up my meeting with him. Would I have waited at a window, or on the front porch of my house until I saw him come along El Dorado? Did I carefully, morning after morning, time my arrival at our meeting point to coincide with his?

Why did we never speak? The silence must have been awkward for both of us. A bit weird even. But there was some sort of silent communication, because we walked together quite often. Sometimes I was driven to school, but I never invited him to join me in the car. If we had ever passed him on the street—which never happened—I'm sure I would have stopped to pick him up. When we arrived at school after walking there together, he went his way and I went mine. We were in different homerooms and we never shared a class. Nor did I ever find him naked in the gym showers, which I very much hoped to do.

In time he found some friends. But they didn't belong to any sort of group or clique that meant anything. He was not an athlete, nor a scholar, nor social. I never saw him at one of the school dances. But he attracted me and wove a kind of silent web of desire around me on those mornings of my sophomore year when we walked to school together without ever exchanging a word.

By my junior year he was gone. I never knew his name.

Jimmy Boyd

For some reason—it may merely have been that we were "sharp" dressers, with the right sweaters and shoes and Arrow starched shirts in muted blues—Jim Boyd and I became attracted to each other in high school, and then close friends. "Attracted" is the word, though not in its more usual erotic sense, but rather to our careful ensembles that caught one another's eye. For me, there was for sure the expected physical attraction: Jim would be voted Cutest Brunette in his class yearbook of 1945. He was certainly that: handsome, with wavy hair, not too tall, but trim, with a soft, come-on look in his brown eyes. He wasn't brainy, had no interest in sports or school politics, but he was always "cool." As I've said earlier, that overused word had the same meaning in the 1940s as today, and Jim exemplified it. He ran around with the clique of other senior boys who had as little interest in team sports as he (and I) had, and who were also cool: Jack Anker (Best Dancer), Chuck Perry (Most Poised), George Bell (Most Sophisticated), and Nicky Demetrokas, who was killed in a car wreck early in his senior year but mourned by the whole school as a darling. These boys were a year ahead of me; in no sense did I belong to their clique (I had my own), but I developed a special relationship with George Bell and Jim. With George I had a sort of edgy love-hate affair. Our personalities attracted each other, and there was a kind of respectful interest in what one another did and said (often catty) and how we presented ourselves to the world. We knew that all three of us were stars of that high school's social scene, and had the pick of the cutest girls. Not me—I had no interest in going steady with anybody. Both George and Jim went with sophomore girls, who again had their own clique.

Somewhere along the way, during my junior year, we gravitated toward each other, Jim and I—two Jims, or two Jimmys, among many of that name. I invited him to our cabin at Lake of the Woods, and he came; he and I for some reason took a train trip down to Oakland, California, together and stayed with his aunt, sleeping—again together—in a double bed, where one morning I ejaculated during a dream I was having, the signs of which, when I woke up, I tried to hide, without losing my own cool.

Jimmy Boyd

I seem to have had many of these overflows when sleeping in a bed with my friends, as with Ted Reeves in Ashland. But that

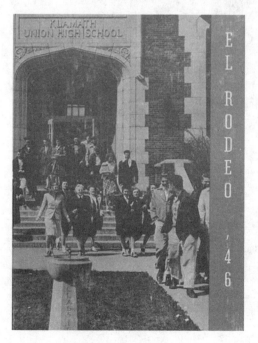

one was prompted by a wide-awake desire, while this time in Oakland it was the work of my subconscious as I lay sound asleep. Sexually of course Jim *did* interest me, but that sort of thing, while imaginable in fantasies, was indeed unspeakable, to be kept hidden. All you could do back then was to hope that sooner or later the object of your desire would undress in front of you in order to get into or out of a bathing suit, or, even better, shower with you in the school's gym; at such moments it was imperative to be on hand without seeming to be, in order to make quick visual contact at least, the only kind available, if not too prolonged. One summer day before a swim I timed it right. I can remember the Cutest Brunette's uncut dick exactly—as I can see that of the yearbook's Best Dancer, also a sharp dresser, with its dangling, pink foreskin that I still recall, shaped like the ones on ancient marble statues illustrated in our copy of Will Durant's *The Life of Greece*. I remember the Best Dancer when he was clothed, too: he liked to wear pale, cool-looking pastel

YUP! THEY EVEN wore shoes . . . and socks too! The honor of being most stylish this year goes to Charlotte Carter and Jim Ivory.

sweaters and had platinum blond hair. Most Sophisticated was cut, observed by me in Klamath High's locker rooms and showers, or undressing in the corrugated iron shed where the men and boys changed at a local swimming hole in Olene, on the way to my father's sawmill at Bly.

In the 1946 yearbook, *El Rodeo* (The Roundup), I would be voted

Most Stylish, though I aspired to be Most Witty. The truest wits, however, were invariably girls (now, as old women, they can still make me laugh). I must have glimpsed the naked male bodies in Jim's class of the Most Studious, Best Executive, and Most Ambitious. But neither their bodies nor their personalities attracted me. These were people who generally lacked looks and style—"star" qualities I went after, even then. Jimmy Boyd and his worldly gang had these.

Sometime in my senior year, Jim had to go into the armed services. He had picked the navy, and left one wintry dawn on a train from the Southern Pacific station in Klamath Falls. Of course I went to see him off, as did his girlfriend, Lynden King. World War II had ended in the summer of 1945, so Jim must have been going to a reserve call-up of some kind. He was certainly not going off to fight, but his leave-taking was as full of drama for us as if he had been. It was an awkward scene on the platform. We embraced stiffly, if we did—back then men did not embrace, certainly not one's male high school friends. On thinking about this again, probably we only shook hands, Jim and I. Lynden kissed him as passionately as

Lynden King

decorum allowed. One thing is certain, though, and that is I, too, wanted to kiss him goodbye, and on his lips, like Lynden, and—most likely—after Lynden had, in order to assert (wrongly, madly) some preeminence I felt. It should have been me to kiss him last.

But Jim—did he sense my madness?—jumped aboard when the train first moved, and Lynden and I had to run along beside it, waving to him as he stood in the open doorway. She must have been

thinking, Why the hell is that stupe Jimmy Ivory seeing my boyfriend off in this way! She had called me a "stupe" out of exasperation
when she inscribed my yearbook.

The train was taking him out of my life and away from hers, actually. I received many letters from Jim written while he was going
through basic training. I haven't reread them, because I can't find
them, though I never throw letters like his away. But I remember
one or two of them as being surprisingly emotional, and surprisingly
affectionate. I imagine that Lynden eventually told him that she had
begun to date someone else. He would have been homesick and fed
up with being in the military in peacetime, and sick as well of his
navy uniform, being always such a sharp dresser.

When he returned in a couple of years, I was already at the University of Oregon, which he chose as well. He at once pledged one of
the grandest fraternities, Phi Delta Theta, but I remained an Independent. Our friendship, which seemed to draw away from us mutu-
ally then, like a familiar shore receding from a boat, had one curious
detail that still bound us together: we shared a pair of dark blue dress
slacks. I have no idea how it came to pass that we owned a pair of
pants together. Maybe they were mine. But sometimes he needed to
wear them for a big occasion—for what? a date? an alumni dinner?—
and when he did, I arranged for him to get them without my actually
delivering them to the Phi Delt house personally. When *I* needed the
pants, he brought them back. Neither of us seemed to see the humor
in this joint possession or recognize the irony in this sharing of a
dress-up garment which we alternately wore and which each of us
had to open in order to pee.

Jim never invited me for a meal at the Phi Delt house, although it
would have been easy for him to do that. Fraternity members
did it all the time, with no special view to pledging a friend,
though that, too, was done all the time. I suspect that an older
member found this borrowing of a pair of pants unseemly, if not
even somewhat weird, especially from an Independent. But Jim
had little money when we were in high school, and the Boyds lived
in a tiny house on a main thoroughfare of Klamath Falls that could

not even be called a neighborhood. He must have been attending Oregon on the G.I. Bill. So it might have seemed natural for him to share an old friend's pants, and instead to spend what money he had on some new, cool garment—another Arrow shirt, or a smart belt. How it was that those pants fit us both I have no idea. By the time we went to college I was an inch or two taller.

This is what he wrote in my 1945 yearbook:

> Well "Smoothy" this is the end of my school days, so I will expect you to carry on. I'm really sorry I didn't get to know you sooner. I think you are really one "sharp" boy! I will be around for a while and maybe we can get together and have some laughs and some good times. You seem to be "in the know" around here and there are lots of things I would like to ask you, but it can wait. Well Jim I'll see ya around so best luck to you and everything you do! Your pal always Jim Boyd.

It's now more than seventy years since we graduated from the University of Oregon—me, a real weirdo, from the School of Architecture and Allied Arts; he, I learned, from the business school. If he is still alive, it would be easy to find him through the Phi Delta Theta alumni of the Oregon chapter. What questions did he want to ask me in 1945, I wonder? I looked on him and his buddies at Klamath Union as having all the answers and being "in the know." Would he ask them now? Would we have a laugh about our pair of pants, or the morning I came all over his aunt's sheets? When I find his letters from boot camp, as I know I eventually will, am I going to discover a confused, homesick boy, or the cool seventeen-year-old I thought I knew, who found me so smooth?

I think that gradually, over our first year at college, the shared dark blue pants became for me a symbol of our fading friendship, and came to possess magical properties of connection between us when seemingly there were no longer any others. That is why I was happy to go on lending them to Jim, and became disappointed when he stopped calling me to ask for them.

Those pants sometimes passed from hand to hand in the dark corridors and nooks of the university library, which stood exactly across the street from the Phi Delt house. It would have been easy to steal an unseen kiss there. Handing my pants over to Jim was that forbidden kiss.

Fraternity Sickness

The undergraduates at the University of Oregon were divided socially into the Greeks and everybody else. Since I had come from a small-town high school that had been dominated socially by a number of cliques, and I had belonged to the one that counted most in my class, I assumed that when I arrived on the Oregon campus I would naturally take my rightful place among the freshman fraternity pledges. There are several reasons I did not do that—partly a matter of timing, partly a matter of personality, and partly because there was no one who could sponsor me—no father or older brother who had belonged, no older friend I had known in high school who could explain, endorse, maybe browbeat.

The matter of timing was like this: 1946 was the first year in which able-bodied men went to college after World War II. Freshly graduated high school students enrolled, and so did thousands of ex-G.I.s, most of whom had the G.I. Bill to pay their way (otherwise, they might not have gone to college at all). So the Oregon freshman class was enormous. Competition to get into a good fraternity was intense. There was also the matter of finding somewhere to live. The university threw together some makeshift dorms to house the overflow. I had my heart set on a mock-Tudor frat house. The older fraternity members were returning veterans who had been drafted into the armed forces in their sophomore or junior years when the United States entered the war. Now they were twenty-four or twenty-five and were serious, often ex–combat men, sometimes ex-officers, who had seen the world, and whose perspective was very different from that of someone like me.

What does that mean: "someone like me"? Now I come to the

matter of personality: I was reed thin and unathletic, without having had good grades in high school to compensate. No one could claim I was a "brain"—least of all myself. I had an offhand, rather smart-alecky way of speaking and liked to put weird twists to some slang words that I'd heard at the movies, which, with my somewhat high voice, must have sounded affected. While accepted maybe as witty in high school, I soon got the idea I wasn't being listened to at the all-male fraternity get-togethers I did get invited to, where a lot of beer was drunk and girls and sports were discussed. Though I had been voted Most Stylish, my clothes somehow called attention to themselves. They were perhaps too neat and too carefully "coordinated," and so understated they ended up having an unfortunate look of preppy costliness about them that was way out of place on the slobbish Oregon campus, where just keeping dry became one's main concern. Finally, I was in the art school. Admittedly, in architecture, but Greeks traditionally stayed out of there. And vice versa. Students in the School of Architecture generally wanted to have nothing to do with the Oregon fraternities and sororities, considering them basically uncongenial, nonserious, anti-intellectual, and even anti-art.

Whenever I was invited to lunch or dinner at a fraternity in my freshman year, I was tense and withdrawn, with an anxious expression, and had nothing much to talk about. I've rarely mixed well in large groups of gregarious men; I felt excluded from their physicality, expressed most often in roughhouse or sports. I was an odd duck—so odd, in fact, that once at a Beta Theta Pi dinner, to which I had been asked by the dashing elder brother of a friend at a different university, and having to pee after downing several beers in hopes of loosening up, it was my bad luck to be struck by some sort of temporary bladder failure as I stood next to him at the urinals—a worldly, blond ex-aviator with movie-star looks—where not so much as a drop would come out of me. A kind young man named Dick Igl, he probably thought little about this collapse of my system, but I never returned to the Betas and gave up all hopes there. Supposedly it was the grandest fraternity of all, with a glamour the others lacked, recruiting its pledges from the best "old" Portland families.

All my freshman year and all of the next one, I became more and more conscious of what I understood to be a kind of inferior social status. I even thought I heard it in the way people spoke of my being an "Independent," in the upward, as if questioning, lift of the penultimate syllable of that now detestable word. I could perfectly well see that friends of mine who had not pledged a fraternity were having a great time anyway. Being a fearful snob, I was contemptuous toward those fraternities that didn't rank in what I'd learned from other snobs were the top half dozen houses, and I turned down their invitations when I got one. This ate away at my heart until I felt I had to pledge a good fraternity even if it meant changing schools.

My father had been in Alpha Chi Rho at Syracuse University in New York. I believed that if I transferred there and let it be known I wanted to join, they would be more or less obliged to take me in.* I would be leaving all my old friends, going three thousand miles away to a state I didn't know, and to a university that had a less strong art school than the one at Oregon I would be leaving—all to enjoy the dubious status of a "spook," or inherited member, of a house I knew nothing about as well. It was unthinkable to ask "Dad, how would you rank Alpha Chi Rho? Was it in the top half dozen houses? No? Yes?" My father was in fact opposed to this move, though he didn't forbid it. He felt I would be sorry if I did not experience a cumulative four years at one school; this outweighed for him the fact that I was unhappy at the University of Oregon. Perhaps because he had joined a fraternity himself and had been the kind of young man who is always and automatically accepted in that sort of world, it did not have much importance for him, whereas the fact that his own education had been split between Purdue and Syracuse did. In the end the admissions board at the second-rate art school at Syracuse turned me down, feeling I had little, or not enough, artistic talent. The drawings

---

* Years later, on a visit as a filmmaker to the Syracuse campus, I figured out why, I think, my father had wanted to pledge Alpha Chi Rho: it was exactly across the street from the School of Forestry, where he would be spending most of his time. It was an attractive-looking house, however. Not mock-Tudor, but something older, something with deeper roots. I can imagine my father running out the front door, tying his necktie, two minutes before his first class. In 1915 a slobbish look would not have been encouraged by anyone.

I had dashed out at a summer job in Utah in order to show what I could do were certainly very dreary. So I remained at Oregon.

I was now a junior and decided, against all advice, to go through Rush Week. Juniors were sometimes pledged to fraternities if they transferred from a school that did not have them, or if they had done so well in athletics or got such tremendous grades that they enhanced the house record of scholarship by joining. But I had done neither; I hadn't become desirable Greek material. Friends told me I was much better off living in a dormitory—even friends who had joined a fraternity as freshmen. They were starting not to like that sort of communal living and tried to obtain space in a dormitory themselves. They were fed up with all the horseplay and constant hazing of the younger men, which they found brutal and stupid; they hated sleeping in a common dormitory on the freezing third floor of the frat house, where other members kept shouting and came in roaring drunk sometimes and threw up, or—in some wild outburst—turned over the beds with people in them. They also complained of not being able to study quietly, and of the endless number of chapter meetings, and of the pressure alumni sometimes brought on them to pledge some unlikable creature (like myself, I suppose, but I never had the benefit of that). Worst of all, and felt by some members to be a kind of moral outrage, was having to blackball somebody they *did* like, because he was Jewish. But no one could talk me out of my, by this time, unseemly desire to be pledged to a good fraternity at Oregon. I knew that I had to rule out some of these. There was no hope I would be asked to join Sigma Chi, Alpha Tau Omega, Phi Delta Theta, or the Betas, who would remember my standing so long at the urinal for no evident reason. These houses were the Big Man About Campus houses—the Metro-Goldwyn-Mayer, Warner Bros., Twentieth Century–Fox, and Paramount of the Oregon Greek world. But I had closely monitored some other houses over two years and it seemed to me I might like life in one of those. I admired their style. The best of these was Sigma Alpha Epsilon, called "the Sleep and Eat Boys," because they were graceful second-raters who never competed very much and didn't give a damn. Some of the members were extremely good-looking, others were rich, and their house was a substantial

mock-Tudor. Nationally, this was one of the oldest and best fraternities. I had researched it.

In the first week of September 1948, I arrived in Eugene in a new, yellow Pontiac convertible, with a carefully thought-out slob wardrobe. It was unusual in those days to have a new car like mine, because it was so soon after the war. The American motor companies hadn't gotten back into full swing. My father had maneuvered someone, somewhere, and I drove up to Eugene from Klamath Falls, black canvas top down, with an ever hopeful heart. I wasn't too put off by the jibes of my friends, who told me that the main reason I would be pledged was that I owned a new convertible.

In the beginning the Sleep and Eat Boys didn't disappoint. All the fraternities held an open house on the first night where you could be looked over, as well as have a look. Then, if they liked you, you would be asked back for another look. Would-be pledges went every morning to Johnson Hall on the campus to pick up hoped-for invitations to return. We were weeded out with astonishing speed and there was

no way to be asked back once you had been blackballed. Each fraternity went down the list, saying yes or no. But the two houses I most
liked had asked me to return:
Sigma Alpha Epsilon, and Phi
Gamma Delta, whose laid-
back style resembled the Sleep
and Eat Boys, though their
ramshackle house wasn't as
nice. Other houses also asked
me back, but ever the snob—
and recklessly—I turned down
their invitations. And omi-
nously, one or two of the houses
that I felt were probably not
too bad, and that maybe I
could join, had blackballed me.
I did not go back to the house
of my best friend from high
school, Dick Yates.

Dick Yates

I had been blackballed, he told me, by a boy from our hometown
whose father published our local newspaper, and who, it seemed,
had always had it in for me. Certainly, I had to admit as these birds
came home to roost, I'd treated him in high school as he was now
treating me.

I went at dinnertime of the second day to the house of the Sleep
and Eat Boys, where I dodged the football being tossed about on the
front lawn between prospective pledges and older members. Once
inside, I was taken under the wing of a senior member who began
actively to promote me. He took a small group of potential pledges,
including myself, to a Chinese restaurant in town, where he drew me
aside and made me promise I wouldn't act hastily and pledge another
house without giving them a chance to prove how much they liked
me and what Sigma Alpha Epsilon could do for me. I remember this
moment perfectly, as we stood on the street corner together a little
apart from the others. The depth of his wooing seemed almost like
a marriage offer. He was very good-looking, with soft brown eyes

that fixed you with a sincere and even loving look. I made my vow, too fervently perhaps. My heart must have been racing; did my voice crack as I said "I will!"?

The next day, when I went to pick up my invitations there were fewer of them, and Phi Gamma Delta, who had taken me on a rowdy beer bust along the Willamette River, had dropped me. But I didn't care. I hoped that on Friday I would be pledged by the Sleep and Eat Boys, for I was now into the third day of Rush Week, and going back for the third time to the house of my choice. This was an afternoon function, something like a cocktail party minus the alcohol, and casual dress (which meant a sweater and open shirt) was prescribed. I put on a gray-blue cable-knit sweater my mother had made for me, which I had always felt was one of my coolest garments. I had saved it for such an occasion. But somehow when I passed under the Tudor archway and joined the small crowd, who turned to look at me, sizing me up as someone who might be destined to become an intimate, I felt less good about it. Did it fit well? Was it maybe a little too long over the hips, and a little too tight? It was not the preferred slob look of the others. I became uneasy. An anxious expression must have come into my eyes, and I must have turned grim and remote. I didn't shine, was drab, definitely not Sleep and Eat material. My new friend and promoter—I've forgotten his name,* but I could pick him out in a lineup of brothers in an instant—must have tried to help me, but like a junior executive at MGM promoting an unlikely script, he would have felt the wind blowing from the wrong direction by this time and had most likely stopped pushing me for election. I knew I was failing by the minute. Probably I tried to talk to some of the other candidates, and probably they moved away nervously, afraid of contagion. If my new friend tried to make me feel everything was all right, I knew that it wasn't, that it was all over. That night I was blackballed. There were only a few poor invitations the next day; one or two of the less "good" houses threw out their nets in my direction, but for me Rush Week was over and I did not even stay to the end, and got back in my snappy yellow convertible which had failed me, and drove back to Klamath Falls, black top up.

---

* A little research reveals that his name was Don Edwards.

Sigma Alpha Epsilon, home of the Sleep and Eat Boys

From that moment on, I never thought about fraternities again. I took up a new lifestyle at Oregon, that of the artist, and while it may have been a little self-conscious in the beginning, I was soon very happy. Having gotten over Fraternity Sickness, I was free at last to think about my work. Or, perhaps, going through Rush Week was the last episode of my childhood. I was not embittered by not having become a Greek, but I have retained the feeling to this day that I had been unfairly excluded from some sort of Big League activity, and whenever any of our film projects got turned down or blackballed ("We'll pass on this one") by the majors, I again experienced something of what I felt at the end of the Oregon Rush Week, however illogically. I know full well that I was much better off being an Independent then, just as I am now.

At Dr. Zeck's

Me at Dr. Zeck's, 1951

Some notes from Los Angeles from my drive east along Wilshire Boulevard in October 2002, on my way to visit the USC campus: The Wilshire Ebell Theater, to my right, where I saw José Limón's *The Moor's Pavane*, an international dance hit in 1950. What is a pavane I'm wondering, thinking I will look it up;* Perino's restaurant, now

---

* *Merriam-Webster's Collegiate Dictionary* says: "A stately court dance by couples that was introduced from southern Europe into England in the sixteenth century." I would have liked Limón's dance piece, I'm sure; I was just beginning to listen to early music then. The olive-skinned Mr. Limón must have danced the Moor's part. I have a memory of silhouetted bodies moving against a golden background, and that I saw them at a matinée.

closed and forlorn, on the left, still painted in pink and dark green, with its studio-set Brighton Pavilion details in the 1940s Beverly Hills Regency style. The place was dedicated to smart and expensive dining, but as a USC student I never entered there—when I could finally afford to, it was no longer smart and had outlived its usefulness as a glamorous hangout for movie stars and Hollywood big shots, like the Brown Derby, another place I never set foot in. Farther east the old Bullock's Wilshire store, also closed, a fine monumental art deco department store building in green and tan marble, its tower still dominating that end of Wilshire Boulevard, its huge display windows dirty and empty. Bullock's vied with I. Magnin in the days when there was no Saks Fifth Avenue and no Neiman Marcus store in Beverly Hills, which, together, essentially drove the two older stores out.

Dr. Zeck's house at 643 Thirty-Second Street off Figueroa, where I lived when I entered the USC cinema school in the fall of 1951—unimaginably still there, still with a transient population, USC students maybe, or just the poor inhabitants of some now crummy old

José Limón and Betty Jones in *The Moor's Pavane* (1949)

boardinghouse. Who was Dr. Zeck? I must have met him at some point, maybe when I went to his office on the campus to make a two-month deposit on the room I was taking in his house. He was USC's dean of men and would no doubt have dropped in from time to time to see what his student tenants had done to the place. Was it an old family home? If so, it hasn't been painted apparently in the fifty years since I left it. Across the street is the back of the Shrine Auditorium. Whenever the Shrine had some big event, we made pocket money by parking cars in our driveway and on the never watered front lawn. This might be the visit of an opera company like the Met, or the San Francisco Opera. I was once a priest in the crowd in *Tosca*. (I was paid ten dollars and saw Tosca leap, still singing, onto a mattress in the wings next to me where she was caught by stagehands.) The Academy Awards show was also held there—then an event we all disdained, as we beckoned to parkers with our flashlights.

Zeck's was a hothouse of sexual desire—mine, and everyone else's. It was where a prostitute was brought and where Bill Franke put his hands inside my pajamas one fine morning, to my amazement. From time to time we would throw a party, or even a dance, with strange women—not students, but older women—and everyone would get drunk and pass out or throw up. Who were my roommates? Apart from my new friend Bill, there was a rather cool-acting English graduate student named Maurice, whose name we always mispronounced—"Mau-reece" instead of "Morris"—with glossy, slicked-down, black hair; he was working for an advanced scientific degree and sometimes smoked a cigarette in a holder, which he called a "pimp stick." There was a guy with an angular face and a crew cut, with hard little eyes, who clomped around like a Southern sheriff and owned guns. While always the butt of our jokes, he never fired them at us. And there was a slightly older graduate student who was a vet, already going gray. He was desperate to get laid, we knew, and that made *him* the butt of jokes as well. He must have been doing something wrong, because none of the women we saw him with were ever seen again. He had a defeated look, with worry lines, but was polite and civilized.

I painted my walls at Zeck's a very dark blue, so that the room was never bright, even on sunny days. This was phase two of my evolving student-room decorating schemes, the first having come about on the Oregon campus, where I lived in a tiny glassed-in sunporch adjoining the wall of a movie theater, through which came the music and other sounds of the films playing there (like the earthquake in the re-released *San Francisco*). In that room I had a bright yellow floor, an army cot for a bed, and a mauve-colored folding screen that I dressed and undressed behind if I had visitors. My much larger upstairs room at Dr. Zeck's in Los Angeles was more carefully decorated and held the treasures I had brought back from my first trip to Europe in 1950, all on display. This room thundered to LPs of *The Goldberg Variations* and Bach's Mass in B Minor. No one complained very much, not even the Sheriff, who lived opposite me on the landing. Everyone always seemed to be cramming for some big exam except me—calmly going to my examinations smiling nonchalantly, like royalty to the block: you had to be pretty dumb to flunk out of USC.

We all shared the one wretched bathroom. Maurice, deeply English in his tastes, bathed in a dingy tub. The rest of us showered in a rusty stall. The icebox was full of sour milk, ice cream, cottage cheese, and old eggs. Frozen pizza hadn't come on the scene yet. We were honor bound not to touch anyone else's food.

On Sundays, if it was hot, we drove out to Santa Monica to the Jonathan Club—my father's Los Angeles club, which also had premises downtown, near Pershing Square. We drank a lot of gimlets and lay on the beach, and afterward took long showers in the fine shower room, which had an endless supply of big white towels. I don't know what ruse of mine succeeded in getting a bunch of us from Zeck's in there over and over, but we seemed always to be welcome. My father footed the bills and never once scolded me about being overly generous with his club's facilities.

At the center with me in all these excursions was Bill Franke, my friend of friends at Dr. Zeck's. He came from Kansas City, Missouri, and was majoring in journalism and advertising. On the day I first arrived to inspect the Zeck premises, not encouraged by the weeds and dead lawn, Bill answered the doorbell, throwing open the door and offering to show me around.

Bill Franke

I liked him at once and moved in as much because of him as anything else. It was a case of love at first sight and we became passionately attached to each other without quite being lovers. He was straight in the sexual sense and also, I suppose, in the other sense. I thought of myself as the artist-intellectual, and of him as being more at home in matters of business. He had the fraternity man's easy manner and jocklike interests— sports and cars and picking up women. He was trim and quick of movement and quick to laugh at things with me. We made an amusing life for ourselves at old Dr. Zeck's, becoming something of an exclusive pair where all the rest were concerned, much preferring each other's company. Bill was more outgoing, I less so.

How we drank in those days! Martinis and gimlets, and on the weekends all sorts of tropical South Sea island rum concoctions served in pottery skulls or coconuts, gulped down one after the other as accompaniment to Polynesian ribs at the Trader Vic spin-offs—the real Trader Vic's at the Hilton Hotel in Beverly Hills being too expensive for us. These Saturday night drinking excursions were invariably made with some of the others from Dr. Zeck's house, Bill always, and often Maurice, who was funny as he got drunker, becoming more properly English as the night wore on. It's odd, looking back, that no one from the USC's cinema school was ever asked to join us; perhaps it was the beginning of that feeling I have that it is not very necessary to know other film directors. I don't know how we got home or avoided being arrested because of the weavings of my car on the freeway—the

Editing my Venice footage in Los Angeles, 1953

same yellow Pontiac convertible I drove at the University of Oregon. This happy life went on from the fall of 1951 until the same time the following year, when I went off to Italy to make my first film, and our days at Zeck's came to an end.

I returned to Los Angeles in the spring of 1953. Bill took an apartment in the Hollywood Hills that summer and found the girl he would marry, while I moved into a Charles Addams–ish Victorian mansion on nearby Adams Boulevard full of student musicians (where I met my first heroin addict, though I was too innocent to recognize this). There I waited to be drafted while I edited footage I had shot in Venice, Italy, earlier that year, and waited, too, to be laid, which I was by a young string player. In October 1953, I left Los Angeles for basic training at Fort Ord, where, in my zoo of a barracks, the old squalid life at Zeck's—something like a third-rate frat house of mismatched brothers—would be recalled as a golden, luxurious dream.

How did it happen that Bill put his hand inside my pajama pants one fine morning? We were home alone, everyone else having left for his classes. I went downstairs and into Bill's room, where I found him lying in bed. I got in next to him, facing away, and lay there, feeling his warmth. Did we speak? Was he surprised? I don't think so, but after a little time, on a sudden impulse, he reached around, or over me, and took hold of my cock: my first experience of a straight guy's sexual curiosity about me. Then I turned around and satisfied my own curiosity about him, but before we could go further one of us thought he heard some movement in the empty house and we jumped up. I much regretted that this moment—so bold on his part, so eagerly welcomed on mine—was cut short. But it was soon to lead to further intimacy and all pretense that only some kind of lopsided desire existed between us had to be dropped by both of us for good.

There was a hysterical side to Bill, something a little violent that our physical closeness may have triggered while we were living at Dr. Zeck's. One hot afternoon—and I don't know what led up to it, maybe the heat—Bill and I were in his darkened room. He'd shed his pants and was sitting back somewhat provocatively in his white Jockey shorts in the big easy chair where he studied. I urged him to get rid of them, or maybe pulled them down myself. He let me fool around with his dick under the lamplight, allowing me a good look. It was a very shapely American frat-boy hard-on, and to my eye the best of the national norm, complementing his handsome face. I can see us still, Bill leaning back against a many-colored afghan thrown over the chair, the floor lamp shedding its light onto his lap, and my kneeling self, head bent, between his open legs. At first he seemed to enjoy this, closing his eyes as I abandoned myself, using every art I knew to make him come. Then he made me stop. I hear myself protesting, see myself trying to keep him there, and I see him jumping up and pushing past me. His mood was furious as he hopped around the room on one leg trying to get his pants on.

A few minutes later my sister, Charlotte, who was also a student at USC, dropped by for a visit, and the three of us went out to where she had parked her car. She liked Bill; they had a kind of buddyish relationship—drinking buddies, that is. We often took her to the Trader Vic–like places to get smashed with us, which was not at all good for her. Bill always seemed to like her. But now he burst out with a lot of insulting language laced with four-letter words—an unheard-of thing. He was in one of those enraged American male moods when you smash the wall with your first as your angry mixed-up thoughts collide in your head and on your lips. He became someone else, someone neither of us knew. He went back inside and I tried to comfort my shocked sister, who had done nothing to provoke his outburst, yet seemed to be the exclusive target of it. For some reason he never attacked me, even though I felt it was me he was mainly angry with, and I knew enough college psychology to guess that his permitting me to give him a blow job had churned up all sorts of puritanical, midwestern guilt feelings. I think he liked the idea of seducing *me*, without having to work at it, but the idea of being so enjoyably seduced himself was somehow unacceptable. Of course I couldn't explain Bill's crushing behavior to Charlotte in order to comfort her, and we sat in the car for a long time with my arm around her shoulder as she dried her eyes.

IT WAS DECIDED one day that a prostitute—or maybe two—would be hired to service the inhabitants of the dean of men's house: all horny young men who were desperate for sex with a woman, any woman. Except for me. But I played along. A Saturday night when no one was expected to study was set and a girl was found. Where she came from I was never told. Maybe a call girl, maybe a streetwalker.

It was also decided that Bill's big double bed on the ground floor would be the setting for all the fun being planned. A cleaning lady was brought in to spruce up Bill's room and a lot of beer was laid on. Rubbers were bought. We drew lots to decide the order. I was to be number two. After number one came out looking pleased—it was the Sheriff—I was more or less pushed into Bill's room by the others and the swinging door closed (the room had once been the dining room). The girl sat naked on Bill's bed, very composed, smiling in welcome. I was naked, too, under a bathrobe, which I got out of. The dark room hid my shyness, and we sat on the bed facing each other. The girl, who was probably in her twenties, had big breasts and I experimentally touched them, lifted them. Their weight and fullness surprised me. She began meanwhile to fondle my penis, pulling on it over and over as if she were milking some resistant teat, while we sat there a bit inanely. There wasn't the semblance of an erection. We might have been playing in some icy stream together. To gain time while she worked on me I tentatively touched her large nipples—first one, then the other. They weren't soft, but hard, even leathery. I became something of a dispassionate observer but I couldn't bring my hand lower than those nipples. The prostitute was sympathetic; I think she called me "Honey" as she tried to stimulate me. Perhaps she had introduced many young men to sexual intercourse. Some of these must have been fine, robust successes, others would have been a fizzle, like me. After a while there seemed to be nothing left to do but thank her, stand up, and apologize with vague words about not being in the right mood. I left her so that number three could come in. Of course, everyone asked me, "How was it, Jim? Was it great?" I don't think— rather, I know—that I ever owned up to any of them, including Bill, that at the age of twenty-three I was still a virgin where women were concerned and that this status had not changed on that night. When I read in biographies how famous young men—kings and artists and composers—are led to a courtesan for their initiation into sexual life, which may turn out to be very eventful, I think of my roommates at Dr. Zeck's standing outside the door in the shadows like so many knowing courtiers to greet me as I came out. I contributed my share to the kind working girl without letting on to them that from their point of view it had been a dismal experience. Funnily, it had not been at all, and I don't think of that night with any shame.

Bill's double bed figured in another somewhat enigmatic scene, also played out in the dark. One night, very late, after some party or other form of carousing, he and I had something to talk over—an issue of some kind. Perhaps it was our "relationship"—openly homosexual on my side, hetero (but maybe tottering a bit) on the other. Bill lay stretched out in his pajamas in the dark on his bed and I stood at the foot of it, leaning over the footboard. I could easily have reached down to seize a bare foot or leg and he kept them there almost ostentatiously within reach, as if tempting me.

We talked and talked, our mood was affectionate, and Bill lay there—waiting, I felt sure, for what I would do—but I never touched him or made any movement suggesting I might. I had made a decision when I came in not to take advantage of him as he lay on the bed. Was this shortly after the aborted blow job and the scene with my sister? Had we been rehashing that? Was he in fact trying to make amends? Was this his way of trying to put things right, by offering himself again? I considered the pros and cons of reaching down and grabbing him, or walking around the bed and taking him in my arms. But that might have led to another terrible scene, more crazy shouting. So finally I said good night and went out.

Bill pondered this bedtime scene and my unexpected walking away from him. We spoke a few days later of what had been passing through our minds then. I said, "I absolutely know you were waiting for me to pounce on you, expected it at any moment." He answered, "You son of a bitch!" and laughed. "Yes I was." And I answered, "I wasn't sure what you'd do, so I couldn't risk it." I think he didn't know himself what he would have done. I think he recognized that he had very strong feelings for me, feelings that didn't entirely exclude the sexual. But he knew that the sexual part was also forbidden, dangerous, and associated with despised faggotry. He was afraid—other straight men with whom I've been intimate have said this to me, that they feared they might become "changed"—he would like the sex too much, that it would somehow take hold of him and he would slip over into the ranks of fairies he saw cruising on Hollywood Boulevard, with many imagined unhappy consequences.

Yet he enjoyed the sexual teasing, pushed it further; the flirting, the nudity, our showers together at the Jonathan Beach Club, where I gazed at him in open pleasure; our erections, which need not be hidden but were exhibited—and, finally, the hushed, emotionally throbbing moments when he lay quietly on top of me, absorbing my—what? My essence or something like that—as I absorbed his: moments that I think had to be the most serious of all between us, the most truly loving, even the most truly sexual. Did he ever analyze why he chose to do this with me, as our hearts beat together?

BILL AND I never managed to go all the way, but, as I say, there was a lot of fooling around. After we left Dr. Zeck's, he'd go bounding about his little apartment in the Hollywood Hills stark naked and I remember one afternoon hooking a shirt on a hanger over his erection—the kind of silly image most homosexual men like to recall of the straight, would-be boyfriend, having very few of a more charged kind. One night, sitting in his car looking down at the lights of Hollywood, he at last proposed that we "go all the way." But not that night, another night, and a date was set two weeks in the future. When this moment arrived, he was ready to go through with it—as a philosophical experiment perhaps, like Voltaire agreeing to sleep just once with Frederick the Great. He lay invitingly on his bed stripped and spread-eagled, as if to say—well, he *did* say, "Take me, I'm all yours." But then I committed a grotesque tactical error: instead of stripping also, I got into bed wearing my shorts, so that his hands in the dark came up against a barrier of cloth instead of my eager flesh. This was for him a turnoff; our moment was spoiled and he never got himself up to that point again, although we went on messing around in our jokey and pleasantly adolescent way until I was drafted into the army a few weeks later.

But there *had* been something else for us, something much

better. Long before the unexpected morning episode at Zeck's that I previously described, which had led the way to our later intimacies, we had found together a kind of satisfying physical communion—or "sharing," as the Edwardians called physical closeness between two men. Somehow—I don't remember how this first got started—Bill and I began to lie on a daybed in my room, I underneath on my back, Bill spread out on top of me, more or less face-to-face. We would lie like that, his weight pressing down on me—it wasn't too great, I could support him—absolutely still and quiet, not speaking, until finally it became uncomfortable for me. He didn't lie on me in any sort of aggressive way, pushing me down as if trying to master me. We didn't kiss, or embrace, or fondle each other, though I was agreeably conscious of his half-hard penis pressing against mine through our pants, for we were always fully dressed. Nor did we ever become fully aroused. Once or twice we were conscious of the possibility of that, but it was less important than the arousal of our feelings for each other, which could be expressed in this way while remaining mute. These charged minutes—only once or twice a month—were the most emotionally stirring we ever had, and the manner they were brought about for me was unique in my life. No one else ever did this. How did Bill come up with such an idea? Was it a survival from another close male friendship that, like ours, had an element of secrecy, of furtiveness about it, adding to the sexiness of things? Luckily we were never interrupted during these sessions of lovemaking, for that is what they were, quite literally. Taking place usually in the middle of the afternoon, when no one else was at home, they can only be described as "hot"—hot in every way: emotionally, and in a way physically, as two grown young men lay tightly, one on top of the other, shooting an energy into each other that was utterly affirmative.

More than sixty years have passed since then. Bill has died* and I expect all his thoughts on our friendship—if he ever put them down on paper—are lost. The world has come to accept almost any degree of closeness between men, every form of physical and emotional intimacy. Our unions are blessed by ministers and civil authorities.

---

* Bill Franke died of Lou Gehrig's disease in his midsixties.

Nothing is condemned anymore, except denying one's sexuality, whatever it is. That is where the sin lies today in the minds of most enlightened people, and not even the most enlightened. Bill's form of being a "prick teaser" was not reprehensible: it was actually advertising in the only way he dared that he was open to whatever little frissons of the forbidden sex he (a straight man) and his best friend (a gay man) might think up together. At crumbling old Dr. Zeck's, he and I managed to live most romantically for many, many months. It is this romance that prompts me to write at such length about our friendship, one unlike any other I've known. I feel sure that he would say the same if he were alive, although the words "romance" and "romantically" might not be the ones he would choose to describe the way we were together. I know I had never before been so close or on such intimate terms with anyone else as I was with Bill at Dr. Zeck's. When I left for Venice in the fall of 1952, aged twenty-four, I would wait a full nine years before I fell in love again.

Another Bill

On a Tuesday morning in the early summer of 1977, old Mr. O'Neill fell over and died in his upstairs hallway. He was on his way to see Mama—Mrs. O'Neill—and was being led to her by his nurse. He had become like a little child again. When he collapsed, Mrs. O'Neill could see him lying on the floor near the head of the stairs. An ambulance was called and the police tried mouth-to-mouth resuscitation, but he had suffered a massive coronary and was dead by the time he reached the hospital. His son Bill telephoned me in Claverack that evening. There was to be a wake the next night in Port Chester with the funeral the morning after—all pretty fast, but Catholics aren't buried on Friday, and moreover this Friday was the Feast of the Assumption.

It wasn't a very big funeral. Mr. O'Neill's casket stood in the front of the church covered with a white pall, which made me think of little children. His family and a few friends filled up two or three pews in front. The rest of us were dotted here and there behind. I was late and took a place in a back row. The priest—actually a bishop—was just breaking the Host. It was bright and clean and cheerful and business-like in there. Electric fans mounted on the walls whirred and rotated. Bill was standing in the front row at the aisle and he had to let the others pass by him to take communion. Bill did not join them, which didn't surprise me. He stood straight and tall in a dark suit and he'd had his big head of curly hair cut short so that he looked altogether more sober and serious than usual.

Jack Steers came back from the communion rail, passing down the side aisle and crossing behind. On his way back up the main aisle to his pew, he stopped and shook my hand with his usual aplomb. Even on his way from receiving his Lord in His House he carried a far from unattractive hauteur, smiling down like an old-fashioned swell. The bishop put on a white miter and went down to sprinkle the casket with holy water. Six thuglike pallbearers in dark suits stood waiting, three and three, in the back, and when the bishop had finished his blessing, they went up the aisle to wheel Mr. O'Neill out. A little procession formed: the clergy, the altar boys leading; then the thugs with the casket on wheels, pushing it along; then the family— brother Paul, looking very middle-aged indeed, and sister Kathy, and then Bill, who took my hand as he passed; and finally a little cluster of mourners, mostly Maryknoll nuns from Kathy's order. I watched them pass out of the church and the thugs get to work, picking up the casket to put it in the hearse. I thought, Oh Lord, how we are lifted up! and I thought of how swiftly life passes, and how fast our youth flies away, so that I became a little emotional, with a lump in my throat. When Jack Steers's mother took my arm, I turned to her in a daze, and couldn't focus on her, so that Jack had to introduce us.

They led the way to the O'Neills' and I followed their old Cadillac to the house on Putnam Avenue, which was being repainted. There were boys up on ladders and I thought, That's a strange note. I went inside and found Mrs. O'Neill sitting in her living room with two ladies. She had not been allowed to go to the funeral; but it was only a formality anyway. She was very composed and her manner was that of a hostess receiving her guests for a party. She had on a black dress and a necklace of small crystal beads. She held her old head high, with its almost turn-of-the-last-century upswept hair, showing a very Italianate profile, but when she opened her mouth to speak, it was pure New York. In fifty-seven years of married life, she was saying, her husband had never once—no, not once!—complained about her food, or ever grumbled when she had put some dish in front of him.

The room filled up as everyone came back from the cemetery and it was very soon full of priests and nuns. The bishop sat in a wing chair with his long legs spread, not speaking. He was an old man with white hair and he kept looking into the dining room, where the funeral luncheon was being set out. I remembered, twenty years or so before, on a bright sunny day like this one, while his mother napped upstairs, Bill sitting in the same wing chair, legs also extended, the light from a window streaming in on us, as he ejaculated copiously into my clean, folded handkerchief, which afterward I stuffed into a rear pocket before catching my train back into the city.

When the good sisters from the Maryknoll Convent were introduced to me, they wouldn't let go of my hand so that I had to disengage myself. Perhaps, in tending the sick and looking after the dying, they get used to having some hand in theirs, even an inert one, and forget they're still holding it. They soon moved off and sat in a group on the sunporch; they looked like an all-female consciousness-raising session, except for their Superior, Mother Eucharista, who had stuck to the old ways, and to her old-time gray habit. All the others wore sensible frumpy outfits, but Bill's sister, Kathy, had plucked her eyebrows. What nun would pluck her eyebrows? The priests had long sideburns and one of them was wearing a cowboy belt with a big silver buckle.

Mr. O'Neill's brother came in. He was a merry little man who had had some sort of operation on his voice box; he had to wear a little microphone in a hole in his throat, which was hidden behind a scarf. He told cheerful stories in the tones of a frog. Bill led me outside to meet the painters. One of them was his special friend Joey. Bill introduced us, Joey on top of the ladder, me on the ground. "This is my friend James, the film director." Later the two boys were led into lunch. There's so much food, the ladies were saying, why should it go to waste? We stood about eating dainty sandwiches and Italian hot pickles and drinking iced tea. Kathy had firmly decreed, No liquor. I looked at all those plain, unmarked women, unsexed and somehow undeveloped, and vowed to myself that I would never ask for the comfort of my religion, or whatever it's called; vowed, too, not to call a priest with sideburns to my deathbed in order to make my last confession.

Bill took refuge on the back porch with his young men; I went to pull him out and make him walk to my car with me. We strolled along, two old friends. He said, "Joey got a hard-on just sitting there with me, in front of his friend. Well, I still have that effect on people." We said goodbye under a droopy pine branch and I told him to trim his mustache and that he was as good-looking as always. "I appreciate that," he said. He moved off, tall and dignified, a year away from fifty. He was on probation for dealing drugs. He had to make money because Paul, his stockbroker brother who managed his portfolio, scarcely kept him in small change—and anyway, it was exciting. He supplied his teenage friends with marijuana, and some of the town's young matrons, dealing out of his studio on Port Chester's Main Street, where he painted and sculpted.

I USED TO drive out from New York to see Bill in that studio in the years after we returned from the army in Germany. In a way, it was because of me that Bill had set it up. He became intrigued by the work I did for Special Services, where I designed and produced posters for the GI's live entertainment with the aid of a new and very professional German silk-screen printer installed for my exclusive use. I was going through my Matisse cutout phase then, which I put without shame to advertising our Foch Kaserne's Puerto Rican band, for instance.* Bill decided, as he watched me at work

---

* Foch Kaserne was the headquarters of the Second Armored Division, located in the town of Bad Kreuznach.

in my attic atelier, where I also painted, to become a full-time art-ist on his return home, and after his discharge in Bad Kreuznach, where we had been stationed, he stayed in Europe and entered an art school in Florence. I had also opted to be discharged in Germany, but I chose to go see Greece and Egypt before returning home. If you did that, you forfeited your ticket back on the troop ship that sailed from Bremerhaven.

I visited the pyramids and allowed myself to be picked up by a young American with a mustache named Ben, as we stood together one night between the extended limbs of the Sphinx. A tall stele cov-ered in hieroglyphics rose up, hiding us from the guides and fortune-tellers. It had been erected by a youthful pharaoh named Thutmose a thousand years after the immense head above us was carved out of the living rock. The young warrior-king had fallen asleep there, and was informed in a dream as he lay resting in its shade, by the spirit of Cheops, that one day he would be great.

As I was reflecting on this story, which the pharaoh had put onto the stone stele, and which I happened to know—and was wondering if perhaps Napoleon had also lain down to rest there—Ben pounced. I said okay, but not here in all this sand, and we went back to our hotel, called Mena House, down the road. We met up again soon after in Athens, where Ben hired me to do a rendering for his ar-chitectural firm, there being no one else in the city, strangely, who did that sort of thing (he said). I was paid one hundred dollars and with it bought an air ticket to Rome, where Bill was making a trip to see me.

Bill came back after his Florentine studies to Port Chester to live with his parents and concentrate on printmaking and sculpture. When I visited him there, sometimes he asked my advice and showed me things he'd done. Sitting side by side on a mattress covered by a sheet on the cement floor, we would catch up on our lives. I was often away, mostly in India; he mostly stayed in Port Chester. Set out in front of us were the things he was working on; these would be life-size clay busts of his family and friends, or his own silk-screen prints. One day I found he had done me the compliment—or was it a challenge?—of taking a pen-and-ink drawing I had made after

Veronese's painting *La Bella Nani* and come up with an image of his own miles beyond mine in its abstract and rather wacky bluntness, which he then printed in stark black and electric blue. I was never once shown a single image expressing a gay eroticism and I don't think he made those (or needed to, maybe)—not even in the life drawings of his male models, who always seemed, on paper anyway, chastely professional, though I have no doubt he slept with most of them there on his mattress.

Sooner or later our informal, yet serious, quasi-critical sessions would become casually sexual. He didn't seem to mind that my hand rather quickly found its way inside his pants as we sat talking of Art. He probably didn't even feel it anymore, and I wasn't put off that by thirty-five or so he'd become a bit enervated from all his cruising and his hundreds and hundreds of conquests. Most of these were local boys like Joey, the house painter I met on the day of Bill's father's funeral. Bill seemed never to worry if someone were to walk in while we were fooling around, and never bothered to go and secure the outside door. I had remained attracted to him and he would always respond, perfectly good-natured. Due maybe to the rough work he did making sculpture, his hands were calloused and dry, and sometimes smeared with white plaster of Paris. He was a master at finishing me off. No one else has ever done it so enjoyably, so deftly, and in so little time.

He must by then have given up his relentless cruising. He told me when he was younger he used to hitchhike on a section of the road between Port Chester and Greenwich, going back and forth, where he was always picked up right away. When he and the driver had finished, he was dropped back on the road for his return, where he again stuck out his thumb I guess, and waited for some other good-looking man to stop.

BILL AND I became friends soon after he'd arrived at Foch Kaserne, during my final months there. I'd given him a ride back from Wiesbaden one Saturday night in my crowded little car; over six feet tall, he took up most of the room in it. But something clicked between us then, so that the next time we were together in my car, alone and unobserved, it could all begin. He was marvelously handsome and eager; I didn't believe my good luck. But Bill was the sort of new lover-friend who, once he'd had you, lost interest and went right back on the prowl. Unfortunately, I was the opposite type: once I'd had someone—especially someone as good-looking as Bill—I couldn't wait to do it again. I remember a Saturday night right after we'd met, when we were together on a three-day army pass in Bingen, when he got up from our bed, gave a quick dash of water at himself in the bidet, and went straight down into the raucous German street. While checking into our little hotel with me, he'd spotted another soldier from our base he'd been interested in and had hopes for. It was hard for me later on to understand his attraction to some of my rivals; they seemed to be the opposite of me in every way. I would not have wanted to go after them myself. But since they were in no way like me, I strangely felt no jealousy and just hoped he'd be done with them fast and get rid of them.

We were soon taking longer leaves together, once even to the South of France, where I continued to lust mightily for him, my advances meeting with success whenever he was in the mood and not distracted by somebody else who had wandered by. Did Bill's

With my silver-blue Volkswagen in Germany, 1955

presence in the vicinity send out a kind of exciting aroma, attracting other young men, like bees to certain blossoms? We had similar interests when it came to art, if not to sex. We would drive miles to see a church or to visit an out-of-the-way museum with some reputed treasure on view. On one of these trips I took along my college friend Bob Luoma, from Oregon, who was stationed nearby in Frankfurt. The irrepressible Bill had to have him right away of course, then and there, on the backseat of my silver-blue Volkswagen convertible. I slouched down in front and pretended to be asleep, worried that the prowling military police might slide up to my striking-looking car with its U.S. Army license plates, parked in a dark cul-de-sac between two bombed-out buildings, and throw their floodlights on us.

Bill O'Neill

And yet Bill was maybe not that highly sexed in a physical way. He didn't seem to delight in, or care to prolong, sensation. His urges were more psychological than physical ones seeking bodily gratification, and they could never be satisfied. Not once did I hear him say that a soldier he'd slept with was a "great lay." The act was got over with fast, and in itself wasn't of much interest to him. You wanted to say, Slow down. For Bill, a soldier's greatness in bed would have been a matter of numerical ranking, like Don Giovanni's conquests: number five hundred, or—had it been possible in his lifetime, and maybe it was—five thousand. I would, in retrospect, never call him a sensualist. It was the *having*, the stranger's total capitulation, that brought on his passion, and the quicker the better. Then his eyes flashed and his hands flew, and his deep voice rumbled in anticipation, as all defenses fell.

Me at Foch Kaserne, Bad Kreuznach, 1955

Because of Bill, I came under suspicion at Division headquarters. There was a question going around about the nature of our relationship. Bill, at over six feet and endowed with a very deep voice, was without a trace of effeminacy. He would, however, stride into the PX restaurant where everyone mingled—officers, wives, and enlisted men—shouting campy things like "Darling! Where have you been?" To these mostly straight people he may have seemed ruggedly masculine. I, apparently, did not, and I was far prettier than any soldier in a tank division ought to have been. To make matters worse, I outranked him. These lunchtime encounters—and maybe others—had been noticed by our superiors, which led to some sort of an inquiry, unknown to me. I was never summoned for questioning, but my boss, Harry Paul, a Department of the Army civilian, was. He vouched for my manliness successfully, but afterward, when he was telling me of the concern at headquarters, he shook his head in resignation. Might he have come under suspicion himself?

I was due just then for a promotion to the rank of sergeant, and this episode, plus a driving infraction reported to my commanding officers (the failure to signal as I turned in to the PX from the main road in my attention-grabbing car), must have been responsible for my remaining a corporal until my discharge a few months later. My promotion was put on hold. In the peacetime army after the Korean War, promotion was pretty automatic if one didn't fuck up;* it was not the result of showing any kind of military prowess and came with adequately serving one's two-year term. So, to a snooty, college-educated draftee, born into the officers' class, ultimate promotion to the rank of a sergeant, one of army life's perennial comic characters and a target of disdain then from types like me, seemed laughable and a preposterous joke. But paradoxically, the withholding of my third stripe stung me.

IN 1988, WHILE I was in San Francisco making a commercial for Ralph Lauren's household line—in their minds, crazily, to be based on *The Philadelphia Story*—I had a sad call from Bill's brother, Paul, who told me that Bill had died. He was only fifty-seven and had cancer. I'd just been to see him in the family home in Port Chester after a long absence. He was lying in a four-poster in his parent's old bedroom. He asked me as I came in, "To what do I owe this honor?" He had undergone many bouts of chemotherapy, but his thick, dark, curly hair had never fallen out. Instead it had gone straight. When I'd vis-

---

* What were some of the ways of fucking up? Being caught while sleeping on guard duty was one of the greatest offenses. In peacetime that would lead to a reduction in rank at least; in wartime the traditional punishment for that was the firing squad.

ited him in the hospital, he was laughing and flirting with his doctors. He died on the Monday after I'd seen him at home, exactly a week later. He had his last meal with me, it seems. His helper made us two chocolate malteds and brought them to the sickroom, and I shall not forget Bill's lusty sucking on the straw after the last drops were gone. He never ate anything else again.

Bill O'Neill, Cologne, summer of 1955

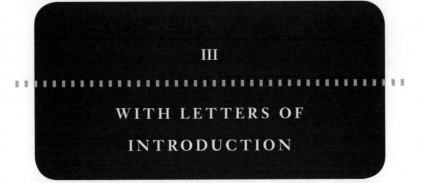

III

WITH LETTERS OF
INTRODUCTION

Venice

My Venice

Where and how did I spend my very first night in Venice? Italy in the summer of 1950 was hosting the first Holy Year after the war, and the biggest wave of foreign tourists to arrive in the country since the beginning of the Second World War in 1939. I had come to Venice by train from Paris with no more than fifty dollars in my pocket and put up at a student hostel someone told me about. This turned out to be a dormitory on the upper floors of a religious organization. The beds were steel army cots set up in rows in a big room with many windows, through which the clanging of church bells woke me at 6:00 a.m.—that sound is still perhaps my deepest memory of Italy. The bathing arrangements were primitive, and one was not expected to spend much time in this place during the day. You left your suitcase under the bed and hoped it wouldn't be rifled through while you were sightseeing. There was a curfew, and a lights-out. I turned in on the first of my two nights there exhausted, but happy to be at last in fabled Venice. I was awakened suddenly by an explosion of high spirits: a party of stark-naked, very pink young Scotsmen, like aliens from outer space, were whooping and leaping about over the beds where we lay, turning the sleepers onto the tiled floor, from which they sprang up ready to fight. These invaders had switched on all the lights and I can see and hear the scene to this day: a melee of muscular legs and bare prehensile feet, fists, balls, clan yells, and vomiting, until two harried-looking priests ran in clapping their hands for order, when the Scots at last finally fell down or passed out.

I took a train to Rome, with only ten dollars left, but unharmed:

First passport, 1950

a slim, serious young American with a high forehead, carrying his first of many, many passports safely buttoned inside his coat breast-pocket, wearing a two-piece, grimy Brooks Brothers seersucker suit and sweaty white shirt, whose ever generous father in California had promised to wire some more money, care of American Express, Rome.

I would return to Venice two years later to make my first film. In the meantime I needed to go back to the University of Oregon for my final year at the School of Architecture and Allied Arts in order to obtain my degree. I was draft age, and liable for calling-up because of the American war in Korea, which had begun in the summer of 1950. I would be exempt from the draft if I continued my schooling, so, after graduating from Oregon, I enrolled myself in the cinema school at the University of Southern California in Los Angeles. I was aiming for a master of fine arts in cinema. But, in the two years I was away, I couldn't get Venice out of my mind. I had to return, no matter what. I concocted the idea—seemingly a novel one for my instructors at USC—of making a film in lieu of writing a master's thesis. This was agreed to, and my father said he would fund it. I would write, photo-graph, and direct the film myself, even though I had never operated a motion-picture camera before. I was full of that kind of enthusiasm a young man can often generate in himself and others when he has an idea, but which sometimes is not very well thought out.

I proposed to tell the story of Venice through art. I was not an art historian, or a cameraman, but I was jumping right in to make a very ambitious film that professional filmmakers might have approached with more caution, after a lot of homework, and with an experienced team. Who was going to be on my team, my instructors asked? Why, I said, the painters Gentile Bellini, Carpaccio, Veronese, Titian, Tin-toretto, Canaletto, Tiepolo, Turner, Monet, and Whistler—what a roster of great names, of big stars!

Undaunted, I set out for Venice in the fall of 1952 with a new 16mm Bolex camera with three lenses, a light meter, and a tripod. What I could not carry myself, I was determined not to miss. I knew no one, and did not hire an Italian assistant, and could speak very little Italian. For practical as well as social reasons, that was a mistake. I have always thought of myself as someone other people have found easy to meet, to know, so my self-created solitude in Venice during the winter of 1952–1953 seems strange and uncharacteristic now. People had always wanted to befriend me—that had happened in France when I made my first trip there two years before, and I palled around the city of Tours, where I was supposed to be learning French when I wasn't in a swimming pool, with an enjoyable gang of foreign students. So why not in more convivial Italy? I could see that Venice was teeming with attractive people my own age who might be fun to know, as well as useful; why did no one come forward? They

The Pensione Calcina

moved in groups through the narrow streets laughing and joking, even brushing against me.

I settled in the Pensione Calcina, on the Zattere. A plaque by the door said John Ruskin had stayed there a century before, but I had not read him. The guests at the Calcina were better behaved than the naked Scotsmen at the hostel. Conversation in the little dining room was a low, genteel hum, mostly in Italian. Some of the pensione residents had moved out of grander quarters to save on heating bills. There was a very distinguished, slow-moving old lady in a long black dress that fell to the floor. She resembled, in her stateliness, the dowager Queen Mary of England. She was accompanied by a younger

Acqua alta

companion, who spoke to her a bit too sharply sometimes, so that the rest of us looked up from our plates to glance discreetly. The food at the Calcina was a tasty and classical three courses of soup or pasta, meat or fish, and dessert—most often (too often) of stewed fruit. But I was always ravenous after my exertions and ate up everything, including the tasteless white hard rolls.

My dinners may have been lonely, but my days were full. If you have all Venice for subject matter and you own a good movie camera as I did, you quite quickly become a cameraman and develop your eye. I was out every day, in wind, rain, high tides in Piazza San Marco, which you had to cross on little, slapped-up, jiggly bridges during the *acqua alta*, when the square is flooded. I was mostly happy, if alone, and sent off roll after roll of exposed film to my lab in Los Angeles. These contained images of what might be called Eternal Venice: the trembling reflections of marble church façades in the canals; the battle-axe prows of tethered gondolas bobbing up and down; Whistler-like distant views of the lagoons at dusk. Clichéd images for those who knew the city, but magical when you did not, like me.

Permissions were needed in order to shoot views of the Venetian medieval and Renaissance past seen in the mosaics of St. Mark's and the series of enormous paintings by Gentile Bellini and Vittore Carpaccio in the Accademia. How I went about that I no longer remember. Certainly I came prepared with a letter of introduction from the

Filming in the Accademia, 1952

USC cinema school, which must have gotten me in. Once admitted, I realized that I would need lights to photograph the paintings, the dark surfaces of which absorbed all of the daylight even on the brightest of days. These I was able to rent from the Scalera Studio, a defunct movie studio that had operated in Venice some years earlier. They provided me with six enormous lamps and furnished a pair of electricians to augment those of the Accademia. These lamps were terribly heavy and stood on adjustable stands. They threw a very hot light on the pictures I was most eager to shoot, like the St. Ursula cycle by Carpaccio. The museum *soprintendente*, Signor Moschino, fretted that my lights would damage these very popular star pictures, and indeed they would have if placed too close or kept on for too long.

It is unimaginable today to subject ancient paintings like those to such stress. No picture gallery would allow it. But a lot was allowed at the Accademia in those days. One day I was handed Giorgione's dreamlike little picture *The Tempest* to hold. It had been taken down off the wall for some reason while we were shooting. Everybody's

Giorgione's *The Tempest* (1508)

hands being full, I took it. I remember studying it closely as I held it in my arms in its frame until someone was ready to hang it up again. I've read since that ephemerality and vulnerability are said to be the subject matter of *The Tempest*.

The *soprintentendre*, a nervous man with good reason to be, paid periodic visits to us every day in order to reassure himself. His assistant, however, a much less nervous man named Mario Franceschini, organized things with the guard at the museum office next door so that he would be telephoned on our set whenever the *soprintentendre* was on his way. This was a half century before mobile phones. Then the lamps would be turned away from the picture we were working on in the direction of a stone-cold one. When the boss arrived, he would walk up and touch it and say "*Va bene.*" My co-conspirator,

A detail from Vittore Carpaccio's *Arrival of the Ambassadors* (1498)

an unflappable, kind, and charming younger man, put in charge of the day-to-day matters of the shoot, was present at the horrifying moment when one of my top-heavy lamps began to rock, and then topple over toward the middle of one of the big St. Ursula pictures. Before it could tear through the five-hundred-year-old canvas it was caught in the arms of the gang of electricians, a burning-hot, massive weight. This was a very sobering moment for all of us. If my lamp had continued its course, ripping through St. Ursula, I would have been expelled from Italy as "an enemy of art," and kind, openhearted Signor Franceschini, my one true friend in Venice, would have lost his job. So, too, would his boss, who would soon have discovered how mercilessly he had been tricked by us, and so ruined.

WINTER NIGHTS ON the Grand Canal: When I was not shooting in the Accademia, from where I could easily walk back to the Pensione Calcina with my equipment, and had set up in some other part of the city, I would take a *vaporetto*—or a *motoscafo*, which was more expensive—and return in stages to my quarters on the Zattere once it had gotten too dark to shoot. Most nights were very cold, but I didn't want to sit in the boat's cabin, where everyone was smoking. I stood instead on the deck and looked into the brightly lit windows of the passing palazzi. Sometimes I saw into what seemed to be luxurious rooms: modern-looking living rooms with smart contemporary sofas and big lighted lamps, with shadowy, wonderfully painted beams above. As the weather was so cold, the big windows I looked up into were mostly shut, so I couldn't hear the owners' talk or laughter, or music from the radio, or from phonograph records (the first LPs had recently come on the market everywhere), or hear any convivial sounds of ice clinking in highball glasses, or the popping of champagne corks, as you can in summer—all sounds I supplied myself as I peered in. Sometimes I could see the lucky occupants moving about. I was the eager outsider with my nose pressed against the glass, looking in with longing eyes, as my *vaporetto* crisscrossed the Grand Canal from stop to stop.

I could not foresee that entire floors of some of these palazzi I was

Palazzi on the Grand Canal

passing—the best and most luxurious floors, the most beautifully painted ones—would someday be given to me to inhabit and throw parties in, in my persona to come of a notable foreign film director, one invited to the Venice Film Festival. Or that I could one day be standing on what was temporarily my own balcony, leaning there nonchalantly with my friends, glasses of champagne in our hands.

After spending all winter in Venice shooting my first film, and enduring an American presidential election there, when the beloved Adlai Stevenson was defeated by General Eisenhower, and the reaction to this in the Calcina dining room was a mere shrug, I went back to California. But during my last fortnight in Venice I finally became acquainted with a group of young Venetians, students like myself, who quickly became my friends. One night we all took a box at La Fenice to see *Il crepuscolo degli dei* (*The Twilight of the Gods*). My new friends alternated between necking on their gilded chairs and hooting in derision at the inadequate stage effects of Wagner's collapsing universe, but I liked them very much. They spoke acceptable English and I tried to make jokes in the Italian I'd learned. I hated to part from them so soon.

I came to Venice one more time in my twenties, while on leave

Venice, 1955

from the army in Germany in 1955. I shot more footage for my still unfinished film, now called *Venice: Theme and Variations*. Then I vanished for eight years. I turned up in 1963 with my father and my partner, Ismail Merchant. We stayed at the Palazzo Gritti and had brought with us a print of our first feature film, *The Householder*, which we had made in India. We had hoped to enter it in that year's Venice Film Festival, but either the selection committee didn't like it or we had turned up too late, or both, and it was not chosen. My father asked to be shown the Pensione Calcina and I took him there, but everyone I'd known was gone.

AFTER THAT I did not go back to Venice for more than twenty years, until 1986, having spent much of the intervening time in India making films. On this trip the rooms behind the closed windows on the Grand Canal opened up wide for me. I was coming in triumph with *A Room with a View*, soon to take on almost an Italian identity and to be renamed *Camera con vista*. Ismail rented a palazzo belonging to the ancient Marcello family, who had several of them, some on the Grand Canal, some not. Ours was in the San Marco area. At night I lay in a rococo bed, in what I recall was a pale green and gold room resembling the famous Venetian bedroom from the Palazzo Sagredo in the Metropolitan Museum, with my windows wide open to the summer nights. There was an extraordinary muniments room, as they're called in English castles, containing centuries of records of the Marcello family: rolls of parchment with dangling seals, and great leather binders stamped with the years standing on shelves from floor to ceiling.

This was to be our custom when we were invited to the Venice festival, as it was at Cannes, when we happened to be going there, where we would rent a villa by the sea or in the hills. Ismail always filled up these grand establishments with our actors and cameramen and editors and writers, and also our office employees from New York, London, and even Bombay. And when I say "filled," I mean "filled"—god knows where everybody slept. We all had to work. On your way to do press interviews you might be asked to come back via the market to pick up bags of rice because the numbers of journalists who had been asked to dinner had been miscalculated and Ismail knew he needed to throw together some Indian *keema*, *daal*, and rice. One year at Venice, Ismail served on the festival jury but he somehow managed to entertain lavishly, giving orders to the cook in the morning before he went to the Lido in his speedboat. Those left behind had to fan out to search for a particular spice that would be needed, or go buy more vodka for the press and the newly befriended celebrities that were expected. Somehow it all came together.

This was Merchant Ivory's unvarying festival routine, and everybody liked it and looked forward to it. Five times at Venice: *A Room with a View* (Palazzo Marcello); *Maurice* (Palazzo Giustinian Brandolini); *Mr. and Mrs. Bridge* (Palazzo Albrizzi); *A Soldier's Daughter Never Cries* (Palazzo Dona delle Rose); and *Le Divorce* (Palazzi Mocenigo). And eight times at Cannes, but the names of all those villas escape me now. Except for the Villa d'Andon at Grasse, which we took when we presented *Savages* at its world premiere in 1972 at the Directors' Fortnight. My comfortable room in the villa that night had been given to some important guest by Ismail, and I returned when the festivities were over, in my tuxedo, to a cell I had been assigned in

The Palazzi Mocenigo (above) and the view from the balcony (below)

a freezing turret, with a stone floor and a mattress of straw. But I didn't care, and fell asleep exhilarated by the fact that our first film at Cannes had been a resounding, sold-out succès d'estime.

Merchant Ivory's most recent visit to Venice was in 2003, when we came with *Le Divorce*, and virtually its entire cast, including Leslie Caron. Many of us stayed at the Palazzi Mocenigo at San Samuele.

Like the Albrizzi palace, the Palazzi Mocenigo has a wonderful art deco bathroom, which was again my luck to draw. Those early 1930s, very elegant Venetian bathrooms should be celebrated in their own right and possibly transported to the Metropolitan Museum, too. Their designers (and their patrons) liked sumptuous combinations of red and black and silver, with many mirrors and generous numbers of light fixtures to make the whole place sparkle. There was a stupendous view from our balconies, right, left, and across: Ca' Foscari, Palazzo Balbi, another Palazzo Marcello, Palazzo Persico, Palazzo Barbarigo—a study in style from the gothic to the eighteenth century. Directly across was the San Toma stop of the *vaporetto*. How often I had gotten on there in the evenings after packing up my camera and tripod, and looked across to the lighted windows of the twin Mocenigo palaces! Now I seemed to have come full circle and to have traded places with the starry-eyed young people in the passing boats below, who perhaps might have come to Venice for the first time, and who, if they were looking up, might have noticed a white-haired man silhouetted in front of an inviting room, leaning on the balustrade. He would be wearing, yet again, a Brooks Brothers seersucker jacket, in style as immutable, and unsusceptible to change, as the balcony itself. He would be looking up and down somewhat idly. Possibly his thoughts would be—as theirs might be, too—full of gratitude at being in Venice, full of wonder.

The Stranded Gondola

In 2006 I made a film in Argentina based on the novel *The City of Your Final Destination*, by the American author Peter Cameron. It told the story of a rich German Jewish family named Gund, who immigrated to Uruguay in the mid-1930s. Among the possessions they brought with them was a real Venetian gondola—symbol of the lost European world they fled and a reminder of their honeymoon happiness in Venice.

When we shot our film, we needed to have a genuine Venetian gondola; it was an essential prop. But there were none to be found in Argentina and surrounding countries, and of course no

Charlotte Gainsbourg and Omar Metwally in
The City of Your Final Destination (2009)

gondoliers. But we were able to buy, for five thousand dollars, a real Venetian gondola from its owner in Venice, and we found it on eBay. This lucky purchase must have been at the time when all the old gondolas in Venice were replaced by a fleet of new ones. Otherwise, what gondola owner would agree to sell the principal means of his livelihood? Our gondola was shipped to Buenos Aires and then brought up the Río de la Plata to where we were shooting; it was in good shape, and seaworthy you might say, and appears in the film as dictated by the story of the Gund family. But then a new problem arose: what to do with the gondola when we were done with it? I couldn't bear to abandon it in the South American jungle, so I had it shipped to my home in upstate New York, where it lives now. Unused, alas, as there are still no gondoliers to propel it over my big pond at Claverack. Does anyone need a gondola? Who will give it a good home? I've offered it to Central Park in New York City, but they already have one, and a part-time gondolier.

The story of the Gund family gondola, whisked away from the set of *The City of Your Final Destination* in Argentina to upstate New York, has a happy ending. Here it is, written by the new owner, my friend Sean Wilsey:

"I grew up skateboarding, which made me a vandal in the eyes of society. When I visited Venice, I recognized gondoliers as fellow skateboarders and was determined to become one of them. They glided through the streets, ducked bridges, casually placed their feet on canal-side buildings and pushed off, as if all the beauty every-where was just so much asphalt to them. So I called the gondolier's union and asked for an apprenticeship. Someone there put me in touch with a rowing club on the island of Giudecca, where a heavyset man in his fifties took twenty-four dollars off me, and held up a white V-neck T-shirt with burgundy trim, emblazoned front and back: ASS.

"Gliding around with the word ASS on your chest was the defini-tion of skaterly. It was a perfect shirt, the hint of insolence invisible to—and sanctioned by—the Venetians. Wearing it, I felt an unfamil-iar feeling: wholeness. Then I apprenticed with a gondolier named Gino Macropodio. At sixty, Gino wore his shirt unbuttoned to the navel, and a solid-gold lion of St. Mark on a chain around his neck. His pinpoint pupils were set in eyes so shockingly blue that they seemed recently dredged.

"Though I left Venice to become a writer in New York, there is no object I have ever admired and desired more than a gondola. The boat that *is* Venice. But when Gino 'put down the oar' and offered me his gondola, I said no. I had other ambitions in another city, and Gino's offer, the most generosity anyone had ever shown me, did not also include the audacious act of shipping a gondola to the United States. Who would, or could, even contemplate such a thing? And a gondola requires constant devotion. I was devoted to a job at *The New Yorker* magazine. But my longing for a gondola of my own *never* abated.

"When I heard of Jim's boat, and then astonishingly it came into my care, I fixed her up, painted her burgundy and gray, and took her out to Orient, New York, on the end of the north fork of Long Island. I row before it gets windy, around 5:30 a.m., in a bay where the shore is laced with grass-lined canals. The other day, my teenage son, a skater too, sent me a picture of myself on the gondola from last summer.

"'Dad,' he said, 'I love this picture of you. You're smiling so wide and you look so happy.'

"'I was thinking about Jim Ivory,' I answered.

"Thinking about Jim means thinking about beauty. His gondola gives me an adult version of that feeling of wholeness I felt putting on that ASS shirt. And with this gift Jim has made beauty so tangible you can stand on it."

About the time all this was happening with my gondola, I began work on a new

The gondola, under wraps, in Claverack

script. It was based on the Henry James novella *The Aspern Papers*, and our longtime screenwriter, Ruth Prawer Jhabvala, was writing it with me. Our plan was to update the original story, first published in 1888, to the 1950s—to the time when I first went to Venice. It was to have been a full-length feature, and if it had been made, with certain adjustments necessary because of the updating, it would have been my only full-length dramatic film to be set in Venice.

On a visit there in 2010, I was shown the large garden James is said to have had in mind when he wrote his story, adjoining the Palazzo Gradenigo where a friend, Toto Bergamo Rossi, lives. In James's original story, an ambitious American biographer wheedles his way into the crumbling palace of the aged mistress of a long dead poet, someone like Lord Byron, in hopes of extracting letters the famous poet may have written to her half a century before (in our version he would have been someone akin to Ezra Pound). The

American biographer energetically applies himself to the task of bringing the old lady's neglected garden back to life in the hope of ingratiating himself and earning her confidence; her drab spinster niece falls in love with him. All his plans end up failing drastically, however, as did mine for the film, when I fell down some stairs and broke my leg. In time, the leg mended itself, but Ruth Jhabvala had by then stopped her work on the script and couldn't return to it.

Sometimes it's in the nature of planning a film that you end up after a lot of work with the ephemeral and vulnerable—what Giorgione's *The Tempest* is said to so beautifully embody—something to be dreamed of and pursued, into which you pour yourself for a time before you are forced by events to turn elsewhere.

Kabul

Progress and Prohibitions

In 1960, when I first went there, Afghanistan's goal was to modernize, and the image of the country presented officially to the outside world was to be one of progress in all matters. For instance, the seclusion of women ended by decree; women could—or should—hold jobs, go to university, and move about in public without fear of censure.

The chador, the full-length veil covering them from head to toe in yards of billowing pale blue material, was abolished; hence it no longer existed, and so was not to be commented on (outside Kabul, the capital, women never left their homes without it). "Westernized" or "modern" Afghan women went out into the city streets in dark, trim suits and Italian shoes, silk scarves tied over their heads, wearing dark glasses, which perhaps preserved a suggestion of privacy. But traditional women—doubtlessly urged by their males—kept their chadors on. To a documentary filmmaker trying to shoot an atmospheric film about old Kabul and beyond, veiled women, moving like undulating ghosts through the adobe lanes, seemed far more photogenic—or cinematic—than unveiled ones. My attempts to film them, however, were frustrated by the little "crew" assigned to assist (and guard) me, who sometimes put their hands in front of my lens: the chador did not exist, so there was no need to film it.

At that time, Afghanistan and Pakistan were virtually at war over a large territory to the east of Kabul, a part of Afghanistan called Pashtunistan, the homeland of the Pathans. Afghans tried to make their claims and their boundaries, drawn by the British in the nineteenth century, even more legitimate by teaching Pashtu, the language spoken by the Pathans, in their elementary schools (government officials who did not know the language had to go back to school to learn it). All sorts of accusations and counteraccusations were made by the two countries in the General Assembly of the United Nations. For instance, Pakistan was accused of putting out propaganda, aimed at persuading the Pathans to secede, that the Afghans were becoming godless in their quest for modernity and were not good Muslims anymore. In the center of Kabul, by the river, there was an old mosque that was being pulled down. It was to be rebuilt in a larger, safer form, for the brick walls were full of cracks and the minarets tottering. I was forbidden to shoot this demolition: Pakistani enemies would use my footage as evidence that in Kabul the mosques were all being torn down. I did manage to shoot it, but on the sly, and guiltily, for there was something of an honor system at work in my relations with my Afghan hosts—not to mention with my helpers, who might be held accountable for my actions.

One day, standing on a bridge in the middle of town, I saw some boys in the river below playing water soccer with heads—goat heads, not human ones, though in 1960 such a possibility was not that far in the past. I hastily set up my camera and began to shoot, and once more a prohibiting hand was placed over the lens. That is the way it was throughout my stay in this land seeking a new identity, where the past and its traditions were often proscribed, and the present— already outmoded—was eagerly awaited.

A Foreigner in Kabul: Spy or Prince?

When I landed in Kabul in May 1960, I was taken to stay in a rambling sort of place called the International Club. It was a collection of ram-shackle bedrooms with primitive baths attached, arranged around a bar and dining room. The bar, in officially dry Kabul, was the club's great drawing card. The place was said to be a nest of CIA spies. No doubt it was, but as far as I know I didn't meet any, for the bar was not a very congenial place and I didn't spend much time in it. I was put in a room with another American, a young man named Dee, college educated like myself, but, unlike myself, hearty and something of a jock. He used to go flopping about our room naked, to the consterna-tion of the scandalized room bearers bringing tea in the morning. He was completely unaware of the grave offense he was giving in such a traditional Islamic country; they stood with averted faces while he, totally nude, joked with them, trying out his new Farsi phrases and rummaging around in search of his dirty laundry to give for washing. One day Dee and I were having lunch in the club dining room when I discovered a fat black slug in my salad, then another. I called over the manager to point this out. He barked at the waiter, who removed the offending dish. A few moments later there were loud howls and groans coming from out back, and I asked Dee what these might be. Oh, he said, that's our waiter being beaten.

Athletic, high-spirited, open-faced—could Dee also have been a spy? A nice guy like that—had he been enlisted by the CIA? And was he asking himself the same questions about me? Most of the Americans I met in Kabul were somewhat evasive about the work they did there. Some of them were actually called "observers" for the mission, but what was "the mission"? The only American mission it seemed to me was to save Afghans from themselves—the main objective of American foreign policy in all underdeveloped countries. I remember showing Dee some of the things I'd bought in India, like Rajput miniatures. He himself was looking for rugs, but nothing unusual had shown up in the bazaar; he hadn't made the right contacts yet. What about antiquities? I asked. Anything like that was always smuggled out of the archeological sites, he told me, and was too hot to buy, unless one was a diplomat. "Don't think the Afghans don't know what's going on, or don't know what they have." Another American I met in Kabul told me a story about the high-profile French archeological mission, which had discovered superb objects in their excavations in the Buddhist *stupas* but were prevented from sending any of them off to the Musée Guimet in Paris by their Afghan hosts. They had been allowed to keep only valueless lumps—aesthetically speaking—out of their (heavily French-financed) digs.

I did not stay in the International Club very long, although I wouldn't have minded if I had, as I was getting used to its atmosphere and its ever changing clientele. I was never given any reason that I was moved to Kabul's Grand Hotel on the main street. Perhaps it was to keep an eye on me—probably more of a protective than a suspicious one. The hotel was a large, unfinished shell of a place, smelling of wet concrete. While I was in Afghanistan with the blessing of the Ministry of Culture, and with letters of introduction to high officials, I always felt that my presence in that hotel was of negligible importance to the staff. I got no calls or messages. No one answered my room bell. The front desk had little interest in my requests or needs. Often, the waiters forgot to bring my meal to the table. And it went on like this for most of the summer.

Then one day my status changed for the better. In order to go around the country on my own, I decided to rent a Land Rover. After I had obtained an Afghan driver's license, a very sturdy, reliable vehicle was turned over to me by an international car rental company that supplied the capital's foreign aid workers. I went everywhere in it—to Bamyan, through the Khyber Pass to Peshawar, and to all sorts of inaccessible sites—in order to shoot my film. The vehicle never gave me any trouble. But one day in downtown Kabul, near the hotel, the engine began to smoke alarmingly. So I turned in to the hotel's rear compound—a place intended as a garden but more like a dusty playing field. I pulled up at the back or "garden" steps and hopped out. Afraid that the vehicle might explode, I moved off in a hurry, to watch what was going to happen from a safe distance. There were a number of Afghans lounging about who also watched. The smoke grew denser, blacker. Then one of them got up, and waving the smoke away from his face with a long sleeve, went closer to inspect. He reached for the ignition key and turned off the motor. The smoke died down and soon blew away. I felt somewhat foolish. The man who had turned off the ignition now opened the hood and the other men got up and came to look. So did I, halfheartedly. After decades of driving, looking under hoods has never made me any wiser about motors. The men muttered to one another and poked here and there. After a while, bored, I went inside the hotel. From that hour on, I was treated there with new respect. I was the immensely rich foreigner from a land of uncountable material blessings, who had indifferently abandoned his smoking car, almost with a wave of a nonchalant hand and a toss of a carefree head. From then on, the hotel staff, who had at last taken my true measure and had recognized that in my own land I was without doubt a great prince, tried to satisfy my every wish.

Watercress

I always felt while I was in Afghanistan that I was on the verge of starvation, for the food at the hotel was appalling. There was nothing to buy in the bazaar except Afghan *naan*, a flat bread that had a gritty substance in it like ash, or even sand. Once I was given a tin of French pâté by somebody and I spread it on the *naan* and that was a great treat.

I particularly missed green vegetables. There was a waterfall at a public garden just outside Kabul; as in a Persian miniature, the water flowed prettily over large, sharp gray stones into a crystal pool. The edges of this pool, and the course of the cascade as far as one could reach, were lined with luxuriant clumps of watercress. When I saw this deliciously edible plant, I put out my hands at once to pull it up in order to augment my hotel diet.

"Stop! I wouldn't do that if I were you," an older woman standing nearby warned me in English.

"Why not? The hotel can make me a salad."

"Sure, who wouldn't want a watercress salad in this place? But you'll get amoebic dysentery or jaundice. Think where that water has been, and all the stuff that's been added to it."

I withdrew my hand.

"Are you American?" I asked.

"No," she replied, looking displeased. "Canadian."

"But you sound just like an American," I persisted.

"Really? Well I'm not."

Frowning, she moved away from me and the tainted watercress, which seemed preternaturally large and growing larger every second, as in a horror movie, its beckoning leaves like brilliant emerald *fleurs du mal*. When I got to Delhi a few months later, I had lost more than ten pounds. India seemed like the land of milk and honey to me. I gorged myself on hot Indian food, especially spicy vegetables, and ordered ice cream via an obliging room service in the middle of the night.

My Hat and a Rose

I decided one day that I would buy a Persian hat and from an Afghan friend got the address of a high-class hatmaker. When I went there—to a small shop with a show window and a glass door set in a mud wall—I tried on a selection of fur hats called *garagoli*, mostly brown, black, and gray. This popular fur, when acquired in Central Asia, sometimes has a rank smell when it gets damp because the pelts have not been well cured. But I didn't know about that. When I could not decide which hat to buy, the shopkeeper brought out one from a hiding place. This fit perfectly, and was a silky gray of luxurious softness. I said at once I'd take it (for about ten dollars). As he was wrapping it up, the shopkeeper told me that he had been keeping my hat for another buyer, a government official who would no longer need it. I asked why not. The hat man drew his index finger across his neck in the universal gesture for throat cutting. I used to wear that hat in winter in New York until it disappeared, and it was often very smelly.

One afternoon in Kabul I went out from the club to take a walk on a long straight road that was lined with the high mud walls of Afghan family compounds on one side and open fields on the other. I hadn't gotten very far when I saw a diminutive young man dressed in nondescript rags coming toward me. He was smiling as in greeting and carrying a pink rose. His head was shaved and he wore a dirty, embroidered skullcap on it. As we drew abreast, he suddenly shot out the hand holding the rose, which he offered to me. I took it of course, somewhat astonished by this unexpected gesture of friendship from a stranger. He went on, still smiling and without breaking his stride. I smiled back and we continued on our ways, the pink rose now in my hand; I think—being sentimental in these things—I pressed it between the pages of one of the many books I lugged to Kabul.

Bamyan

I made my first trip to Bamyan soon after I arrived in Kabul. I went in a hired car with a young Afghan called Yusuf, who had been assigned to me by the Ministry of Culture to make sure that I didn't get into trouble. Yusuf was short, with a turned-up nose and a gap between his front teeth; he always wore one of the dusty-looking second-hand American dress suits that could be bought in the bazaar. Those suits (and overcoats) came with every kind of American department store label still attached and were imported by the thousands into the country by enterprising Afghan old-clothes dealers. Who gathered them up in the United States for resale? I wondered. I once saw, spread out on display in the bazaar, one of those Brooks Brothers herringbone tweed overcoats with velvet collar that had started its life on Madison Avenue on the back of a stockbroker.

Yusuf was unfailingly cheerful and, within his instructions to police what I shot, helpful, but he wore an anxious expression most of the time. His was the only home in Kabul I was ever invited to visit on my first trip; I went there for tea. I remember meeting brothers and older men in that house, but no women. I never met a single Afghan woman while shooting my film, or spoke to one. Later, when I went back in 1965, I met several, for by that time *purdah*, at least among the upper classes, was less strict. Yusuf must have had a mother, aunts, perhaps sisters; I know he had a wife. But none of them came out to meet me. In contrast, in India at that time, even the most orthodox families, whether Muslim or Hindu, were far less strict about a woman meeting a young foreign man.

The trip I made with Yusuf to Bamyan was a long and dusty one, over rutted roads winding through mountain passes. The rugged landscape reminded me of Arizona, and Colorado, with red cliffs jutting up at sharp angles against a bright blue sky. What looked like rock formations in the distance as we jolted along sometimes turned out to be abandoned strongholds said to have been sacked by Genghis Khan. Occasionally our car had to follow overloaded buses or brightly painted trucks carrying men sprawled on top of heaped-up goods. When we stopped for a tea break, my companion telephoned ahead, or back, to say we'd reached such and such a point, for the road passed through many fiefdoms more—or less—loyal to the central government. I have to say this about the telephones in Afghanistan at that time: they were very good; far, far better than in India. That is because the lines had recently been installed by Siemens, the German company, for the first time linking the whole country together with up-to-date equipment.

Arriving at Bamyan in the late afternoon, we drove down into a beautiful fertile valley bisected by a much photographed avenue of white-barked *chinar* trees. The hotel stood on a rise overlooking the valley; carved into the distant cliff opposite were the defaced colossal Standing Buddhas, which at the time were Afghanistan's main tourist attraction. At the dubious-looking hotel, I was offered a choice: a room inside or private tent outside. I chose the tent. In my luggage was a paperback copy of *Swann's Way*. I remember lying in that tent on my cot, the early morning sun beating down and distant sounds of the Bamyan valley coming up to me, while I tried to savor Proust's remembrance of his childhood and to keep straight his multitude of

The avenue of white-barked *chinar* trees in Bamyan (above);
the Standing Buddha (below)

characters. Every distant sound pierced the web Proust was spinning so that even now, when I think of his famous madeleine, I can still hear Afghan donkeys braying.

Proust's late-nineteenth-century world seemed as far removed as any could get from my Central Asian country—which was then stuck perhaps in the thirteenth century, and now may be in the fifth. Everything Proust described was missing, had never been there, and could never come to Bamyan or Kabul: not the highly developed social rituals, nor the physical world of soft white beds and madeleines, or the cafes, mansions, theaters, and streets. Not the sea, of course, nor the soft landscape like Balbec's. My senses were starved after nine months in Asia. I didn't know it, and would not have agreed if anyone had said so—especially since India, I thought, satisfied ev-

Hazara men celebrating Eid uz-Zuba

ery craving. But even then I knew that Afghanistan satisfied almost none, except a sense of adventure and my taste for a rugged terrain that evoked the American west I came from. So I held my book and tried to read until the buzzing flies in my tent made me get up and go outside.

The Hazara people were celebrating Eid uz-Zuba in the bazaar in Bamyan. "Hazara" means "thousand"; the name comes from the thousands of horsemen of Mongol descent brought by Genghis Khan when he conquered Afghanistan in the thirteenth century. The "thousand horse" people are an ethnic minority in Afghanistan, and they were definitely looked down upon in 1960 and kept apart—as they are today. Tall, fair as any European, often with red hair and blue eyes, only their Mongolian eyelids declared their origin. Afghans used to tell me that Afghanistan had never gotten over the Mongol invasion, and that until that time the country had been as prosperous and enlightened as Persia. Perhaps the prejudice against the Hazaras stems from that: unwanted invaders who brought ruin to a fair land. They have lived in the Bamyan valley for centuries, where they try to lead a decent rural life. But in Kabul, the Hazaras do all the dirty work, most commonly carrying backbreaking loads, like animals. Few ever save up enough money to make the pilgrimage to Mecca. I used to see the men and boys lined up along the river-bank, before they went to pray at the mosque, washing their scrawny white backs and legs and their patched brown rags in the surging brown waters of the Kabul River.

Picnic

One weekend I was asked to go camping by a high official in the Ministry of Culture. This was the gentleman most responsible for my safety and well-being, who would be obliged to answer to his superiors if I ran amok with my camera and shot compromising things. He arranged to pick me up at my hotel on Saturday afternoon. We drove through Kabul and made a second stop at a compound on the outskirts, where a foreign woman, a bit older than myself but younger than my host, got in, carrying an overnight bag. She turned out to be an Australian aid worker. We drove through barren hills until, about sunset, we arrived at our campsite in a little valley, which had been carefully picked for its beauty and for its seclusion in an unfrequented part of our host's lands. Three white tents had been set up in a grove, through which a stream ran. One tent was for me, one for dining, and one—apparently—for my host and his Australian friend. Bonfires had been built, cushions and carpets laid on the ground (much as in the scene in my film *Heat and Dust* where the Nawab entertains Olivia), and servants moved discreetly in and out of the shadows carrying platters of roasted meat. The most delicious melons I have ever eaten were served; they had the crunchy consistency of the flesh of apples. There was some chilled wine and a bottle of scotch. We had a good time, but not a relaxed one. It was all extremely dignified, our host's face ever watchful by the firelight for his guests' comfort and—most likely—for unseen intruders beyond the illuminated circle of the camp. I no longer remember his name; I will call him Naseem. He must have been in his early forties.

Olivia (Greta Scacchi) picnics with the Nawab (Shashi Kapoor)
in *Heat and Dust* (1983)

Unlike the actor Shashi Kapoor, who played the Nawab in *Heat and Dust*, Naseem was neither strikingly handsome nor did he bother much to charm us with small talk. He was another kind of character from a film, one encountered more frequently: the ever alert, taciturn sheikh of the oasis camp, who studies the night skies and sand dunes for hidden signs, and intently listens to the rustling and lowings of his herds for clues of danger. In time—not sharing his concerns—I withdrew to my tent and fell asleep in the cool air.

The next morning, after bed-tea, I decided to go out on my own— without informing my host, who had not yet appeared—to shoot a bit of rural footage for my film. I walked along the stream until I found some old men with long beards pulling mulberries down out of a tree to eat. They were happy to be photographed gorging themselves on the long purple berries, staining their fingers and white beards. I climbed up a hillside and was setting up my camera when a man passing on the dirt road below called out to me. What was I doing? he asked. Who was I? Where did I come from? Why was I taking pictures? I waved vaguely at the empty, almost featureless landscape of brown hills. Apparently satisfied, he went off, and when I finished, I climbed down to our camp with my camera and tripod. My host was relieved to see me. I impulsively told him about meeting the man on the road. His mood darkened. Who was the man? Where was he from? What did he look like? How was it that he knew English? That was not at all good. Our tents were struck and we headed for Kabul. I had not done a good thing, Naseem said as we drove, to wander off unaccompanied with a movie camera. Questions might be asked. Bad things might have happened. He frowned all the way back to town, and his friend—never the jolliest of Australian girls on this outing— frowned, too.

Perhaps it was really all very simple, I thought, having only to do with his official responsibilities. Or perhaps it was murkier. Had I been asked simply as a chaperon? But if my host and his girlfriend needed a place to tryst, why not fly over the mountains to Tehran, then a wide-open city full of foreign tourists? Why drag anyone along, especially an unreliable young American with a movie camera? Of course, none of these things might have anything to do with Naseem's unease. The reasons could be far beyond my Western imaginings. I was never again offered his hospitality and do not know what became of my companions of that weekend, or how—together

My host and his Australian friend

or separately—they breasted the tidal waves of woe that swept this way and that across Afghanistan in later decades.

A Sick American

The Americans and Russians were competing for Afghan affections in 1960, each country trying to move Afghanistan into its camp. The Soviets were constructing a highway down from their border, and the Americans were backing another, from the Khyber Pass in Pakistan west to Kabul. The joke going around was that this highway, being built with American money, would later be used by the Russians to invade the Indian subcontinent. That had always been the fear of the British, back in the days of the czars. The American presence in Kabul was bustling and large; to me, it had something of the quality of the American frontier about it, with visions of lands soon to be annexed beyond the wild, desert horizon—a horizon that always strikingly resembled those of the American west.

The United States Information Service put out a four-page mimeographed news sheet to keep Americans in Kabul informed of world events, for there were no newsstands, no *Herald Tribune* or *Time* magazine. So we read in it that Kennedy had been nominated for president, and all about the abortive Gary Powers spy mission. This newsletter was just about the only link I had with my countrymen in Afghanistan. An American not officially connected to the American mission was on his own. Once I got an intestinal disease and went in search of an American doctor at the Mission hospital. No one would examine me there, no matter how much I waved my passport around and dropped the names of my New York patrons at the Asia Society, including Mrs. Rockefeller. An American friend had heard that the British were more cooperative, so I went next to the British Embassy

The Khyber Pass

doctor. He turned out to be a florid, very easygoing sort of man—civilized, as the British would say—and he gave me some antibiotics. I can see him still in his rather bare clinic, silhouetted against a window as he scribbled out some instructions for me. I felt I might have been his only patient that day. I've never forgotten this act of mercy, or quite forgiven my hard-nosed countrymen for their lack of compassion—and imagination, for back then one could die quite soon in Asia if untreated, or go blind, or lose a limb to gangrene. No doubt there were excellent Western-trained Afghan doctors in Kabul, but I didn't know any.

I made a trip in my Land Rover to Pakistan, crossing the Khyber Pass to Peshawar. I took a passenger along, a youngish Englishwoman who lived in that city. She had come to Kabul to have her hair done, as—god knows why—the best hairdressers were there. We left early and she chattered away brightly, as that kind of Englishwoman does; she was the wife of the British consul general in Peshawar. She asked me if I had seen the production of *My Fair Lady* that the English little-theater group had just put on in Kabul. When I said I had not, she said that was a great pity; it had been so professional, the singing first-rate. Her husband had warned her that on no account were we ever to stop driving while in the Khyber Pass. Terrible things happened to the unwary who stopped to photograph, or to picnic. If anyone tried to hinder us, I was to put my foot on the accelerator and charge right through. This was not an easy trip for me. I had picked up a rash that went right across my stomach at the level of my belt, probably from a dirty towel in my hotel. The rash itched horribly, and looked like a bad case of poison ivy, red and weepy. The hotter it got as we descended toward Peshawar, the more uncomfortable I became. My passenger had nicely asked me to dinner, and to stay at the British residence, which I accepted. But once installed there, where I washed off the grime of the trip in the luxurious bathroom (and no doubt infected my hostess's towels), I asked to see a doctor. This was soon arranged, but when I explained what was wrong with me, my invitation to stay the night was revoked—for the good of her children, my hostess explained. A room was booked for me at Dean's Hotel, an icy air-conditioned room, the kind I love. I was visited by a Pakistani doctor, who prescribed a tincture of gentian violet for painting my stomach. I returned to the British residence for dinner; the evening was endless, the heat stifling—something like 100 degrees at ten o'clock that night.

A Stranger on the Road

I spent a week in Pakistan, then drove back alone. I broke the consul general's rule about stopping in the Khyber Pass. I felt as if I might be getting sunstroke; as I drove through the jagged canyons, the sun's heat beating off the stone scorched my face. The gorge was like a fiery red mouth lined with long, sharp teeth. Sometimes I passed figures wrapped in rags, carrying huge burdens on their backs. At one point I pulled over and ran pell-mell down to a stream. I threw myself flat on the ground, like the raving characters in movies who get lost in a desert, and lapped the cool water like a dog. This water was perhaps carrying every germ in the medical books, but I didn't care, nor did I care about being kidnapped. At the border I presented my passport to Afghan officials who knew no English and—most oddly—tried to speak to me in German, while a border guard kept me back with the tip of a bayonet pressed against my stomach.

That evening, as the sun was beginning to set, and when I was still fifty miles or so from Kabul, I stopped again: this time to pick up a hitchhiker, who suddenly appeared at the side of the road, starting up out of a gully and making frantic waving motions at me. He was a middle-aged man, with a still youthful and handsome face crossed with many fine lines. His black hair was cropped close, and he wore the familiar old suit jacket. He spoke enough English to ask me for a lift into Kabul. The times I have picked up a hitchhiker anywhere in the world, including the United States, can be counted on the fingers of one hand. Reason told me to be unaccommodating, but this man's personality attracted me, so I told him to get in. He knew more English than I first thought, and began to ask me questions about America. He must have liked what I told him, and liked me, too, for in a mood of sudden, personal exultation, he began to recite the Gettysburg Address in a loud voice. He knew it by heart and he shouted out the great phrases exuberantly.

Sometimes he misplaced the stress, or mispronounced, and Lincoln's rhythms got lost in the chant he made of it, as he emphasized "*Of the* People, *by the* People, and *for the* People." There was a sweetness about all this, nothing mad; my new friend's brown eyes were stretched wide open and were untroubled. I could imagine him shouting these words into the wind of an Afghan hillside, amid his sheep—a biblical patri-arch who had heard Jehovah speak, telling him to lead the People out of bondage.

We drove fast over the unpaved road the Americans were build-ing, throwing up dust and gravel into the mauve-colored evening air. On Kabul's outskirts he got out. He told me his name, I told him mine, and then he walked away. I had asked him to take dinner with me, but he said he had an appointment to meet a friend on a bridge.

IV

MAKING MOVIES

What I Do

Satyajit Ray (center) on the set of *The Postmaster*

In 1959 I was commissioned by the Asia Society of New York to make a documentary about Delhi, and traveled to India. I wanted to meet Satyajit Ray, whose film *Pather Panchali* I had seen at the San Francisco Film Festival, and which had stirred me very deeply. I managed to make his acquaintance—an Indian friend in New Delhi said to just call him up, that his number was in the Calcutta telephone directory. I did that, and he invited me to his set of *Two Daughters* (or *Three Daughters* as it was originally called; one of the stories was cut by Ray's American distributor because it was too long). I remember getting up at absolutely the crack of dawn to be out there on set in the country. It was the last day of work on one of the stories, "The Postmaster," and I just watched and watched. It was the first time I had ever seen a director at work. We never visited a Hollywood film set in all the years I was at the USC film school. I didn't know what a director did until I went on Ray's set and saw him communicating all sorts of things to the actors in various kinds of ways, and muttering things to his cameraman. At that point, he had begun to operate his own camera, which is something his cameramen were not thrilled about, but they could hardly stop him. And I understand now why a director would want to operate his own camera if he can, especially Ray, who couldn't do a lot of takes because Kodak film was so hard to get in India at the time. He would know at once whether he had got what he wanted out of his actors in terms of timing and composition in a way the cameraman could not.

Me and Ismail and Leela Naidu, the first of many, many leading ladies, during the filming of *The Householder* (1962)

And in 1962, when I came to Delhi to do my first feature, *The Householder*, in Delhi with Ismail, we were able to hire Ray's cameraman, Subrata Mitra, and about fifteen of his crew, including his first assistant. So in a sense, what they knew was what I learned during the nuts-and-bolts part of making a movie. I had never done a breakdown of a scene or a shot before then. It was like jumping into cold water, but I had to be able to do that.

I think *The Householder* naturally benefited from the fact that I was with Ray's longtime collaborators, and aesthetically there was further benefit, because I was looking at a scene through the eyes of his cameraman. When we came to editing the film, as we weren't happy with it—it was long and draggy and not cleverly edited—Ismail and I asked Ray if we could show him the film. We put ten reels of sound, ten reels of picture, and a lot of rushes in some big tin trunks and went on a train from Bombay to Calcutta. He liked the film and agreed to help us shape it, but on the condition that he do it freely with his editor, Dulal Dutta, and we not interfere. "Leave me alone for two or three days," he said. Anyway, he worked out a whole new framework for the actual story and shortened it considerably, and gave it the flashback form it has today, within bookends. When we did *Shakespeare Wallah* later on, we again showed it to Ray, who suggested how we might tidy it up a bit, and he agreed to do the music.

I feel that I have never really found a better way to set my scenes than as Ray taught me, or a way I like better. Somehow unconsciously

Satyajit Ray and actors on the set of *The Postmaster*

and without a tremendous amount of analysis on my part, simply seeing his films over and over has worked on me so that, although I'm dealing with different kinds of subject matter and in countries thousands of miles away from India, I feel his influence very strongly. Some years after I've finished a movie and I'm looking at it, I realize that I wouldn't have done it that way if it had not been for Ray's lingering influence.

I never talked to Ray about this, but I feel he must have had similar ideas about working—in that I feel that if you hire good actors, then they are artists through and through, and what they give you is the gift of their talent. A director is crazy not to recognize this and accept it. There are times of course when actors get on the wrong track and you have to guide them back. But I've always felt that actors are very deep and not wide—that they go into the depths of their own character to create this new character for you. And on the other hand, directors are wide but not deep, because a director has to deal with hundreds of things going on horizontally and he must deal with all of these things confidently, but he may not be able to deal with them in the depth that he would like. He hasn't got the time; he has to spread himself more thinly than the actors do. But that makes for a good balance, and it carries over into his working relationship with his other collaborators. A director, for example, can't remember every fine nuance of every single take, whereas the editor has an incredible memory for that and knows exactly where any shot goes out of focus or where an actor stumbles on a line. It's impossible for a director to know all that—anyway, I can't. I'm famous for my sets and costumes, but I don't begin to know how the designers come up with these things. I just get very good people to do them, and I let them do what they know best.

So I think I work with actors rather as Ray did: I have a tremendous amount of respect for them. It's hard for me to understand how some directors can push actors around and humiliate them—and I hear terrible things from actors about the most famous directors. I couldn't work in that way. I don't tend to shove people around or yell and scream. There was a now famous actor we worked with once who had too-long fingernails, and I felt that the character he was playing wouldn't have such long nails. It was very hard for me to bring it up without saying "Goddamnit, just cut your nails," so I didn't say anything, and there he is in the film with long nails. Sometimes you can't get your own way because you will offend the actor and disrupt something else that they're doing, which is not worth it. It's better to have long nails and wonderful performances. A director sees a million things. A leading lady might think that one angle of hers is better than another, yet you see that the angle she thinks is bad is really her best angle and you have to work to maneuver her in such a way or into such a position that the camera will take advantage of the better angle, which she hates. Often you have to work secretly with the cameraman to do something or other like that. There's a lot of secrecy that goes on all through the making of a movie to enable the director to get his way.

When I'm casting, I've learned to be more open-minded than I used to be. There have been casting mistakes in some of our movies—more in the earlier ones—and one has to be more receptive to suggestions from agents and one's friends about actors. What I'm always looking for—and this is true even when casting a well-known star—is a kind of individual distinction. I don't like actors to be too

Daniel Day-Lewis, the actor with too-long fingernails,
in *A Room with a View* (1986)

conventional in appearance or personality; I want there to be some additional thing that brings some extra life. When we're casting new, young actors, we rarely choose some pretty girl or good-looking guy. Leelee Sobieski (in *A Soldier's Daughter Never Cries*), for example, was only fourteen when we cast her, but she doesn't look like your average teenage girl. She's about seven feet tall and has a marked aquiline nose, which gives her face a kind of strength and character that an ordinary pretty girl wouldn't have.

Leelee Sobieski in *A Soldier's Daughter Never Cries* (1998)

We always intended to have long dialogue scenes in our films. Earlier on, when we worked with Subrata Mitra, we would very often do a whole scene in one shot, a combination of tracking and zooming and so forth and we'd get all the dialogue in one shot. Later on, I did less of that. Such shots were difficult to edit. With conventional scenes from one viewpoint, such as the actors acting Shakespeare in *Shakespeare Wallah*, we have always worked in the classical way, which is to light for the long shots and then, on a particular angle, go in closer and closer to the tighter shots, and then reverse and light the other way and again get closer and closer. That's pretty traditional, and Ray's crew had been trained to do that. We still stick to that way of shooting. In India, it was very hard sometimes to do elaborate tracking shots because they didn't have good dollies, and the floors were often uneven so it was difficult to lay rail—or sometimes we didn't have enough rail. Nevertheless, in *Bombay Talkie*, we made very good use of long traveling shots, which Mitra and I worked out carefully and which really paid off.

There are all kinds of ways of breaking a scene down. If it's a straightforward dialogue scene with people moving around a room and alighting here and there and sitting and standing, it's all rehearsed before we start and we don't need these tracking shots. The scene is broken down into shots so we know what we're going to do, and we follow that plan. But sometimes the scene is covered in one long master shot, which we then break into with closer shots for emphasis.

Paul Newman and Joanne Woodward in *Mr. and Mrs. Bridge* (1990)

I'm considered to be a perfectionist, but I also don't believe in doing too many takes because the actors hate it, and chances are they've given their best already and from then on, they get worse and worse.

Because of the kind of money we have, it's very rare to be able to bring the actors together for rehearsal before a shoot begins. Emma Thompson literally arrived on *The Remains of the Day* the day before we began shooting because she had another film going. There are

only two films where we've had proper rehearsals—*Autobiography of a Princess*, which was very short, but we were able to plan rehearsals with James Mason and Madhur Jaffrey that really paid off; and *Mr. and Mrs. Bridge*, where we were able to have a proper two-week rehearsal period because we were all in New York. Also, Paul Newman and Joanne Woodward wanted very much to get to know the actors playing their kids. We even blocked some of the scenes, although I remember that when we got to Kansas City to shoot, I threw them all out of the window

Kate Beckinsale in
The Golden Bowl (2000)

because they didn't apply to where we were shooting. I'm sure the rehearsals helped the wonderful performances in that film. Usually we do read-throughs beforehand, and when we're going to shoot, we rehearse thoroughly on the day.

For example, when we shot the scene where Maggie tells the Prince about her dream in *The Golden Bowl*, it was Kate Beckinsale's second day of work. But she felt confident and so we went into the room and rehearsed it several ways. She ended up sitting on that couch at the foot of the bed with him down on his knees in front of her. I think there's a logic to any scene that is set in an existing room with furniture in it and doors and windows. You have to man-

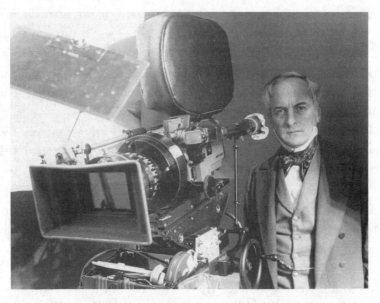

Me on the set of *The Europeans* (1979). Many of the male members of our
film crew wanted to put on the 1850s costumes, have their hair teased
appropriately by the hairdressers, and appear as extras—as I did, too.

age something within that—it's not like a set where you can take a
whole wall out or shoot from above. It's therefore slightly inflexible,
but the actors always manage it. You just rehearse it over and over
until they're happy that they've moved about in a way that seems
logical. It's an actor's logic. I have very good cameramen who, if the
actors want to do their lines under a bed, will find a way to shoot it.
Anyway, after we've organized a scene and the actors are satisfied,
they then go into makeup and costume, the lighting is arranged, and
we shoot it when they reappear.

Ruth Prawer Jhabvala and I continue working on the script right
through shooting. She rarely comes on set because she doesn't
like to: she always feels she's going to get in the way. But we keep in
close touch over the phone and fax or by letters sometimes, and she
watches the rushes all the time. She often picks up on things that feel
repetitive and rewrites scenes we haven't shot accordingly, or if I tell
her that someone is not working out as well as we thought, she will

simplify speeches—or vice versa; if someone turns out to be brilliant, she will pump up their part. Sometimes she'll think we don't need a scene and will tell me to look at it again carefully because it could be a waste of film. That happened in *The Golden Bowl* with the Prince, Maggie, and the little boy asleep in the bed at the end—that was originally two scenes.

When I'm making films based on very well-known novels, I am not keen on actors improvising all over the place, nor am I keen on their taking the novel and suggesting we reinsert scenes from it. When we were making *The Europeans*, everybody had a paperback copy of the book and was wandering around reading it all the time. Ruth knows exactly what she's doing; she's thought it out five hundred times, and on the whole there is no need not to speak lines as written. Most actors tend to respect that, although any director's a fool if someone comes along with a better idea for a line and he doesn't accept it. Ruth also gets involved in the editing room. I change the film enormously in the editing. The first full screening is usually a vast, shapeless monster, and we do a lot between then and the final cut. There's stuff in the movie that isn't first-class, but

Me, Ismail, and Ruth on the porch at Claverack, 2004

sometimes you are forced to keep such scenes in because they help the story. You must find a cut to present them in the best possible way. We don't reshoot. It's never as good as what we did the first time, even when it was done badly. We do add scenes sometimes, like the scene in *The Golden Bowl* where Maggie is reading the letter in the courtyard, which strengthens a particular strand of the story, and which was shot months later.

Critics of course only respond depending on whether we are in a fashionable or unfashionable phase in our career and reputations. We have been in and out of favor numerous times the whole forty years we've been working. It all just washes away finally. We just carry on making films, and what we do is often the only thing like it out there. I do feel that we're a little bit like aliens in a way—from outer space.

What a film director does—and does not, or cannot, do as he shoots his film—was wonderfully described by Jean Renoir in his memoir *My Life and My Films*, written in 1974. This is how he puts it:

> To me a script is simply a vehicle to be modified as one draws near to the real intention, which must not change. The intention is something that the film-maker has at the back of his mind, often without knowing it, but if it is not there the end result is superficial. The film-maker establishes his characters by making them speak, and creates the general ambiance by building sets and choosing locations. His own inward conviction only gradually appears, and generally in collaboration with the artisans of the film—actors, technicians, natural settings or artificial sets. We are subject to the immutable law whereby the essence is only revealed when the object begins to exist.

And:

> The film director is not a creator but a midwife. His business is to deliver the actor of a child that he did not know he had inside him.

I learned later that Ray had hung around Renoir's set of *The River* when he was a young man working in an advertising agency in Calcutta, as had the sixteen-year-old Subrata Mitra, who later was Ray's cameraman on *The Apu Trilogy*, and was the cameraman for the first four of Merchant Ivory's Indian features.

In the big classroom at UCLA that I visited with my friend Mindy Bagdon, Renoir had set his students a problem. He described a dialogue scene with a certain amount of necessary action and necessary moving around. What would be the best and most interesting way to do that? he asked. There was a kind of low stage, and his students then got up on it and walked through the imaginary actions of Renoir's scene. Some of the students didn't bother to go up on the stage where Renoir was standing, but indicated from their seats with a wave of their hands how this or that character might move about. Some sat silent, eating yogurt. I sat there thinking, My god! Do these guys know who this is? But then I remembered my own classes at the USC's film school years before and how unimpressed we had been by the eminent, mostly retired, once stellar figures who had been induced to come and talk to us. One day it had been the great art director William Cameron Menzies. I should have been trembling with awe and curiosity but was not, as these louts at UCLA should be now.

Afterward, outside, I went up to Renoir. I wanted to bring news of his old friends Satyajit Ray and Subrata Mitra, with whom I had just been working on *The Householder*. I spoke of my admiration for *The River*, and of how much it had meant to me when I had become interested in India—or rather, besotted by that country and its people.

In 1963, in Southern California, one still went out often in the daytime in a jacket and tie. I was wearing a necktie that had a traditional design of tiny mangos. Renoir (also in coat and tie) looked at it, and I think even touched it. He said then that when one eats a mango, all the delicious sweetness of India you may have been seeking is concentrated in a ripe mango's taste, like no other fruit. Just as when one eats an apple from Normandy, all the sweetness and flavor of France is concentrated in its crisp flesh. I am sure he had said this before, especially while in India, in the most beautiful French, which my translation above must not be compared to. His use of the word "sweetness" was not literal. He was talking about other spheres of sweetness that were as much about emotion and thought, and a hoped-for, remembered goodness—the special sweetness of a place, and now perhaps for an elderly Frenchman living in Southern California, of home.

This was my only meeting with Jean Renoir. He was still at work, making a string of color films after *The River* through the 1950s (of which my favorite was *The Golden Coach*, starring Anna Magnani), and had just made *The Elusive Corporal* in France. In 1969 he made his last film, *The Little Theater of Jean Renoir.*

Jean Renoir filming *The River* (1951)

Standing By in Bhopal: In Ismail's Custody

Ismail relaxing on the set of *In Custody*, in the
crumbling *haveli* of the Begum of Bhopal

A short cast list, in order of appearance:

Tony Korner: The publisher of *ARTNews*, often associated
with some of Merchant Ivory's earlier films, such as *Savages*.
Humayun: A young friend of Ismail Merchant. Humayun
was also the name of the second Mughal emperor, who fell
down the steep steps of his palace in Delhi and cracked his
skull. He was replaced on the throne by his son Akbar, the
greatest of the Mughal emperors, in 1556.
Shabana Azmi: *In Custody*'s female star.

Raquel Welch: The star of MIP's *The Wild Party*, who used to loudly ask her acting coach after a shot what her best takes were whenever she was dissatisfied with my choice of prints.

Shashi Kapoor: The male lead of *In Custody*, playing the poet, Nur.

Sunil Kirparam: The accountant in Merchant Ivory's London office.

Nirad Chaudhuri: The Bengali writer and polymath, about whom we made a documentary for the BBC in 1972.

Kathryn Martin: The production coordinator of *In Custody*.

Wahid Chowhan: Ismail's brother-in-law and the producer of *In Custody*

Sultan Khan: The great Indian classical musician and sarangi player, who often provided music for our Indian films.

Shabana Azmi, *In Custody*'s female star

For once, I'm not paying much attention as we land. There is a tremendous smack as we hit the ground; I felt the plane should have broken in two. The plane has veered sharply, its wing almost hitting the ground next to the runway. The passengers exchange looks.

It is 1993, and I am once again in India.

When we get off and go into the airport, there is Tony Korner, about to board another plane. He comes forward to greet me. Is he, too, dreading dying soon in an Indian plane crash? Anyway, these two ships pass in the night. He had come to visit Ismail on his set. I find my things and get into the car MIP has sent for me. Bhopal seems rather sanitized—none of that terrible smell of ordure following you everywhere. The roads are clean and refuse clear, the sky pure, the air—well, who knows now about the air here?*

The hotel is a modern construction overlooking a vast, man-made lake—almost an inland sea—that is a thousand years old, around which the city was built. I ask to be shown up to Ismail's room. There are twin beds in it, and a handsome young man is fast asleep in one of them. This is Humayun, I learn later, whom Ismail has befriended, and I look down at him. He's rather dark for a North Indian Muslim, and his eyes open, startled, as he sees my face above peering into his. I make calming gestures with my hands, as if to say go back to sleep, and begin to stow away the things I've brought Ismail from London.

I go to the room reserved for me, unpack, and wait for him. Quite soon, having wrapped,† he dashes in for a few seconds. He doesn't have much to say yet and soon rushes out, not taking, or even looking at, all the mail I've brought him. Later on, there's a long session of viewing rushes on a VCR and he frequently leaves it to answer the telephone. There are many foreigners in the crew—I'm surprised at how many, all young and eager: from America and England, Switzerland and Belgium, South Africa. And many of the old faces from *Heat and Dust* and even *Bombay Talkie* days. *Very* old faces now. I did not recognize the handsome Ahmed who was once Shashi Kapoor's driver in Bombay and is now some sort of security guard, creaky and lined. Rambali from MIP's Bombay office, one-eyed and irrepressible; Gianchand, our head grip, who threw Jane Buck, my script supervisor on so many films, into a swimming pool, etc. As the days go by and I meet—or remeet—these old-timers, I feel how terrible it

---

* The Bhopal disaster—a gas leak at the Union Carbide pesticide plant in Bhopal on the night of December 2, 1984—is considered among the world's worst industrial disasters. More than five hundred thousand people in the surrounding area were exposed to methyl isocyanate gas, a highly toxic substance.
† Finished shooting work for the day on a film set.

would be if I were not to recognize them. I imagine myself sitting on the set and vaguely looking about and wondering.

The set is a vast, crumbling *haveli** beside the lake, belonging to the Begum of Bhopal, the only hereditary female ruler in all royal India. Downstairs is the production office with direct dialing to London, New York, and Claverack, plus fax machines disgorging the latest magazine articles about MIP, all set up within a disintegrating marble colonnade. Policemen, very thin and lethargic, keep out the crowd—never very big, actually. Two lady constables have been summoned because there have been cases of sexual harassment on MIP's set, where there are many lady onlookers. Strangest is Shabana Azmi's confidante, an emaciated, unsmiling Anglo-Indian named Alice. She has a bony back poking through her blouse, no doubt often struck by a wrathful hand.

Shabana has a very good shot—not in the script—on Nur's terrace, in which she rushes out in a rage and frees all of her husband's pigeons, then collapses. We watch from below and applaud as the birds fly up into the sky. Ismail says he likes the takes, but Shabana calls down: "What does Jim think?" I say loudly that I, too, like all three takes. I don't want any of that sort of thing when I visit Ismail's set; she reminds me a bit of Raquel Welch during *The Wild Party* at this moment, and I wonder if Shabana is up to some kind of mischief. I decide to stay away from her shots and only to be there for Shashi's.

The set is wonderfully cool, fly-free, and on the whole uncontaminated by ancient drains. The crew toilets are on the roof, and have long since run out of toilet paper; the spigot with water for the plastic *lota*† is dry. We caught the kitchen helper refilling the unsealed Bisleri water bottles from the tap, so now everyone guards his own, breaking the seal in the morning and carrying it around all day, or until it's used up. Then new ones are brought out of a locked cupboard, as if they are vintage wine.

The Begum has some extraordinary books. They have been lent for the revolving bookcase in the poet's room called for by the script. There is *An Irish Beauty of the Regency*, the *Unpublished Journals of the*

---

* A grand home, or palace.
† The little metal pot to hold water that Indians use to clean their bottoms with.

Honourable Mrs. Craven, and *The Autobiography of Charlotte Amélie, Princess of Aldenburg,* the latter labeled "No. 244 in the Private Library of H. H. the Begum." I hope Ismail's camera did not linger long on these. Nur's taste in literature may seem to be, especially for an Urdu poet, very recherché indeed.

A conversation with Ismail in the car: He is saying how negative and frightened our cameraman, Larry Pizer, is, and how when the riots started,* he was afraid he would be done in. I try to reassure Ismail, feeling his displeasure may next be turned on me: "Oh, but he's so involved and interested in everything," I say, and "How he loved doing Shabana's pigeon shots," etc. Ismail looks darkly out of the window and says impatiently, "Pigeons are pigeons." He tells me at every opportunity that I must not "tax" him, that he will send me away the next day, and that generally I am a great vexation falling on him when he has so many other things to think about. Sometimes he is deliberately and abominably rude, as if he is trying to prove something—not unlike the days when he perhaps was trying to prove something to

Nautch girls, circa 1870

---

* There had recently been terrible Hindu-Muslim riots in the neighboring state of Gujarat, with many deaths.

Dick Robbins (but what?). Now, however, Dick is no more,* so what is he trying to prove? Something to himself (but what?).

Muslim girls of good family have a new fashion I haven't seen before. I'm talking about the smartly dressed ones. They tie a *dupatta*† diagonally down over one shoulder to the waist, a bit like a diplomat's sash of honor. But this is also the style of the old-time Nautch girls,‡ as seen in Victorian photographs. I wonder if they know this, and that the old-time nautch girls were little better than prostitutes.

If you are a very restless, energetic, and physically active male, you make a film that has those qualities naturally. Ismail's best scenes reflect that side of him. If, on the other hand, you are relaxed, easygoing, and comfort seeking, are happiest when lolling about without a single practical thought in your head—or with perhaps many thoughts in your head, all more or less of equal importance, then maybe your films—that is, *my* films—naturally reflect those qualities.

Bette Davis in *Juarez* (1939)

More about the Begum's library: three further books. *The Duchess de Chevrenne* by Louis Baliffol; *The Story of a Beautiful Duchess* by Horace Bleackley (its subject being the Duchess of Hamilton, who was a predecessor of Emma); and *Imperial Twilight*, by Bertita Harding. This last author is someone I read as a teenager. She wrote a book called *Phantom Crown*, all about Maximilian, the emperor of Mexico, and his empress,

---

* Richard Robbins, our longtime composer, and Ismail had been inseparable for many years but had recently fallen out.
† A long, scarflike piece of diaphanous cloth that Muslim women in India and Pakistan drape over the shoulders.
‡ Hired dancers and songstresses.

Carlota. A movie was made of their sad story starring Bette Davis, Brian Aherne, and Paul Muni as Juarez, their nemesis. Just the kind of movie I liked then: the French Napoleon III installs a puppet king from the Hapsburg family in Mexico. The Mexicans don't want him, neither does President Lincoln, busy with the Civil War.

Then Napoleon III gets bored, abandoning Maximilian to the firing squad (painted by Manet). Carlota comes back to Europe to plead their case, but even the Pope won't take her call, and she goes mad. Bette Davis, in black lace veils, eyes bugging ferociously, goes to pieces in the Vatican. Carlota further endeared herself to me by having been born on my birthday, June 7, and she lived on crazy right up to my time. Inside *Imperial Twilight* there was a note in a fine hand: "Historical— very interestingly written." Was this the Begum of Bophal's opinion?

To spend time in one of these many-terraced, multilayered stone Indian houses built before the Industrial Revolution is to know how it was to live in ancient mansions of Rome or Greece—the multiple courtyards, the stairs going steeply up a wall, little rooms stuck into towers and turrets with views down onto the water, the massive solidity of the construction, which is no doubt why the ruins of Roman villas still exist in a semi-intact way.

Sunil arrived from London with a plastic sack full of all the Sunday papers—or, all but *The Independent*, the one I really wanted to read. These were snatched up by the English crew members. But there wasn't any real news in them, as Nirad Chaudhuri remarked so long ago when we interviewed him: how in England nothing of any real importance ever happens anymore. Just scandals and lawsuits and parliamentary bickering and tips for the home and garden—and of course pages of sports news. How they love to run down President Clinton, calling him "Silly Billy," and treating him as if he were some sort of airhead! *The Telegraph* is the worst. And when he was running for president, even though it was clear he would win, they cooked up stories about how his support was draining away, or all imaginary. There must be nothing worse for a certain kind of English person than a populist American president from some down-home place like Arkansas. Now their prime minister, who publicly backed the wrong man, must go to Clinton almost as—no, *as*—a vassal, in order to restore the "special relationship."

Today Kathryn and I went into the bazaar to buy cloth. We went to the stall that's been supplying the film with demented-looking printed fabric to decorate the brothel. I bought yards and yards of different kinds of Matisse-like cotton cloth, in spectacular colors; so did Kathryn. The shop owner kept pushing discreet, rather traditional choices on us—"For export, sir!"—but we stuck to the wildest patterns, not to decorate the set, but in fact to take home. I wonder if we have set the fabric designers here back decades: distinguished old sahib comes in with nice young English memsahib who go into ecstasies over kitsch, buying like mad. There is nothing like the refined Western eye, running amok in an oriental bazaar. Then all this stuff is dragged back to one's rather austere rooms, and you don't know what to do with it.

There is now what might be called the Battle of the Bisleri water. Waheed Chowhan, Ismail's brother-in-law and the producer of *In Custody*, has decided (backed up by Ismail, it goes without saying) that the crew is abusing its Bisleri water privileges, and that too many bottles have been seen with too many members of the Indian crew— three, four, a day! The Indians cry out that they, too, have delicate stomachs. It's not just the English who do, and that withdrawing their Bisleri water makes them second-class citizens. Bisleri water bottles have become the status symbol on the set, as if they were bottles of Perrier, and then later, Evian in the West. A sort of compromise has been reached: two bottles will be put in each hotel room; everybody else can drink *agua minerale*. What everybody liked was breaking the seal on his or her private Bisleri bottle.

What can one do when nine hundred million people suffer from an inferiority complex? And what can you do if nine hundred million people are antisocial, in the sense of having no regard for, or interest in, others that they don't know, or aren't related to, or who belong to a different caste? A perfect example of this national Indian character defect: a man eats in a hotel restaurant, goes after his meal to the men's room, fills his mouth with water from the basin, rinses his mouth out, spits the debris into the basin, then leaves without washing it out. Later on, in the course of his day, he will spit a lot of bright-red betel* juice on the walls of any stairwell he's descending.

Sultan Khan Sahib told us that any Muslim music teachers who regularly went to luxury apartment blocks in Bombay to instruct their young Hindu students have been told not to appear anymore. This breaks a five-hundred-year tradition in India. On the deepest level, that is what Ismail's film *In Custody* is all about.

Today I do a short interview with a Toad† who has been gushing that she would treasure my autograph in her copy of the *In Custody* novel. As I didn't write it and I'm not directing the film, I sign it: "Standing by in Bhopal. James Ivory." She says to me, in the course of the taped interview, that of our Indian films—or even our later non-Indian ones—she likes only *The Householder*. She wrinkles up her nose when she speaks of *Heat and Dust*. I ask her if she's ever seen *Shakespeare Wallah*. She hasn't. She is quick to tell me that the Delhi press had not much liked *Howards End*. They had found it too "picture-postcardy" and too "literary." I say to her, "No film can ever be 'too literary.'" Did they mean to say "too literate"? She thinks about it and says they'd actually written "literate"! So then I say, "Well no film can ever be too 'literate.'" But I'm glad I've met with her. It has taught me not to let down my guard for a second when I do my press call for *Howards End* after I return to Bombay tomorrow. Such Toads are to be treasured, and like certain Indian pickles, counted on to spice up a long, dull day.

Ismail's young friend Humayun is a sweet and modest young man with perfect manners. He has been put to various small production jobs so he can earn a little money. Was he not one of the enraptured youths

---

* Red juice created by someone chewing *pan*—betel nut wrapped in a leaf.
† Too often a spectacularly beautiful and well-turned-out Indian woman who has very little upstairs. From the family vocabulary devised by Ruth Jhabvala and her husband, Cyrus. The male equivalent, who may appear at first to be a formidable, dark god, they called a "stone." Prime Minister Indira Gandhi was referred to as "the Prime Toad" by the Jhabvalas, who had long known her. She was neither young nor beautiful and had no elegance. But she utterly lacked that nimbleness of mind that they prized in women, and so became a Toad candidate—though, as it proved, a crafty and manipulative one.

Me, Emma Thompson, and Anthony Hopkins shooting the too
"picture-postcardy" *Howards End* (1992) in Simpson's in the Strand, London

taught to cry out "Wah! Wah!" during the evening musicale staged in a
haveli we see being torn down later? He's not only desperately poor, his
family is difficult and quarrelsome. They see him as the breadwinner,
and are enchanted that a great sahib, a famous man, has taken him up.
Ismail wants him to go on with his studies and Humayun promises
he will. Ismail wants him to improve his English, and he tries to do
that, writing notes to him in English with fulsome salutations but not
much else in them, ending always in the hope that God will keep Ismail safe. As he is woefully educated, I can guess his letters are written
by a scribe in the bazaar. He is socially several steps up from the sort of
boys there who are quick and personable and streetwise, who can look
after themselves and aren't sad and hopeless-seeming like Humayun.
I saw that there was a tinge of exasperation in Ismail when he read
Humayun's letters.

Today I am on the second-floor balcony of Ismail's new Bombay
apartment looking down into the street because I hear some sort of
bawling song—not the song that so entranced Dick Robbins when
he made his film about Bombay street musicians. And sure enough,

three beggars appear: one sort of crawling along; the second a leper, sitting in a cart being pulled; and the third, not maimed or deformed but tall and good-looking, and even rather smartly turned out in a *lungi,** bright shirt, and scarf. Perhaps they work as a team. I signal to the party and the tall man enters the compound through the gate. The *chokidar*† tries to stop him, but I yell from the balcony and wave a fifty-rupee note. But when I try to throw it down, it flutters through the bars of an open window into the apartment below. So the *chokidar* goes to get it. He's gone quite a long time and the beggars wait patiently. When the *chokidar* returns, he gives the beggars the note. But I can see that it's not my fifty-rupee note, but a ten-rupee note. At this moment Waheed appears below and I tell him what's happened, and how much I threw down. Waheed straightens it out for us, threatens the *chokidar*—even raising his hand as if to strike him—and gives the correct amount to the beggar's leader, who does *Adab*‡ with his hand courteously, and withdraws. The song resumes.

---

* An ankle-length tube of cotton or silk worn around a man's waist and knotted to keep it in place, usually worn at home; poorer Muslim men often wear it in the street.
† A gatekeeper.
‡ A salutation, usually by Muslims, like a salute, the hand raised to eye level. The *Adab* is also used as a farewell gesture of respect.

Maestro

The Alien*

Satyajit Ray, the Bengali cinema director, was in town recently, en route from Hollywood, where he had just concluded a film-making deal with Columbia Pictures, to Calcutta, where he lives, and where he has made nearly all his movies—*Pather Panchali*, *Aparajito*, *The World of Apu*, *The Music Room*, *Two Daughters*, *Devi*, *Charulata*, and many others, some known here and some not seen outside India. We called him and asked him if he could bring us up to date both on his current projects and on his future plans, and he invited us to go with him on

---

* This section originally appeared in the July 22, 1967, *New Yorker* where, from time to time in the late 1960s, I wrote "Talk of the Town" pieces.

a shopping expedition, during which we could ask him anything we liked. We met him shortly afterward on a quiet street in the East Fifties, and began walking with him toward Fifth Avenue. The day was sultry; our progress down the street was steady and purposeful, with only one pause, in the middle of Park Avenue, to take a photograph.

Mr. Ray, who is in his forties and is a very tall man, with a strong face and commanding voice, told us about his Columbia film, which will star Peter Sellers. "Science fiction has always been an interest of mine, and I've written a good many science-fiction stories," he said. "A lot of them were for a children's magazine that I put out—well it's not really for children; it's for fourteen-, fifteen-, sixteen-year-olds—and, naturally, I've often thought of making a science-fiction film of some kind. In Calcutta, we have a science-fiction-film club, with over fifteen hundred members and a long waiting list. On behalf of it, I wrote a letter to Arthur Clarke, the science-fiction writer and the co-author, with Stanley Kubrick, of the screenplay for *2001: A Space Odyssey*, which Kubrick is at present directing. We asked Clarke for his good wishes—for his blessing, you might say. He wrote back expressing admiration for my films, and we began to correspond. Clarke put me in touch with Michael Wilson, my producer—an Englishman who is living in Ceylon. Wilson came to see me in Calcutta. He thought we might be able to do a science-fiction film together—my direction, and Clarke collaborating with me on the screenplay. It sounded good. We talked over an idea that I had, and I did a quick treatment of it. Mike was confident from the start that we'd find backing, but I had doubts. To me, the biggest stumbling block was the fact that the film would have to be in Bengali and English. I was afraid this might not go down very well. And then I knew we needed a much bigger production setup than I usually have, with many more facilities. The film would require technical treatment of a fairly high order. Special effects and processing would have to be done abroad. All this meant big-studio backing. I wasn't sure. But then Peter Sellers joined our team."

Just how *had* Peter Sellers happened to be cast in the film, we asked.

"When I wrote the part of Bajoria, the Marwari philanthropist— Marwaris are businessmen who have a special reputation for shrewd- ness—I felt that there was no Indian actor quite right for it," Mr. Ray replied. "I mentioned to Mike how good Peter Sellers would be in a part like that. Mike was entranced with the idea. Of course, the part *would* gain by having Sellers. He just happens to be one of the greatest virtuosos that we have, you see. Mike asked me if I was very sure, and I told him I was. So he sent off a telegram to Sellers in Lon- don. He had to get the address out of the *Artists and Writers Year Book*. Luckily, the Oxford Bookstore in Calcutta had a current copy. The telegram went something like this: 'Please inform soonest whether you are interested in principle playing serious role in Vedic science- fiction subject to be shot in India.' Sellers's agent intercepted the tele- gram and wired back in a few hours to say that Sellers, who was in Switzerland, *was* interested. We made plans to go and see him. Mike had a feeling that, in case Sellers didn't know my work, it would be a good idea to show him one of my films. We managed to get a print of *Charulata* in London—a very *bad* print, by the way; all the night scenes looked like day scenes—and we flew off to Paris with it, where we met Sellers and a screening was arranged, but even before the screen-

Soumitra Chatterjee and Madhabi Mukherjee in *Charulata* (1964)

ing Sellers indicated he was interested in playing the part of Bajoria.
After that, Mike went on to Los Angeles, with a commitment from
Sellers, and I went home to Calcutta. A few weeks later—sometime
in May—I received a cable from Mike saying that Columbia was interested in financing us. By that time, I had written the script—not,
as it turned out, with Arthur Clarke—and I left for Los Angeles with
it. There's only one drawback to all this. Sellers isn't free until October,
1968."

We asked Mr. Ray to tell us something about the story.

"It's called *The Alien*," he said. "A spaceship lands in a lotus pond
somewhere in Bengal and begins to exert a powerful benign influence on the flora and fauna all around. Only the gold tip of the roof of
the spaceship can be seen above the surface of the pond. The people
in the neighborhood—mostly quite uneducated—think the space-
craft is a sunken temple. Bajoria—that's Sellers—wants to salvage
the temple. He has hired an American engineer to drill a well for
him, but he decides maybe the American—that part isn't cast yet—
can be put to better use. Meanwhile, the people are beginning to
pay homage to the new deity. A lot of complications follow, as you
can imagine, leading to a climax, which I think one ought not to talk
about, and the spaceship leaves. The interior of the craft will be like
a living organism. Instead of control boards, with dials and knobs and
flashing lights, there will be veins and nerves, under a parchment-
like surface, through which colored liquids will be moving. When
the alien, or the inhabitant of the ship—who will be played by a
ten-year-old boy—wants to operate it, he presses on the veins and
nerves. The center of the floor pulses."

The two of us arrived at E. J. Korvette and went into its cool, bright,
jam-packed interior. Mr. Ray pulled a typed list out of the pocket of
his shirt—it was a black-and-white striped sports shirt—and consulted it. He quickly bought two ladies' tan wallets; four rings, at the
costume-jewelry counter; two jars of Yardley's solidified brilliantine;
a long-playing record entitled *Magnificent Movie Music*; a flexible toy
man called Gumby; a Scrabble set; and two eight-millimetre films—
The Mummy, with Boris Karloff, and *The Adventures of Batman*. Going
out, we crossed Fifth Avenue and headed down Forty-Seventh Street

to the Dumont Stamp Shop, where Mr. Ray bought a stamp album. Then we took a taxi to Macy's. On the way, Mr. Ray told us how he intends to use his time between now and October, 1968.

"First of all, I have to finish a film I'm working on now, called *Chiriakhana*," he said. "There are only six more days of shooting. It has taken fourteen months to make—longer than any other film of mine except *Pather Panchali*. Uttam Kumar, who's playing the lead, had a heart attack at the beginning of the last shooting schedule."

We asked what the film was about.

"It's a detective story, written by Saradindu Bannerji," Mr. Ray said. "He writes the only good detective stories in India. Nothing is cribbed from Sherlock Holmes or Agatha Christie. The characters and situations are genuinely Indian. The scenario makes for quite a dense film. There are lots of interesting characters. It's good. It could be a popular film. The lead—Uttam Kumar—is Bengal's most famous leading man, and there are all kinds of associations of the romantic hero connected with him. I wanted to change that, to make him seem more daring. I thought of the idea of his having a pet snake. I went to see my uncle, who has a kind of menagerie—mouse deer, blue scorpions, hedgehogs, that sort of thing. He had a snake called a baby python, which never grows longer than three feet. It looks like a very poisonous snake that we have called a *bora*. Now, I'm not terribly enamored of snakes myself, and I didn't want to touch it, but I knew I had to. So I just plunged in and grabbed the thing. I took the snake to the set, and of course the crew were terrified of it, but I had everyone there handle it. I used it in the very first shot, where we see it coiled around Uttam's wrist in a big closeup."

At Macy's, we went straight up to the luggage department, and Mr. Ray bought a large suitcase. He dumped his earlier purchases into it and consulted his list again. Then he very rapidly bought a madras windbreaker (size 14) for his son Shandit; a brown cowhide belt (size 28), also for his son; a small can of powdered gold leaf; a pair of embroidery scissors, which the saleswoman told him should be used only for sewing; a lady's comb in a folding case; two little mirrors with handles, to put in a purse; and a small handbag. All these went into the suitcase, and we were out in the street once more, this time on the way to the West Forty-Ninth Sam Goody's.

We asked Mr. Ray whether he would be making any other film before starting on his project with Peter Sellers.

"Oh, yes," he said. "Two of them. I'm doing the first one this September. It's a low-budget film based on a novel by Bibhuti Bannerji, who wrote *Pather Panchali*. It has the same setting—a rural village. It's about a family. After that, I'll do a fantasy—a sort of children's film I've been working on for a long time. My grandfather, Upendra Kisore Ray, wrote the story, and it's a wonderful subject for a film. It's a fairy tale, set in two kingdoms—one with a good king, and one with a king whose Prime Minister gives him potions every day to make him evil. The film ends in a shower of sweetmeats, with the famished Army—nobody eats except the wicked Prime Minister, you see—marching over the Prime Minister's body. Even the horses are badly fed; we'll get a lot of rickety horses from the tonga wallahs— the pony-cart drivers—for the Army to ride on. I have composed six songs for this film. I promised my son Shandit I'd make it, and next January we'll be going to Rajasthan to shoot it."

In Sam Goody's, Mr. Ray produced another list, and, after looking at it and browsing awhile, sent a salesman off to get Haydn's "Lord Nelson Mass" and "Mass in Time of War," a television sound track from *Batman*, a recording of cantatas by Alessandro Scarlatti and Telemann, and Couperin's "Leçons de Ténèbres."

Outside again, we told him that his recent *The Big City* has been advertised here as a "comedy-drama." How would he classify it, we asked.

"Really, how can you describe the film?" he replied. "*The Big City* is certainly not a comedy, though it doesn't lack humor. The domestic aspect is very strong. I really don't know what it is. I've never tried to classify any of my films. I once thought of calling this one, in English, *A Woman's Place*, but nobody seemed to like that."

Knowing that Mr. Ray is a friend and admirer of the French director Jean Renoir, who directed the classic film *The River* in India, we asked if he had seen Renoir while he was in California.

"Yes," he said. "The producer Kenneth McEldowney gave a party for Renoir and me, after a showing of *The River*. Before the screening, Renoir and I had to go up on the stage and carry on a little conversation about the making of the film, which I had watched being shot in Bengal many years ago, when I was still working in an advertising agency. The man who introduced us to the audience said, 'Ray owes a lot to Renoir.' But Renoir told the audience, 'I don't think Ray owes anything to me. I think he had it in his blood. Though he's very young still, he's the Father of the Indian Cinema.' At the party, later, I asked him if he was writing any more books. He told me that he is writing a book for young directors who are just starting out. He said, 'I don't want young directors to make the mistakes that I have made. It's a book of warning.' He remembered all the members of his Indian crew, and asked after them. He told me he had loved *Two Daughters*, the film I made based on a couple of Tagore stories—mainly 'The Postmaster.' I asked him where he had seen it. He answered, 'Somewhere in the world.'"

The Maestro

Early in our friendship with Satyajit Ray, Ruth and Cyrus Jhabvala began calling him "the Maestro." This was in 1963 when he helped me recut our first feature, *The Householder*. We were conscious of our inability to pronounce his name properly in Bengali, which would have come out something like "Shoto-jeet Rye." He made several short visits to New York from Calcutta and sometimes his American distributor, Ed Harrison, would put him up modestly in a Manhattan hotel. It should never be forgotten that in those days—the sixties and seventies—India's greatest artist was often not given any foreign exchange by his government when he traveled to the West.*

---

* When we began working in India in the 1960s, India had to conserve its foreign exchange—foreign money. Indians going abroad had to manage somehow, since they could take no foreign money out of the country. The lack of foreign exchange especially affected the film industry, as the only decent film stock was manufactured by Eastman Kodak and had to be imported and paid for in U.S. dollars. Once India became an industrial powerhouse some decades later, all that changed.

One summer we put him up ourselves in our one-bedroom apartment. Another time we put him in the Hilton Hotel on Sixth Avenue, which he hated because of its noisy, crowded lobby and slapdash, impersonal service. We'd thought he might like being up in a New York skyscraper, but the Midtown view from his window did not compensate for the general tumult of that commercial hotel chain. When he stayed with us, I have a memory of him lying on the bed next to mine covered by a sheet, his large, dark feet sticking out at the end (Ismail slept on the floor in the living room). On another occasion, this time properly funded by some host—perhaps Co-

lumbia Pictures, with whom he was developing his science-fiction film *The Alien*—he stayed in the Barbizon Plaza Hotel on Central Park South. I went to see him and he invited me up to his room overlooking Central Park. While I was there a large chocolate cake was delivered in a box from some fancy Manhattan cake shop. It had been sent by Richard Avedon, who was hoping to photograph Ray for his series of illustrious film

Pauline Kael

directors, most of them pretty old. "I'll never agree to that," said the Maestro, opening the cake box. "He'll make me look like a senile old man" (Ray was fifty then). He'd seen the portrait Avedon had made of Ray's beloved friend and mentor, Jean Renoir. He then began to cut the cake and we ate it.

Another time I called on him in a Manhattan hotel provided by

Harrison and found the film critic Pauline Kael stretched out on the bed, from where she greeted me. This was before she had begun to review my own films for *The New Yorker*, so I still had friendly, even hopeful, feelings about her.

Also in Ray's hotel room was the usual contingent of Indian journalists interviewing him, and Calcutta friends who happened to be in New York. As she lay there, Kael pronounced caustically, in her high-pitched, little girl-of-good-family, shaking voice, to whomever would listen, on this and that current film she'd seen, and this and that director, omitting for once her usual four-letter words. Her excited feelings were entirely positive about all of the work of Ray that she'd so far been able to see. I couldn't help wondering as she lay there, her thoughts ever spinning, if she was hoping that if they ever managed to be alone, a suddenly impassioned Ray might fling his massive, six-and-a-half-foot frame down on top of her.

Whenever Ray made a visit to Bombay while I was working there in the midsixties I would try to see him at his hotel. On one occasion another film critic dropped in while I was meeting him. This was Marie Seton. She was writing a book on Ray and was pursuing him in Bombay in order to get information for it. He was staying at the Airlines Hotel in Churchgate, another modest hotel. He was surrounded as usual by the little reverent circle of Bengali youths who always managed to get in to see him on the pretext of writing an article or doing some "work" on him. What the Maestro was really doing was giving them a kind of *darshan*—the ancient Eastern practice of potentates who were regularly expected to show themselves to their people. The pharaohs of Egypt could be seen in their Windows of Appearance, similar to Indian rulers later, sitting on the Peacock Throne in Delhi. Indian holy men like to do this. I think the Bengali youths sitting in Ray's hotel rooms were no more noticed than the chairs or ashtrays or bedcovers: they came, he greeted them, they sat in silence, they went. I saw this in many places— Berlin, New York, and in the big Indian cities. Anyway, as it happened, Marie Seton appeared at his door—unannounced, I think.

Marie Seton and Satyajit Ray

She put her head into the room, with her mop of untidy graying hair: "Oh, Shotojeet, may I come in?" The Maestro said to her, "I'll give you five minutes, Marie," so she sat down amid the disciples and interjected a few questions, which he casually answered. Precisely at the end of five minutes, he pointedly looked at his watch and said, "Your five minutes are up, Marie," whereupon she rose and left.

Ray referred to her sometimes as a figure of fun in those days; his cameraman, Subrata Mitra, said her book about him is full of mistakes. Therefore it was with a feeling of distress that I heard that Ray, because of no foreign exchange, had to stay with her at her house in London on one of his trips there, or that he had consented to be the guest of honor at a dinner party she gave.

Marie Seton befriended me when I was first in Delhi in 1959. The Jhabvalas could not stand her. They avoided her whenever possible. Once the Jhabvalas and I had driven from the Civil Lines in Old Delhi, where they lived, to the Ashoka Hotel in New Delhi, a distance of about ten miles. And on the dusty road there, making her plucky way along it in the hot sun and on foot, we saw Marie. They didn't want to pick her up, but I made a fuss, so we stopped and she climbed into the backseat and began to tell us her thoughts, her hair, tied up in a knot, bobbing for emphasis. Ruth fanned herself and stared out the window and maintained a silence until we reached the hotel, where Marie was quickly got rid of. At some point that day or later on, I was warned by Ruth why I should not waste my time on people like Marie Seton. No good would come of it. She was just some windbag, spouting the usual nonsense about Indian "truths," while also consorting with politicians like Krishna Menon, and even for a time being a houseguest of Jawaharlal Nehru. To the Jhabvalas, that made her more than ever suspect. All this was perplexing to me as a foreigner who knew very little about Indian politics. I understood only that the Congress Party was "good" and the rival parties were less good. So why, I wondered, would it be "bad" for Seton to be a houseguest of Nehru, the head of the Congress Party?

Later on (sure enough, Ruth said), when our film *Shakespeare Wallah* came out, Marie reviewed it in *The Times of India* where she declared it to be anti-Indian. Noble, dynamic India was put down in our story: our English characters had all been presented with dignity and compassion, whereas our main Indian characters—a rich

A thirteen-year-old me superimposed on the model of the
Window of Appearances I made for a history of architecture class
at the University of Oregon in 1949 (I got an A on my model)

Me, on the roof of the Jamma Masjid in Delhi, shooting
my first Indian film, *The Delhi Way* (1959)

playboy, a decadent maharaja, and a movie actress (read courtesan,
or even prostitute) were in no way proper representatives of the new
India.

BUT WHO *WAS* Marie Seton? She had first stepped on to the stage of
world cinema because somehow she had—not being a film editor—
been chosen by its American backers to edit the footage of *Que Viva
Mexico!*, the unfinished film of the greatest of all Russian film directors,
Sergei Eisenstein. Who were the backers? The author Upton Sinclair
and his wife, Mary Craig Sinclair; Otto Khan (using the name Kenneth
Outwater); and Hunter S. Kimbrough. Eisenstein was summoned back
to the Soviet Union in the middle of his filming because of his profli-
gacy and sexual carrying-on in Mexico. Seton put Eisenstein's half-
done film together as best she could, despite not having many of the story
elements he'd planned to shoot. But without her work, we would have
nothing, and the film was brought out in 1946 entitled *Time in the Sun.*
And how did Marie Seton happen to be in India after Indian inde-

Shashi Kapoor and Felicity Kendal in *Shakespeare Wallah* (1965)

pendence in 1947? Many displaced Europeans, unlucky and stranded, did this then. Marie was less unlucky than most, having had a career as a writer on the arts in England, but her arrival coincided with that of the refugees. Some opened dress shops; some became art or theater critics; others helped to start up folk-art museums. They made themselves useful in the new Indian capital.*

Ruth often wrote about these wanderers in her earliest fiction, mostly sympathetically. Marie Seton was in some ways one of these people, although her family had ties to India; her father had been a captain in the British army there. Marie brought a wider and superior knowledge of modern Western artistic movements to India:

---

* These people mostly lived the rest of their lives in India—they had no place else to go and eventually died there. Charles Fabri, a Hungarian art critic, is a good example. Fabri was known in Indian artistic circles as the former director of the Lahore Fine Arts Museum, who had insisted on painting the ancient Greco-Buddhist statues in the museum's collection in bright reds, blues, and gold, etc. Fabri maintained that this had been their original coloring. He moved to Delhi later and began reviewing in the English-language papers—musical events mostly, where he could do no harm. When he passed away, he was cremated, but he was so fat his ashes filled up two big jars. Cyrus Jhabvala, Ruth's acerbic husband, told Fabri's widow, Ratna, that she should put some of his ashes into an hourglass. In that way, for the first time in his life, Fabri could be useful. Ratna always liked a good joke, and she laughed.

Sergei M. Eisenstein's *Que Viva Mexico!* (1939)

Satyajit Ray and me at the music recording session of *Shakespeare Wallah* (1965). Subrata Mitra, Ray's cameraman, is behind me, wearing glasses.

film, theater, literature, painting, music. Her word, like that of other Western critics reviewing in the Indian English-language press, was law. Yes or no, up or down, when any new work made its way from London or New York to Calcutta, Bombay, and Delhi—in that order, in terms of receptive appreciation from Indian audiences wanting to be au courant on things cultural in the West. Naturally, Seton made knowing, and writing about, Satyajit Ray—India's greatest artist, with a growing international reputation—her business. And if he were unexpectedly to die before he was able to edit a new film, she, citing her past of bringing *Que Viva Mexico!* to inexperienced Indians, would step in and save it as she did for the great Eisenstein. That was the cynical belief in the ever cynical and ever knowing Calcutta.

Call Me by Your Name

When in the early 1950s I began to make my first films, which were mostly about historic cities, artists, and painting, the Oscar statuette was not the most famous statue in the world. Picasso, Matisse, and Braque were still at work then; Frank Lloyd Wright, America's greatest artist, was putting together the Guggenheim Museum on Fifth Avenue; and Charlie Chaplin continued to make his films. But I think we can now say that painting is one of the sleeping arts, and so is sculpture, despite the gargantuan clamor of Richard Serra's monoliths. Since I started working, however, the reputation of the Oscar statuette has grown and grown until it has become the world's most famous statue. Its fame eclipses even Michelangelo's David and the Statue of Liberty.

So it seemed quite fantastic to me that in 2018, and at the age of eighty-nine, I was handed the most famous statue of modern civilization to keep as my own. Fantastic to me, too, that I was being given it for a piece of work I'd taken up almost casually as a favor for some friends, and for the fun of it. This was the screenplay of *Call Me by Your Name*, a film to be made in Italy, and which I had been asked to codirect by the director Luca Guadagnino.

I liked André Aciman's story well enough; I liked the two young men in it, Elio and Oliver. I felt I could identify with them, and I felt I knew how they would think and act, having known the madness of first love myself. But it was the thought of taking up an Italian life again that really drew me in, and to even write the script on spec—that is, for nothing. I was soon making frequent trips to Crema, the northern Italian city where Luca lived. I was sleeping in his best guest room, which is also his library of film books. The church bells rang nearby in the early morning, and someone ran down stone steps next to my room every day, as I lay on a big, white, square pillow. Luca had a coterie of smart young men and women who shared his life and were fun to be with. They were part of his company, Frenesy, and were helping him finish his new film, *A Bigger Splash*. I was happy to be included in this attractive family. It was what I had signed on for. When I turned in my script to them, it was accepted without any changes or requests for rewrites, and soon money was found to make the film, and to pay me. I looked forward to the shoot. The last time I saw Luca was before it began, in New York, when I still believed I was codirecting with him; we joked about what might happen if we got into an argument on set, and laughed about it. I made plans to go to Crema after the Cannes Film Festival in May, where the restored *Howards End* was to be shown.

And then I was dropped. I was never told why I had been dropped, by Luca or anybody else: it was presented in an "it has been decided that . . ." sort of way. Luca would be the sole director. I didn't care all that much. I could see that it might be very awkward sometimes to have two directors on the set. How would it look to the actors and crew if we had a dispute? Who then would be the real director when one of us had to give way? How many minutes of expensive shooting time would be lost as we argued? But I made plans to go to Crema anyway. I wanted to be there, and I was sure I could be useful. And was I not by this time also one of the producers? Luca was sending a car and driver to Cannes for me. But then I was informed that after the first day of shooting, which I'd been invited to witness, his production company would not pay my hotel bill, and that there would no longer be room for me in his apartment. All this from Emilie Georges, the very hard-nosed French producer, not Luca.

But why hadn't Luca himself picked up the telephone to speak to the person he was dropping? It was a pattern, and by then I should have understood. Perhaps because this would constitute an admission of some sort of masculine weakness that his Sicilian constitution could not bear, or take the weight of. It was my feeling he had made a mistake, and had made others that I also knew of. I had—while still acting as his codirector—cast Greta Scacchi as the mother, and she had accepted the part. This didn't please him, perhaps because he hadn't thought of it himself. But from the point of view of this Italian-French coproduction she was perfect. She had an Italian passport, she was fluent in Italian (she told me once that she had learned it from her father's Italian mistresses), and she is a very good actress. But Luca cast another actress for the part and never called Greta or her agent. I kept begging: Luca, call Greta! Call her agent, at least! He would not.

Shia LaBeouf was also dropped like that. He had been contacted for the part of Oliver. At this, *I* was doubtful. I didn't know much about him, so I watched some of his films. He's an extremely good actor. But as an academic writing about the Greek philosopher Heraclitus, he would be a stretch. Well, I thought, he would be a sort of diamond-in-the-rough-scholar type, like my friend Bruce Anawalt. Shia came to read for us in New York with Timothée Chalamet, paying for his own plane ticket, and Luca and I had been blown away. The reading by the two young actors had been sensational; they made a very convincing hot couple. But then, too, Shia was dropped. He had had some bad publicity. He'd fought with his girlfriend; he'd fended off the police somewhere when they had tried to calm him down. And Luca would not call him, or his agent. I emailed Shia to offer reassurance, but then Luca cast Armie Hammer and never spoke to, or of, Shia again.

Timothée Chalamet and Shia LaBeouf, 2015

Luca Guadagnino and Ferdinando Cito Filomarino,
at Pantelleria, Sicily, 2015

What upset me most over the breakup of my collaboration with Luca was that it destroyed the life—stretching over a couple of years—that I had hoped to have again in Italy, a country I love and can never have enough of. Something like my life thirty years before, when I made *A Room with a View*.

I recall my days in Crema with a pang: the lively evening meals, usually cooked by Luca, his scant black hair flying, who made his own spaghetti in some contraption, putting the *impasto* (dough) through again and again; the sessions of movie watching, while he whispered in a kind of baby-talk over the phone with his absent, gifted young partner, with whom he lived in his big apartment, who was often away skiing with his aristocratic relatives and friends. These whispered conversations, which we all heard, were not off-putting to anybody; despite his sometimes aggressive behavior, they proved Luca had a tender heart. When my services were dispensed with, I missed the trips we had taken to see possible locations for *Call Me by Your Name*. Once we went as far as Palermo, in Sicily. He was always good company, always generous, and a pleasure to travel with.

My bedroom at Luca Guadagnino's that I was kicked out of—where I heard from my bed every morning those sounds of Italy I so loved hearing again: church bells, feet running down the stone steps next to my room, etc.

Despite being expelled by Luca from what was to have been my film, too, I found myself a couple of years later on a huge, garishly decorated stage, watched by millions—or was it billions?—where I was being presented with the most famous statue in the world for my work on our screenplay. Oscar was very heavy; I had to put him down on the floor beside me as I read my acceptance speech, which I held in one trembling hand, my cane in the other. I did not fail to thank Luca for hiring me, and afterward he pulled me close to him, though the bulky object I was holding, pressing up against his chest, could only I knew be felt by him as a dishonor.

I left the stage and was conducted behind it on the way back to my seat, holding my most famous statue in the world by its little gold-plated head. I swung him along a bit nonchalantly, the realization that he was mine growing stronger, as pride—and satisfaction that I had won for writing—filled me while we sort of stumbled together through the wings in the dark.

I was the third in a trio of friends who received an Academy Award for best adapted screenplay. Here with Merchant Ivory's longtime associate Chris Terrio, who had won it for *Argo*. Ruth Jhabvala won the same Oscar twice, in 1987 for *A Room with a View*, and in 1993 for *Howards End*. She was also nominated for *The Remains of the Day*.

Elio and Oliver's lovemaking is explicitly described in my screenplay dated April 17, 2015, and features Elio's bare foot moving rhythmically over Oliver's left shoulder during the latter's exertions. My script can no doubt be found on those sidewalk tables in midtown Manhattan selling old screenplays for a few dollars each. Such a shot, as described above, and if taken, would have said everything an audience might want to know. See my page 78. Luca Guadagnino's seemingly decorous panning away through a window from the two boys in bed to some uninteresting trees needn't have concluded the sequence of lovemaking as blandly as it did. If I had directed the film with Luca, I'm sure we could have come up with a better solution than that for the moment every member of the audience had been waiting for. Both Luca and I were blamed endlessly online when the film came out for the lack of male frontal nudity in it. But Armie Hammer's and Timothée Chalamet's agents made sure in their client's contracts that they wouldn't have to do that. American male actors, with the exception of Viggo Mortensen, maybe, refuse to do it. However, their European contemporaries fling everything off with abandon given the chance, as earlier films of Luca and mine show.

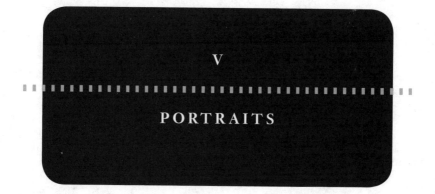

V

PORTRAITS

Kenneth Clark

My diary entry from Saturday, January 31, 1981:

Paris. Angelique Armand-Delille, the assistant editor on our film *Quartet*, comes to get me at the San Régis Hotel. We breakfast there and take a taxi to Gare St. Lazare, but get separated stupidly on the platform and nearly miss the train. This train is like the Amtrak trains from Penn Station to Hudson, which are said in any case to be of French manufacture: sleek and new, with the passengers sitting along a central aisle; the old-fashioned compartments for eight seem to have been done away with. We go from sunshine to a long stretch of fog, emerge into sunshine again at Rouen and reach Dieppe, where Angelique's mother is waiting for us in the station. This is Lady Clark. We set off at once for the lunch we are all to go to, Angelique driving while her mother gives me a rundown on the host and other guests. She is half-American and speaks English like an Englishwoman, and is full of energy. Her descriptions are precise and amusing, a kind of performance, and Angelique looks at me nervously, perhaps afraid that I'll think her mother is going on too long-windedly.

We arrive at a perfect, small country house of the early eighteenth century, built on an H plan. This is the longtime house of Grafton Minor, an ancient and distinguished Bostonian gentleman of leisure. He is waiting for us at the door, in a checked cape. He is eighty-eight. His skin is deathly white, and he looks a bit like Winston Churchill. He has been married three times; his son Alphonse, by now also pretty old, is inside with his wife. They cannot be very good company for the old man; the son is dim and remote and said nothing the whole time we were there beyond murmured civilities. Kenneth Clark soon arrived as we were having our drinks in the little salon; he was accompanied by his stepdaughter-in-law, Jennifer Armand-Delille, an American girl-of-good-family with a broad face and red hair. Kenneth Clark is nearly eighty and has almost as much trouble as Grafton Minor getting in and out of chairs. Nevertheless, it was a fine luncheon party, with the most delicious food, everything redolent of garlic. As I looked around the table, I appeared, for once, to be instead of the oldest or the second oldest person on hand, the third youngest one. After lunch we talked about literary critics. In response to the girl-of-good-family's question whether or not an artist could learn from them, I told her that I thought not, that all critics were a lesser form of life. This went down well. The ancient faces creased in satisfaction.

There was a drawing of Grafton Minor as a young man, in the Gibson tradition. He was in the Harvard graduating class of 1914. I left with the girl-of-good-family in her car; the others went with Angelique.

The girl-of-good-family has a ten-day-old baby. On the way she told me about her postpartum progress, or lack of it: she had bought a milking brassiere in the village, but the shopkeeper told her she could bring it back if she couldn't produce any milk. Bring it back! Already people thought she was a failure as a mother and she found that her mother-in-law (Lady Clark) was watching her very closely. Too closely. She wished she had someone to talk to, "that spoke my language." I asked her if she had depression—what I wanted to ask was, Do you want to kill your baby? She said the fact that the Iranian hostages* had been released the day her son was born had somehow lifted her up, had given her a kind of double joy, and so was probably responsible for her relative peace of mind now. I had to shout at her on the way, Watch out! and *Attençion!* as we nearly drove head-on into other cars. Jennifer Armand-Delille wore a gray flannel suit, the skirt of which was daringly slit very far up her thigh, and when she had relaxed after lunch, the old men could see quite a lot of her white leg. She plans in her spare time to just "whip out" a screenplay of Edith Wharton's *The Children.* I met her farmer husband later, Angelique's brother Freddy, ex–Wall Street: a very healthy-looking and sexy young man in muddy boots, who tramped into his mother's kitchen.

Angelique's family house, which is called Parfondeval and was built in 1610, is a proper château, but seventeenth century, standing on a hillside, with its outbuildings, called *dependencies,* laid out formally. You could see past them to the hillside beyond. Less exquisite than Grafton Minor's house, yet more appealing, perhaps because it is the center of a large working farm. I went straight up to my room under the eaves and took a nap.

SUNDAY, FEBRUARY 1

"The English upper classes have no interest whatsoever in art. But every so often a con man appears who manages to do very well

---

* She referred to the release of the American diplomatic staff imprisoned in Tehran for over a year, who were freed once Ronald Reagan took his oath of office on January 20, 1981.

with things like this—" indicating a bronze heron on a support that was intended to be a fountain but never got farther than the front hall. This is from Kenneth Clark after our morning walk. He took me laboriously up the hillside to where we could see sweeping views; I felt a little guilty that he should have to work so hard.

He lamented not bringing a cane and as he spoke I found a sapling cut down and flung in our path, so I gave it to him and he stumped along with it and felt easier as we plowed through the sticky Norman mud. I had read that when he was a child and living somewhere near the English seaside, he used to accompany the aged and exiled French empress Eugénie, who befriended him, on her walks. I wanted him to describe this scene to me as we tramped along, puffing away, but as soon as I asked him to, I immediately regretted it and apologized, saying that I was sorry, and that I hoped he hadn't minded my question. With his beak of a nose and heavy-lidded eyes, there is something of the look of an ancient and patient reptile, perhaps a tortoise, and last night I heard him groan loudly, so that his wife had to fly to his side. But when I came down in the morning, he insisted on showing me over the property. He explained that the Louis XIII style of the house became popular in Holland, from where it went to England and was called "in the Dutch style." So it is the ancestor of Georgian homes in America, and even of my own house in Claverack.

Empress Eugénie in exile

Maggie Smith and Sheila Gish in *Quartet* (1981)

When we got back from our trek, our Wellington boots completely covered with mud, he made me sit down while he helped me pull mine off first. There was a large family lunch waiting for us, with sisters and cousins and neighbors. I was astonished—but why astonished?—to hear Lady Clark describing the amusingly vivid American colored folk, who so love to sing and dance and who have so contributed to our culture, and did I not agree? I said, "Oh, yes." After lunch I took a nap in the drawing room; when I woke, the late afternoon sun was touching objects in the room with its last rays—things like a terra-cotta apotheosis of Madame de Pompadour, embroidered screens, and Louis Seize chairs.

Angelique and I then went to see the baby lambs, and after that for a long walk up the hill again, but to the other side of it, while I got a history of the hardworking, often unhappy, and many-times-married family members. Kenneth Clark is her mother's third husband. When we got back, we took the train to Paris, where I am now, waiting for the incurious Mark Potter, who had been invited, too, by Angelique, but preferred to stay in town, where we were all working together on our film *Quartet*.

George Cukor

In 1974 it was necessary for me to join the Directors Guild of America. Up to that time I had mostly worked overseas, except for *Savages*, a very low-budget film shot in upstate New York with no pretensions to formal legitimacy. Now we were to embark on a much bigger film, with big stars, called *The Wild Party*. This would be filmed right under Hollywood's nose, in Riverside, California, so Merchant Ivory would be obliged to become a Guild signatory.

In order to join the Guild I had to be introduced, or seconded, by another member who was also a feature director. There was no one I knew to ask for such a recommendation. But then, over a lunch table in Beverly Hills, my hostess, the actress Dorothy McGuire, hatched a plan with Christopher Isherwood, another guest, to ask their mutual friend George Cukor if he would introduce me. He accepted—

he'd liked *Shakespeare Wallah*, he said—and it was arranged over the phone for me to go and meet him at his house the following morning.

The house was in the Hollywood Hills a little way up Doheny Drive, surrounded by a high wall. I rang a bell and was admitted through a gate into a sloping, rather formal garden, down from which was his house, long and horizontal, with many tall doors and windows. Cukor, who was then seventy-four, stood on a terrace. He was silver-haired, tanned, and fit, and casually dressed. He greeted me in the most courteous way and asked me inside. I would have to excuse him, he said, but he was feeling very sad. His dog had just died and it would take him some time to get over this. He hoped that I wouldn't be put off by his too somber manner.

The house was the house of a civilized and sophisticated American artist and must have been built in the 1940s or early '50s. It was understated and cleanly elegant, in the same style as its furnishings. The colors were muted, with floors and furniture—mostly contemporary—shining from care and frequent polishing. There were works of art—again somewhat understated—such as small modern sculptures and, if I remember correctly, some old-master prints and drawings. One could not help imagining Cukor's missing dog asleep on the waxed floor.

He asked me what my film was about. I told him that it all took place at a party in the 1920s, and was based on a poem by Joseph

Moncure March. The story had originally been set in Greenwich Village, but we had moved its location to Hollywood. He brightened up. "Ah, a wonderful, wonderful time then. We had such a lot of fun! There were *such* wonderful parties!" He elaborated: people back then had looked so wonderful, too; they came to parties wearing such beautiful clothes, often all in white, men and women both. No one who wasn't around then could imagine the atmosphere of Hollywood in those days! His face lit up as he described Gloria Swanson, also all in white, slowly walking the length of a long upstairs gallery at someone's party, smiling and waving down like a young queen to everyone below. One could just not imagine how much fun it all had been, the laughter, the informality! And also how close-knit the film community had been when it was still small, and everyone knew everyone else. There wasn't the kind of awful segregation that had lately taken

George Cukor directing Audrey Hepburn
in *My Fair Lady* (1964)

over Hollywood, with actors and their agents on one side, and every-body else on the other. "Everything these days is shrinking. People are afraid to laugh anymore."

He fell silent and we talked of modern actresses. There were still some who shone as in the old days. One star who still shone was Julie Christie; Audrey Hepburn was another. He would be happy to recommend me to the Directors Guild, he said, and wished me good luck. I left him, carrying away something of his vision of shin-ing, sexy young gods and goddesses, all in white clothing, seen as through a gauze or diffusing lens, moving from one glittering en-tertainment to another. His Gloria Swanson provided me with an idea for my film, and at one moment in *The Wild Party*, my own stars, Jimmy Coco and Raquel Welch, also stroll along a railing high up in a grand Hollywood mansion, from where they wave down to their adoring courtiers on the stairs below. But the mood is very, very different: not one of happy nostalgia, but of impending danger.

SEVERAL YEARS LATER, in the late 1970s, I went to meet Cukor again in his beautiful house. Through my agent I had heard he was looking for someone to write the screenplay of a Somerset Maugham story he was interested in, set in a jungle. It was a low time at Merchant Ivory and I wasn't sure what I would be doing next. The Maugham story—I don't remember its title—was a British Raj sort of thing, so I felt well qualified to adapt it.

This time when I rang the bell I was let in by a well-mannered, nice-looking young man who took me inside to meet Cukor. The scene was a very different one from that of 1974. Cukor sat, attended by a second well-spoken young man, propped up on a high-backed sofa against a lot of soft cushions in a position half sitting, half reclining, from where he could not, apparently, get up easily to greet me. He took the hand I offered without, it seemed, recognizing me from my earlier visit. By then he was several years older, as was I. His inquiring look around the room seemed to be asking us all why I had come, whoever I was. The two young men, both in jackets and ties, carefully explained my presence there. They were a bit like very eager young studio executives, who must please their distracted and impatient bosses at all cost.

I'd come on an appointment to talk about the Somerset Maugham screenplay, they said, and he took this information in. I began to tell him my ideas for it, but before I'd got very far his gaze slipped away. Other thoughts had come into his mind and out of his mouth, unconnected to anything I'd said, in a burst of profanity. Picture making today is just shit, he said, twisting about violently on the cushions and wrinkling his beige cashmere sweater up over his stomach. At first I thought he was affecting hip bad language as some other distinguished old men (and women) now do after a lifetime of verbal circumspection. He jabbed the air with his fine hands, letting go a torrent of f-words: agents, studio heads, lawyers, writers—all were best consigned to a special Fucking Hell. He did not seem to be one of those mild old people who become afflicted with Tourette's syndrome and can't help themselves, smiling shamefacedly as they recover from an attack of filthy language. With Cukor there was no recovery; he was never for an instant shamefaced. It was an old man's rant against a changed world and his changed circumstances in it, and night closing in.

The two young men threw me apologetic looks and tried to joke him into a better mood, but as they plumped up his cushions and smoothed down his collar and twisted sweater, he remained in a sort of vexed heap and spat out more expletives. There was nothing for me to do but leave, which I soon did. He had once promised to be my best link as a practicing filmmaker—one able to answer informed questions and make a director's connections—with the old Hollywood, which he had loved and which had loved him, but which had, by slow degrees, turned into some hateful place that was no longer any fun, from which all the beauty had gone, and where everything and everyone was ugly.

IT WOULD SEEM improbable after all the above that George Cukor would direct another feature, but he did. This was *Rich and Famous*, starring Candice Bergen and Jacqueline Bisset, released in 1981. Two years later he died. His directing career had begun in 1930 with a film called *Grumpy*.

George Cukor (second from right, in white T-shirt) filming *Grumpy* (1930)

Lillian Ross: A Day with Wonder Woman

Lillian Ross (holding Erik Jeremy Ross) and
William Shawn, May 3, 1966

May 31, 1966

Dear Ruth,

There's so much in your last letters I want to respond to I don't know where to start. I want to tell you what it's like to be away from India for one year. I want to tell you about a day with Wonder Woman* and all about the christening of her son Erik Jeremy Ross.

---

* Lillian Ross (1918–2017), the *New Yorker* writer, best known for her "Talk of the Town" pieces and for a pointed profile of Ernest Hemingway in 1950 ("How Do You Like It Now, Gentlemen?"). She also wrote an equally acerbic piece about John

I'll start with the christening, which Lillian persists in calling a "dedication." For a long time she couldn't make up her mind about it. Since he was of Norwegian ancestry, Lillian thought Erik should be christened in the Lutheran Church, and she found one she liked out in Brooklyn called the Norwegian Seaman's Church. She never had any idea of bringing him up as a Jew since she herself doesn't practice her religion. So the Seaman's church was settled on. But then she had some second thoughts. Her lawyer was doubtful. And she began to think that to baptize Erik was also wrong. Salinger, who is a kind of mentor and guide in some respects, told her about a minister he knew in Mt. Vernon, outside New York, who was somehow connected with the Dutch Reformed Church.

This man, Pastor Breidison, was Norwegian too, by descent; Salinger liked him because he has experienced "tongue speaking"—a kind of mystic state where you speak an unknown language. By now it had been decided that Ismail and Salinger would be godfathers, and that Garet Newquist, who found Erik for Lillian in Norway, would be the godmother. With Ismail a Muslim, Salinger a Catholic-Jew-Buddhist, Mrs. Newquist a fallen-away Lutheran, and Lillian a fallen-away Jew, Pastor Breidison seemed the best solution. So the day was fixed for Sunday, May 29th. It was a glorious late spring day. Brilliantly sunny and clear, and not too hot. Lillian rented two Cadillac limousines to take us all out to Mt. Vernon, and we assembled at two in the afternoon in front of her apartment house.

We made a rather odd-looking group. Ismail was wearing a long cream-colored *shervani* and *churidar* pajamas, with gold shoes from Chandi Chowk.* Mrs. Newquist, who had arrived the night before from Oslo, was wearing Norwegian native costume—a black wool dress, embroidered with flowers and covered with silver and gold jewelry, with black stockings and black, buckled eighteenth-century shoes. Salinger wore a smart, double-breasted oxford grey suit. Mr. Shawn was bundled up against any possible drafts. And Erik was

---

Huston's making of his film *The Red Badge of Courage* for Metro-Goldwyn-Mayer in 1952 ("Throw the Little Old Lady Down the Stairs!")
* A bazaar in Old Delhi.

wearing the little white shirt you sent, and *churidar* pajamas made by Mrs. Naim, a friend of Ismail's. As we got into the car a telegram of felicitation arrived from Madhur.* Ismail held Erik, so Lillian's new dress—bright lemon yellow—wouldn't get mussed, and Lillian and Mrs. Newquist sat on each side. Salinger and I sat on the jump seats with Amy Gross, a little girl who lives in Lillian's building who Lillian has befriended, and Mr. Shawn and Renata Adler sat up front with the driver. The second car held some other friends of Lillian's, and her brother Simon.

We set out, all of us in a festive mood. Very soon, however, we got into a conversation about *Vertical and Horizontal.*†

Madhur Jaffrey in *The Guru* (1969)

Salinger said it had no business being made into a film when it was so perfect on the printed page. Lillian agreed that it presented difficulties, but she was convinced that we would solve them. Salinger said he instinctively trusted Ismail and me, but still it was wrong. How could it be cast? Who would play Spencer Fifield? Who could

---

* Madhur Jaffrey, the Indian-born actress, food and travel writer, and television personality.
† Lillian Ross's novel, published by Simon & Schuster in 1963, which Merchant Ivory was in the process of adapting for a film.

play such a part? And why try any of this? Think what happened to Jane Austen! (I thought of you and *The Householder*, and of the Maestro* and E. M. Forster.) The film of *Pride and Prejudice* had taken something away from Jane Austen, Salinger insisted. There wasn't a word from the front seat, where two absolute movie maniacs were sitting. Ismail was getting very excited. Who could play Holden Caulfield? Salinger was saying, and I was terrified Ismail would say, "Oh, we've got somebody in mind for him, too." Unfortunately, Salinger hasn't seen *Shakespeare Wallah*, so we have no credentials, other than Lillian's assurances.

Greer Garson and Laurence Olivier in *Pride and Prejudice* (1940)

I told how the Maestro had been rebuffed by Forster, but we all knew he would make a wonderful film out of *A Passage to India*. Salinger said he didn't care about *A Passage to India*, it wasn't so important to him as *Vertical and Horizontal*. Then he said, "I'm just a lemon, I guess," and by that time we had arrived at the church.

I was feeling distinctly cross and out-of-sorts. Partly with Salinger

---

* *The Householder* was Merchant Ivory's first film together, based on Ruth's fourth novel. "The Maestro" was the director Satyajit Ray, who had once approached E. M. Forster for the film rights to *A Passage to India*, which were refused.

(though I suppose I agree with him in many ways) and partly with Lillian, who had put an embargo on any picture taking of Salinger, who doesn't, she said, like being photographed. She had made this very clear over the telephone, and then in the car she announced again, "Jim is going to take pictures*—of some of us." I'm not exactly longing to take pictures of Salinger in the first place, and I don't like being reminded as if I were a child. Also I was cross with Lillian because she hurt my feelings when I gave her Erik's present—a little gold Russian cross. I'd spelled his name with a "c" instead of a "k" and she pointed it out as she opened the card, and not especially gently, but all these feelings were very soon absorbed by the little service Pastor Breidison had devised.

We went into the pretty church, from which a bridal party was exiting as we drove up, and took our places. Lillian, Erik, and the godparents went down in front, and the Pastor told us to come down too. He welcomed us, and a handsome young man sat down at a piano and played a medley of hymns, including some of Bach. When this was over, we sang another hymn, reinforced by some of the choir of the church, who had stayed behind to see the baby. After this, Pastor Breidison read from Scripture. He chose the story of Pharaoh's daughter finding Moses in the bulrushes—another adoption. Mr. Shawn put his hand over his eyes and began to cry, and as the Pastor read on, he began to sob, his whole body shaking. After this a very stout lady in a blue dress, wearing a big cartwheel hat, also blue, got up and sang. She had on a lot of rhinestones and shiny clips which sparkled like a diva's, but she sang very well, and Mr. Shawn stopped sobbing. Then Lillian, Erik, and the three godparents went up to the altar with the Pastor, who dedicated Erik to God in simple words. I think there was another song from the stout lady, and after a few more words it was all over and we went outside and posed on the steps for pictures except Salinger, who stayed in the church.

---

* I took the photo of Lillian, Erik, and Mr. Shawn on page 228 on the day of the dedication. Lillian included it in her memoir *Here but Not Here*, "a remarkable love story of the passionate life she shared for forty years with William Shawn." The photo is captioned: "When Bill and I decided to have a christening ceremony for the baby Bill helped select the church and an actual fat lady who sang."

Mr. Shawn started taking pictures. "Where's Jerry?" he wanted to know, and Lillian told him he wouldn't be coming out for pictures. If Mr. Shawn's not even allowed to take his picture, then who is? Poor Erik, no picture of his famous godfather for his scrapbook. Well, Ismail more than makes up for it.

After the pictures, we all got into the cars and drove back to Manhattan, to a champagne party at the Carlyle Hotel, where Mrs. Newquist is staying and where the Toad of Toads* always stays, and where Kennedy used to stay. The champagne party went on for three hours. Salinger got into a long argument with Mr. Gross, a friend of Lillian's and Amy Gross's father. I don't know what it was all about. Ismail entered into the fray, speaking on behalf of India, five thousand years, and spirituality. Salinger agreed with everything Ismail said, in the greatest good humor. Most of it was quite mad and wild to me. Gross spoke on behalf of his Generation, and five thousand years of Jewish tradition. Mr. Shawn sat at the end of the table, peering at everyone a little like a tortoise from out of its shell, and he and Lillian discussed endlessly whether it was too cold in the room. Mrs. Newquist, who has a long face and seems like a romantic Scandinavian, smoked moodily. Erik watched everything with big eyes, neither crying nor falling asleep. He's a remarkable baby. I have to say so, even I, who never see babies or children. All the fuss seemed absolutely justified.

Afterward we all drifted home through beautiful streets at sunset. Some of us ended up in the penthouse bar of the Beekman Tower, where the conversation revolved around Salinger: IS HE A GREAT WRITER? The consensus was that he is.

You asked whether I miss India. The answer is that I do, a lot. But on the other hand, so much of India is around me, and under my roof, that it's not a form of the homesickness from which Foo† suffers,

---

* Our family name for Indira Gandhi, India's prime minister at that time.
† Felicity Kendal, who starred in our film *Shakespeare Wallah* (1965) and who lived permanently in London after leaving India that year.

but rather a feeling that I am enjoying India somehow from a distance. After all, think of all the Indians around me, whom I see nearly every day. Apart from Ismail, think of Madhur, and S. K. Singh or Nazrul Rahman, and the infrequent visitors like Lochi Glazer and Shama Habibullah, plus old friends like the actor Saeed Jaffrey and Chota Chudasama, Ismail's college friend in Bombay. For almost total submersion, I spend some time now and then at India House. Well, that is being *in* India, I tell you. So I don't feel cut off from India. And I know I will go back. And that everything will be very much the same there. Even our productions will no doubt be the same: just as chaotic, wasteful, and enjoyable as ever, even when there is financing from a big Hollywood studio.*

But I'm beginning to adjust to being here. It still looks foreign to me, but the old familiar drabness contains lively bits of things—strange people, funny scenes, peculiar language, odd sights. There's a lot of "material" here. One could make some very good films. My policeman film† is much on my mind, though I don't work on it these days because of *Vertical and Horizontal.* I just make notes. Someday I'll find the perfect writer to work on it with me and then we'll do a script. At the moment I can't think of a single American actor who is right for the main role. We need a very civilized, upper-middle-class young man with the right accent, the kind England abounds with: sensitive, not too good-looking, masculine, intelligent, and with a sense of humor. But American actors are too much a stock type still: dull, brave, handsome, all-round good guys, the type they send to Viet Nam and interview for *Life* magazine in some village, holding some little Vietnamese boy on his lap.

NEW YORK ITSELF is a great trial to me. In India you have to fight the country—the heat, the bureaucracy, all its blind, dumb things

---

* As was our next film, *The Guru,* by Twentieth Century–Fox.
† I wanted to make a film about Central Park's Auxiliary Police Force, a mounted group of mostly Upper East Side young men like my friend Stephen Scher, who patrolled the park one night a week on horseback, armed, on the lookout for shady types who could be frightened by the big horses.

Smog in New York, 1966

which madden a person. Here you have to fight the city itself in exactly the same way, and it's ultimately just as exhausting and draining, just as apt to break you down and ruin your health, coarsen you,
make you angry, until you just give up and say "what the hell." Then
you relax and enjoy the compensating things. In India, at least for
me, there are the people first, and then the sense of freedom of some
sort or other, and finally the look of the place itself. Here one enjoys
one's friends, though not, I should think, people in general. One enjoys the freedom—the freedom of a huge city where nobody gives

a damn what you do or who you are. And you enjoy the diversions. Lots of good movies, a few good plays, lots of good music, some nice restaurants and shops, and going out into the country to somebody's weekend house for self-indulgence.

The city looks horrible of course: it's as wretched on close in-spection as the most dismal sections of Delhi or Bombay—fearfully dirty, soot on everything and dog manure on all of the sidewalks. Ugly encrustations, the air poisoned, the streets full of careening taxis and huge trucks that can mow you down. Sour faces, shrill voices, nasty language, people hustling after money all the time. But at night all this changes. Then the darkness hides everything and the lights go on. The famous skyline is there—you see it from a distance and you are simultaneously in it. If you're in a good mood, relaxed and happy, it's nice to be in New York, and if you're like me you know there's nowhere else in this country where you can be. Nevertheless, it really gets you down, and I can't imagine living my whole life here. Nor do I intend to. Best to alight from time to time and then buzz off somewhere.

Ismail complains about it, but he also thrives on it. Ceaselessly he grumbles, saying he's going to India tomorrow and never, never coming back to such a hateful place. Then the next thing you know he's enjoying it in the most extravagant fashion, in ways which would exhaust me (the energy he has for socializing and pursuing his goals!). And yet, when you point out that he's doing very well here, and living a life many would envy, he says it's all nothing, and "as dust and ashes" to him. Then he picks up the phone and dials some number. Last night he reached some sort of apogee or something like that. Mr. Shawn asked us to dinner at La Caravelle with Lillian and Mrs. Newquist and Mrs. Newquist's daughter-in-law to be. La Caravelle is a very fancy place I've never been to, much frequented by society types—while we were sitting there old Joseph Kennedy was wheeled in, followed by Teddy K, who looks too young to be a senator, and very self-conscious as he had to walk past the tables from the door—those banquette types from which everybody seated along the walls can see you.

After dessert Ismail excused himself and went off to escort Mrs.

Haupt, his new *bhuddi*,* to a party for Mrs. Johnson† in Beekman Place. Mrs. Haupt is an incredibly rich and well-dressed lady who owns *Mademoiselle* magazine. She looks like a—oh, I can't describe her really. A macaw's face, an eagle's face, both would apply, wearing gigantic jewels. She took Ismail in her Rolls to the party, while

the rest of us went to Arthur, a discotheque. A draft-free table was secured for Mr. Shawn and we enjoyed the spectacle. I did my duty by Mrs. Newquist and the daughter-in-law to be—just as Ismail was no doubt doing with Mrs. Haupt—by dancing, though I didn't feel like it.

Enid Haupt and Lady Bird Johnson, 1968

Mr. Shawn sat nodding to the music (he's a great jazz fancier, and though rock 'n' roll can't be described as jazz, he's very much up on it), while Lillian gave the place a good-natured once- or twice-over.

Meanwhile, Ismail was with Mrs. Haupt, at the party. (The next day, in a tabloid clipping‡ she was described as "one of more than 100 luminaries.") Ismail told Mrs. Johnson she could see *Shakespeare Wallah* at the White House; he would arrange it with the Indian Embassy in Washington. He says Mrs. Johnson thought that this would be a fine idea, but that Mrs. Haupt looked horrified at his suggestion.

By twelve or so we'd had enough of Arthur and got up to go, having given up Ismail, who had promised to meet us there. The

---

* A Hindustani word meaning a rich—and hopefully useful—older woman.
† The first lady, Claudia Alta ("Lady Bird") Johnson (1912–2007), wife of President Lyndon B. Johnson.
‡ This clipping has been lost.

ladies in our party were handed presentation boxes of Cognac and Arthur ashtrays which Lillian tried to refuse, but which the Norwegian ladies grabbed up immediately and began to open out on the sidewalk, to the horror of Lillian, who is like an Indian lady and hates to be looked at. And there were plenty of people to stare, as there always are in front of Arthur—people waiting in line to get in, and other people just waiting to see celebrities. As Lillian agonized, Mrs. Newquist took out each ashtray, regarded it curiously, showed it to Lillian, showed it to her future daughter-in-law, showed it to me. Mr. Shawn was holding a taxi door open, and a line of traffic behind began to sit on their horns. Finally they all got in the taxi and drove off, and I walked the few blocks home.

A little while later however, Ismail, who had dropped Mrs. Haupt at her apartment, but still riding in her Rolls-Royce, arrived at

Arthur, where the doorman saluted smartly and held open the door. Now, as we know, Ismail has his own style and thinks fast. It occurred to him that if we had gone, it would look awful to have dismissed the Rolls and be left standing there on the sidewalk carless, like an idiot, so he commanded the chauffeur to wait, and went inside, dressed in a black *shervani* made in Bombay from two yards of imported Dacron, his white *churidar* pajamas, and the embroidered Chandi Chowk shoes. When he couldn't find us inside, he came back out again, got in the Rolls, and was taken home, where he took off his shoes and socks and cracked his toes.

WHAT A LONG letter this is turning into! I can't quite remember all I wanted to tell you, but I think I wanted to say that America strikes me in some ways much the same as India does you—one part of a vast, sick, mad world, where everything is disintegrating. But I can't write about it now.

I'm so glad you saw an Ozu film and liked it. I think he's marvelous, but I've only seen two of his films. One of them was called *Tokyo Story*, which was so moving. Was that the one you saw?

I saw what John Coleman* wrote, and of course was thrilled, but did you see what somebody said in a Letter to the Editor the following week? The letter writer was full of praise for Godard, calling him the greatest creative mind in the whole world, but that Ivory, Foreman, and Truffaut were blatantly minor artists, though no doubt pleasant and charming. How funny to see all that. I looked at it and could make no connection with myself. I said my name over and over, but it just didn't connect, and I'm sure that's a very good thing.

Please don't tell Ved† a single detail of Erik's ceremony. Lillian doesn't like other people on *The New Yorker* staff to know anything

Me and Ismail, mid-1970s, photographed by Mary Ellen Mark

---

* Film critic of *The New Statesman*, writing a review of *Shakespeare Wallah*.
† Ved Mehta, a staff writer for *The New Yorker*, then visiting India.

about her, and I'm afraid Ved is "other people" to Lillian, sad as it might be for him to know it. You might ask him if he'd be willing to sublet his apartment for two months from July 9th to a friend of mine I can vouch for, who is coming from Paris and will pay 350–400 a month. Will Ved be back? Tell him my friend is very careful and won't smash up the place, and that if Ved wants, he will give him a deposit. Against breakage.

How did you like Wally Shawn?*

Love to you all, Jim†

---

* William Shawn's elder son, the playwright Wallace Shawn.

† Sometime after this Lillian and William Shawn seemed to cool toward Salinger. He had befriended a young woman whom they met on one of Salinger's trips to New York, when they all had dinner together (at La Caravelle, I imagine). She was decades younger than Salinger, and a recent graduate of some Ivy League girl's college. She had tried to dominate the conversation, Lillian told me, and tried to dominate him, and he let her! After that, she and Bill didn't feel like seeing Salinger so much. And maybe they had decided between them that Salinger wasn't a great writer, after all. Around 2005, when Lillian had taken me up again after Ismail's death (and virtually everyone else's death), and I reminded her one time in a La Caravelle replacement restaurant on Madison Avenue (she had gone off high-calorie French cooking by then and had turned to more "healthful," more fresh and pure, less corrupted, Italian cooking), she denied there had ever been any kind of breach between them all. "What about that girl you hated, who talked all the time?" I asked. "What girl?" she answered.

Our silent companion at these occasional dinners in 2005, 2006, and 2007 was Lillian's now grown-up son Erik, in his early fifties, six feet tall, handsome, composed, and perhaps bursting to tell his own story one day, I don't know. He was as enigmatic a figure to me as Salinger grew to be to his millions of fans who followed from afar his every known move, and anticipated reading his every known love letter, including, doubtlessly, those to the girl who talked too much and tried to dominate him.

Dorothy Strelsin

Ismail and Dorothy Strelsin, Benares, India, 1969

For Ruth Jhabvala's sardonic husband, Cyrus, and our principal star in India, Shashi Kapoor, Ismail's *bhuddies* were a subject of a good deal of hilarity. Once Cyrus—or Jhab, as he was called—and Ruth, with Shashi and his wife, Jennifer, went into the lobby of a big New Delhi hotel, where they saw a pair of memsahibs sitting on a sofa together. A memsahib could be any older, respectable-looking lady—often an Englishwoman. Jhab said to his wife and Jennifer, "That's you two, the two *bhuddies*, in twenty years' time." They both asked, "Which one of them is me?" and Shashi answered, "The well-dressed one is

Jennifer." What is a *bhuddi*? Again, the word in Hindustani means "an old woman." To Jhab and Shashi, the word also carried the connotation of a rich, and useful, old woman. There had been a long line of these, starting at the very beginning of Ismail's career as an up-and-coming producer living in Los Angeles.

Ruth and Shashi Kapoor, 1962

He began with the actress Agnes Moorehead, no less. She was the first to make useful connections for him, to rouse her friends to throw parties for him, and to pick up a phone to call some important man. She would be followed by many more whom he had charmed—and disarmed—with his ebullience, his looks, and his glamorous moviemaking ideas. Their husbands were usually long gone, or incapacitated—like Sunita Pitamber's, lying paralyzed somewhere upstairs in her Bombay mansion—all the way down the many years to the very end of Ismail's life, at Susan Gutfreund's Fifth Avenue apartment, where her husband, John, penalized by the New York Stock Exchange for some misdeed, sat quietly among the various socialites and visiting dukes that she had assembled to meet Ismail. He must have seemed to all his ladies to have been the highly

Federico Fellini, Dorothy Strelsin, and Giulietta Masina

Michael York, Rita Tushingham, and Utpal Dutt in *The Guru* (1969)

charged male element their lives needed. Nothing ever came of that, but nonetheless it was there, an unspoken thing.

Dorothy Strelsin was different. She and her husband, Al, knew everybody in New York's show-business circles, and Al formed a company with us, drawing in Twentieth Century–Fox, to make our third feature, *The Guru*, in 1967. But how the couple first came into our lives I have no idea. Perhaps it was at one of their parties, also in a big Fifth Avenue apartment. During the New York Film Festival in the '60s, that apartment was one of the hot destinations. We met Federico Fellini and his wife, the actress Giulietta Masina, there at the time of *Shakespeare Wallah*. Giulietta made the spaghetti sauce in Dorothy's kitchen and then later on read the guests' palms. Al presided, but Dorothy ran the show and, I assume, caught Ismail's eye. He was to take her all the way to the Ganges, to Benares, where she played a small role in the film we were making with Al. Her showgirl energies and blonde Broadway looks were a vivid contrast to the sinister backdrop of the holy city, with its cremation ghats at the water's edge, and its half-burned bits of bodies floating past the film crew.

ONE EVENING SOMETIME after Al's death, Dorothy invited Ismail and me to dinner. When we arrived, I was carrying a rolled-up Matisse rug like a rug salesman; I'd just reclaimed it from my old college roommate, Art Satz, whom I'd lent it to seventeen years before. Dorothy was in her kitchen, cooking. She had left the door from the foyer open and hugged us. She was wearing a kaftan sort of thing that seemed to blend the spots of a leopard with the stripes of a tiger. She had a scarf around her neck and this was entwined with a long pearl necklace, or maybe two (both fake). Her glasses were perched up on her hair. She told us to open a bottle of wine and we made free with Al's bar. I thought I saw his disapproving shade everywhere. He reminded me of my father's old business partner, Gus Luellewitz: the fleshy power and inscrutability, the way he seemed to lie in wait and watch you.

Dorothy served the dinner and we sat at a little round table in the dining room. She told Ismail she knew he was a master chef, but when she had to, she could cook a dinner, too. This dinner consisted of a chicken dish that included half a pear; squash and peas; and a lettuce salad with bottled Italian dressing. Afterward she served some of Raja's ice cream and took Ismail a bit to task for not telling her he owned the Raja shop. She asked if we had liked the chicken dish—"Tell me, honest Injun"—and we said we did.

She talked about her friends, some of whom she had very ambivalent feelings about. She would get up from the table to act out various impersonations. One of these was of Pauline Ney, whom Dorothy was sore at because there had been some little disagreement over a bridge game; when, after Pauline hadn't telephoned Dorothy for a long time, they had met somewhere, Dorothy confronted her, saying, Come out with it, you must be mad at me or something, why do you seem so aloof, etc. Pauline told her that she was feeling neglected and that Dorothy hadn't called her up for a long time. Dorothy told her: Listen, *I* don't have to call *you*; I just lost my husband, I don't have to call anybody, I expect them to call *me*! At which point Pauline went up to her and pecked her on the cheek, or pecked the air actually—this being acted out, Dorothy thrusting her bosom forward and her behind backward and mincing in little steps in imitation of Pauline.

She told us that Pauline was consumed by possessiveness over things—her furnishings, her jewels—and that when she'd invited a crowd of sixteen people to dinner recently, she'd gone to the dime store to buy glasses, afraid her guests would break her expensive goblets. Dorothy said to her, Oh, don't be so goddamned possessive, are you going to take those things to the grave with you? Dorothy told us that she herself had marble floors and couldn't keep track of all the glasses that had been broken on them over the years since she and Al moved in. She had some unkind things to say about Pauline's figure—how she shoved her "big boobs" into brassieres that pushed them up to give her a lot of cleavage, and how she corseted herself to the point of suffocation—and how Pauline had always been so proud of her tiny feet. One day she had her shoes and stockings off and Dorothy said, "Oh, Pauline, what are those awful lumps on your heels?"

and Pauline turned her feet around so Dorothy could see only her toes.

Then she told us about the seven Annenberg sisters (Enid Haupt being one of these), how they gave themselves such airs, but Al had known their old man back in Prohibition days: he had owned a taxi fleet then, and had boasted of his connection with Al Capone. But later on, when he had gotten very rich, he'd cheated on his income taxes and had to serve three years in a federal penitentiary and pay a ten-million-dollar fine. The sisters sort of went into hiding during those years and had never really gotten over this disgrace. Dorothy enumerated what had happened to these women, all stinking rich, but cursed by God—a cursed family, God pointed his finger at them! One had gotten cancer of the nose—which was appropriate, because that sister had tried to deny that she was Jewish. Another one had a daughter whom she loved to distraction, but that daughter killed herself. Another one had a son, also much loved, who gave an overdose to his girlfriend and the girlfriend had died. The boy had stuffed her body in the trunk of his car, but the police had found out. Enid was stupid. She had bought control of all those magazines so she would have something to do—she loved "controlling things," Dorothy said, maybe that was why no man would ever touch her now. Who would want to be Mr. Haupt? The brother was the biggest jerk of all. Everybody knew he'd bought his ambassadorship to London from Nixon.

Then she told us about her friend Foxy, who was Stephen Sondheim's mother. Foxy had gone out to stay with Dorothy in California, but after six weeks Dorothy was tired of her and to discourage her from staying on had instructed the maid to cook only hamburgers. This was not enough to discourage Foxy, however, so Dorothy had to take stronger measures. One night the maid put the hamburgers in front of Foxy, but Dorothy excused herself to go to the telephone to call up friends in New York. Foxy wouldn't eat her hamburger without Dorothy, and after half an hour or so, Foxy began to think all this was a planned insult. She went to sit on the sofa and wait it out. When Dorothy finally finished her phone calls, she asked Foxy sweetly, "Oh, why didn't you eat, the hamburgers must be cold now?" Foxy indignantly said that she wasn't going to be insulted, etc., and that did it, Dorothy had a chance to tell her a thing or two (This is *my* house, I do what *I* like, *when* I like, etc.), whereupon Foxy rushed out of the house and over to the next-door neighbor, saying that she had to call for the police, for help, for a doctor, because it was just terrible, poor Mrs. Strelsin had flipped out, she could maybe hurt herself, etc. When the police came, Dorothy met them, perfectly sane, and they had to leave. So did Foxy, vowing vengeance. She returned to New York to make much evil report of all this, which got back to Dorothy. When Dorothy herself returned from California, she let it be known via gossiping Pauline, who could always be depended upon to carry a bad tale, that she was going to see Louis Nizer, Al's famous lawyer friend, as she intended to sue Foxy for slander. That shut Foxy up.

While we were sitting at Dorothy's table the phone rang. And it rang and rang, but Dorothy wouldn't answer it. She said that anybody who wanted to reach her could always tell the answering service. We went on eating and the phone went on ringing. I said, Dorothy, how can you do that? Aren't you curious? Finally she went to answer it. The call was from overseas, from Paris. At first we didn't listen too closely, and then we began to. Ismail checked his watch—it was 2:00 a.m. in Paris. We listened to Dorothy reassuring someone that Yes, yes, she'd find somebody going to Paris and *send* them, don't worry, tell Mother I'll do it, I promise, etc. She called to Ismail: did he

know anybody traveling to Europe the next day or so, and he told her he could always send things via Air India. Then Dorothy returned, to Mother now, on the phone: Yes, yes, darling, I promise! Only one package left? Oh, terrible! I promise, etc. After many more minutes of this, of entreaties on one side and promises from Dorothy on the other, Mother must have hung up.

Dorothy paused in the doorway and said, "I knew I shouldn't have answered that fucking phone! My

The Maharani of Baroda and her son, Princie, 1948

instinct was right. *You* made me do it" (pointing at me). It turned out that her friend in Paris had run out of L&M cigarettes, which can't be bought there, and had only one pack left. She was growing desperate. Then it turned out that this friend was the famous beauty Sita Devi, the Maharani of Baroda; the first person who had been on the phone was her son, Princie. So the call wasn't from some poor, sleepless creature, alone in Paris with a frightened child, calling up to talk with *someone*, it was Royal India on the phone, demanding that special cigarettes be sent at once.

Dorothy told us at that dinner that she had had a wonderful life, she didn't regret a minute of it. Only she had been so dumb, she hadn't realized what a brilliant, marvelous man she had been married to, she hadn't been tuned in to his needs. I was a very faithful wife, she said, but I was a failure. But we had fun!

Raquel Welch

Raquel Welch in *The Wild Party* (1975)

Anyone would think that Raquel Welch has every right to be proud of her achievements. Here is a small-town, middle-class girl who has become, through her own efforts and energy as much as through her beauty and magnetism, an international celebrity, with fan clubs and a sophisticated cult following. Moreover, through her championing of various causes, she has access to a wider world than that of Hollywood. But somehow, in spite of all this, she does not appear satisfied with herself. It is as if she feels that the route she took to get there—by becoming a movie sex goddess, half Rita Hayworth, half Mae West—isn't dignified enough for her; so she must search for "serious" parts and for directors who will take her seriously, must go to acting school, must learn to sing and dance, all in an effort to realize whatever potential she may have. And this is done somewhat at the cost of her public image, which still feeds and supports her, and also feeds her ego when she is feeling low and isolated.

Nor does she take her appearance for granted: you feel she has to work at it more than many less beautiful women. Since she has come up the hard way—fighting parents, producers, directors, and critics whom she suspected of trying to keep her down—she is like certain self-made men who cannot really believe in lasting success: everything may disappear in an instant. You feel this kind of desperation about her, and you cannot help sympathizing with her attempt to find better ways of expressing herself professionally.

It was in this mood that she accepted the role of Queenie in *The Wild Party* (1975), a film I directed that was, as it turned out, an ill-fated vehicle for her. The part had everything she seemed to be craving: she was to be the glamorous mistress of a failing 1920s comedian—patient, loving, able to look at herself and her fate objectively and to talk about them articulately. Since the film took place during a big party, and her role was that of an ex-Follies girl, she was given an opportunity to sing and dance in a star turn or two. In the last reel she would die in her protector's arms.

As a director, I have the reputation of doing well by the women characters in my films; they have never been mere dumb things. So Raquel and I should have been able to work together on our joint conception of Queenie. But from nearly the first day we were at loggerheads, and no professional relationship, no *working* relationship, was ever established. She wanted to be an actress, not just a star, so I treated her as an actress, and not as a star. That was my fatal mistake.

When people ask me whether Raquel Welch has talent, I'm prompt to tell them that she has indeed, but that it is often eclipsed by her talent for being the Star. During *The Wild Party* Raquel the star fought the film every inch of the way. Her performance in it

Raquel Welch and James Coco in *The Wild Party*

was good, sometimes very good. Most critics saw that at once and said so. But I always felt it could have been 50 percent better, for she depleted her energies in self-defeating battles in which both she and the picture were finally the losers. She appeared intimidated by the arrival in Riverside (where we were filming) of a large contingent of East Coast and foreign technicians and executives, as well as by her costar, James Coco, a gifted and skillful Broadway actor. Imagining perhaps some hint of disdain for Hollywood or for her on their part—some element of threat from what she saw as East Coast elitism—she began to fight with everyone about everything (except with the diplomatic Coco, of whom she was afraid). She fought over costumes and makeup, the interpretation of her part, the lighting, even over matters such as who would see rushes and who would not.

She came to work like the Victorian theatrical and operatic greats are supposed to have done, sending on an advance party of her retinue. It was always a little ominous, as the motorcycle outriders are in a presidential procession: the first to arrive was her dresser, a young woman carrying perhaps a pair of shoes or a hat or gloves and a bag; then came the woman who did her hair, with her combs and sprays;

then Charlene, her personal makeup artist, with her diminutive tins of color and her camel's-hair brushes; then Justin, her personal drama coach, wearing studded Levi's and holding marked scripts against his chest like they were precious, holy books; then her boyfriend and costume designer, Ron Talsky, looking a bit wary. And in his wake, Raquel, in a black satin kimono, flashing looks when she was in a good mood, or staring sullenly down at the ground when she wasn't. The crew, extras, and other cast members would draw back as this procession passed on its way to where the lights and camera had been set up, to where I stood with the cameraman, Walter Lassally.

I would then go over what I wanted her to do, and she would either do it or refuse to do it. If it was the latter, I would draw Jimmy Coco aside, and we would find some way in which my instructions to her would seem to originate with him. He was her only peer. Just before the first take Raquel would make Charlene look through the camera to check how she'd been lit, and after the shot the embarrassed Justin's opinion would be sought to find out which was the best take to print. It was a very strange world, and I suppose I just accepted it after a time; stars were expected to indulge in such antics.

Sometimes when I looked into Raquel's eyes, nothing came back from them; I couldn't make contact. But at other times what I saw there was a look of real suffering, so that I wanted to do anything I could to help her. After a while, though, I came to recognize that this look was often the prelude to some tremendous onstage explosion, to be followed by flight, sobbing, threats to quit the picture, and demands to have us all fired, including Ismail Merchant, the film's producer.

The biggest of these blowups ended rather comically. On the morning of the day we were to do her big love scene with Perry King, I went very early to see Raquel to talk it over. She was about to apply her makeup. Her face was stripped and her mood was threatening. She painted away as Charlene handed her the brushes, and I cautiously put forward my idea of the scene. As I expected, she had her own conception ready, and as far as it went it wasn't bad, I must give her credit: before being unfaithful to her longtime protector (Coco), she would divest herself ritually of the expensive trinkets she was wearing that he had given her. I said okay. What I didn't realize until the rehearsal later on, however, was that once she had done that, the scene was over as far as Raquel was concerned. She had no intention of letting King make love to her; she wouldn't even lie down on the same bed with him. No sex! Everything was to be suggested by the deliberate (and lengthy) removal of her jewelry. And she was adamant about this, though technically that put her in breach of contract. King was furious, and he told me that in the first take he planned to pin her down violently on the bed and hold her there until she threw him off; perhaps in this way we would get something simulating pent-up passion. I agreed and he did just that, but with such force the bed nearly collapsed. Raquel slithered out from under him, barked, "That's it, boys!" and jumped up.

Because the bed had almost fallen down, adding another note of the ridiculous to the scene, I said I wanted a second take. Raquel was fighting mad. What was the matter with the take we'd done? she demanded. Recklessly, I told her that I wasn't convinced of the couple's desire for each other. They should tear each other to pieces; as played the scene was boring. "Boring!" she shouted. "Boring?" She

Perry King and Raquel Welch in *The Wild Party*

rushed out, followed by her boyfriend, Ron, who turned to tell me I should not use such a word to describe a star of her magnitude.

A few minutes later, the news came down that she had left the picture. With some relief I mentally wiped the three remaining scenes we still had to do with her from my vision of the finished film. But the financiers were not ready to do that. There was much telephoning to lawyers and agents before a solution was found: Raquel's "public humiliation" could be paid for only by a public apology from me before the assembled cast and crew the next night. A financier edged up nervously to ask whether I could possibly bring myself to do this. I told him that I could and would. But Ismail could not bear to witness this frightful scene and went back to his hotel.

Quite a few visitors had come to watch us that night. We were going to shoot a dance sequence Patricia Birch had been staging for days with Raquel and Perry. But word had gotten around that something unusual was going to happen. The action was taking place in a garden, and when the lighting was complete, the soundman rigged up a microphone so I would have a recording of this little scene—of this drama within a drama—a record intended as a form of protection in case our troubles escalated.

The moment arrived. More than a hundred people were watching and a silence fell. Raquel stalked up to me in her black kimono, her heels tap-tapping over the garden's flagstones. The soundman angled his boom into position over our heads. She addressed me: "Mr. Ivory, I believe you have something to say to me?" I asked in a loud voice if everyone could hear. "Yes!" the crowd shouted back. I then apologized: "Raquel, if I've offended you, I'm sorry, but you know that whatever I did was only in the interest of the film." She thought this over, evidently decided that it would do, smiled a grim, wintry little smile, and turned away.

Despite the silliness of it all, I rather liked that tiny figure, tap-tapping her way back to the safety of her ladies-in-waiting and the arms of her boyfriend. In this her biggest scene, she had caught the grit and the pathos of Queenie perfectly.

Vanessa Redgrave

Vanessa Redgrave in *The Bostonians* (1984)

Ask directors and they'll tell you there's actress A, B, or C (it could also be actor X, Y, or Z) they're crazy to work with some day. Vanessa Redgrave was at the head of my list, and when Merchant Ivory started to think seriously about *The Bostonians*—or as soon as there was a script—we got in touch with her. She was our first choice for the part of Olive Chancellor, but she turned it down. This was the spring of 1981. Since we were in London, we asked her to dinner in order to talk about it, even though we knew she felt negative about the project.

It was not the first time we had gone to her. We had offered her the part Lee Remick played in *The Europeans*, and there had been much going forward and backward then. She liked the part, but when we were ready, she decided to stand for election as well as to appear in Ibsen's *The Lady from the Sea*. Later, not knowing we'd already shot *The Europeans*, she wrote me a letter to say she would like to play the Baroness Munster if we ever did that film. Something like that happened with *Quartet*, until the part of Lois Heidler was offered at last to Maggie Smith, who snapped it up, whereupon Vanessa announced that she was free after all, but by then it was too late. So this time, after she'd said no I wrote to ask if she were very sure. She came to dinner at Tony Korner's flat, in Cornwall Gardens, where we were staying, to tell us her reasons, trudging up the four flights as she must have done hundreds of times in tall English houses, campaigning or gathering names for some petition. She wore tweeds and sturdy shoes and her glasses.

She had little to say about Olive that night; it was as if she had already put Olive out of her mind and wanted to get to other topics. Olive Chancellor wasn't a woman she could identify with easily, or that she had any feeling for. She didn't see herself as that character. Because Olive was a rich Boston bluestocking? She would not be pinned down.

We then ate dinner. During the salad she began a monologue, not looking at us but staring at the wood of the tabletop, her face half in a shadow. To give a better idea of her here I will quote E. M. Forster's description of how Charlotte Bartlett speaks in *A Room with a View*: "Her long narrow head drove backwards and forwards, as though she were demolishing some invisible obstacle." This harangue, delivered in a low, hollow-sounding monotone, like the prophecy of an oracle sitting in a cave, and mainly about the forces of evil generated by most governments, went on for some time as we—her obstacles?—

nervously plucked string beans out of a bowl. What we could not appreciate was that the style of this piece would be duplicated three years later as Olive Chancellor, with head bent and eyes lowered, reproved the worldly if ill-informed Mrs. Burrage in the following speech from *The Bostonians*:

> OLIVE
>
> You seem to think that I control Verena's actions and her desires, and that I'm jealous of any other relations she may possibly form. I can only say your attitude illustrates the way [demolishing object!] that relations between women are still misunderstood and misinterpreted. It is these attitudes we want to fight. With all our strength and all our life, Miss Tarrant—Verena—and I.

Nancy Marchand and Vanessa Redgrave in *The Bostonians*

The climax of this somewhat dismaying evening (dismaying in that I could not help thinking, Oh, where is the quicksilver Vanessa Redgrave of our dreams, the Vanessa Redgrave of *Blow-Up* and *Morgan!*, the valiant creature that was *Isadora*?) came when she asked Ismail for a substantial donation for the *News Line*, the paper of her Workers' Revolutionary Party. The paper's cost had to be raised five pence per issue, putting it out of reach of many; our contribution, a

Vanessa Redgrave in *Morgan!* (1966)

kind of subsidy, would help make up the printer's losses. The buck was passed to me and I told her some narrow-eyed Yankee lie about seeing what I could do. After this, she left.

Many months later, during a blizzard in London, she called Ismail to ask him to come out and march against Ronald Reagan's Central American policies. He lay in a warm bed, drowsily watching a movie on TV. The wind roared, snow blew about, the windows had iced over, while Vanessa's armies were gathering in—I think—Kensington High Street. This made us a little sad. Brave, noble, wrongheaded being!

Thus ends the first phase of our relationship with, and a way of thinking about, Vanessa Redgrave. We did not do *The Bostonians*, we made *Heat and Dust* instead, while at about the same time she was getting into difficulties with the Boston Symphony Orchestra over—

apparently—having so openly championed the Palestine Liberation Organization. We sent the script for *The Bostonians* out to other actresses for their consideration. We did not have much success with it, which seems strange since Olive Chancellor is certainly one of the great Henry James characters and one of his most fascinating women. Forty years before, Katharine Hepburn could have played the part, but the suggestion of lesbianism within the central triangle of the story would have kept Hollywood away.

At the beginning of the novel James describes Olive's first encounter with her enemy Basil Ransome: "A smile of exceeding faintness played about her lips—it was just perceptible enough to light up the native gravity of her face. It might have been likened to a thin ray of moonlight resting on the wall of a prison." She is last seen by him (and by the audience of the film) in her dash to the stage lectern at the end: "[It] might have seemed to him that she hoped to find the fierce expiation she sought for in exposure to the thousands she has disappointed and deceived, in offering herself to be trampled to death and torn to pieces. She might have suggested to him some feminine firebrand of Paris revolutionaries, erect on a barricade or even the sacrificial figure of Hypatia, whirled through the furious mob of Alexandria." In between, there are fierce confrontations between Olive and a gallery of adversaries—scenes in which good actresses (and even some mediocre ones) may shine: scenes of passionate avowals to a cause and to love, and scenes showing how that love is manipulated, as well as a whole range of jealousies, to find expression. Who would turn down such a role?

Directors like to think that any role they offer an actor is an irresistible one, and when it is turned down, it is often the actor who seems to them to fall short of the mark, and not the part. Directors are in the position of powerful if importuning lovers; rejection hurts, because in offering a part to someone a director has taken an important step, has said in effect, "I trust you." Therefore the rejection of a starring role based on a great figure of our literature seems incomprehensible, a perversity.

The analogy to a spurned lover is not inexact; depending on how

Glenn Close in *The World According to Garp* (1982)

attracted you are, you continue the pursuit, or you move on to someone else. The first of these was Blythe Danner, who turned down the
part; then Meryl Streep, who also turned it down. We hit on Sigourney
Weaver, at that time being groomed by her agents at International Creative Management to be a "big, big star." She kept us dangling for a month
while she fretted. Wasn't Olive a bitter old maid/a probable lesbian and a
man-hating spinster? Wasn't she dowdy? And dried up? Could Sigourney's dashing new image that was being refashioned out of the approving
reviews for her film *The Year of Living Dangerously* accommodate all those
bad words? She was being hailed as the 1980s Vanessa Redgrave.

Christopher Reeve, in agreeing to play Basil Ransome, had con-
sultation rights in the casting of Olive and Verena. He now suggested
Glenn Close as a potential Olive. I'd never seen her work but I liked
the way she looked and spoke when I met her. I went to see *The World
According to Garp* and felt encouraged by the material she'd chosen. In
that film she played a virulent man-hater; compared with this, Olive
Chancellor's views on that subject seem almost benign. But then it
turned out that Glenn Close was also having image problems. The
tragedy for actresses in both the United States and Britain is that by
the time they have established themselves, they're often no longer
young—or they don't *feel* they're really young anymore, so everything they do after thirty is seen in terms of the "right career move"
and of enhancing their image as a saleable commodity.

With Glenn Close, who proved later that she could be winning on
Broadway in *The Real Thing*—could be soft and feminine, that is—
the risk was in doing another castrator. Wouldn't she be typecast? *The
Big Chill* hadn't come out—more cuddliness—but influential people
hadn't seen her in it yet. I began to read her hesitation as resisting me.
Heat and Dust was screened for her. We presented it to her beforehand
as a film with complex characters, a film in which people are seen
in varied lights, good and bad, and still manage to come across as
sympathetic. After the screening we had this conversation in Ismail's
office:

CLOSE
I had some trouble with *Heat and Dust.* I felt you were sort of
removed from your characters.

IVORY
Me? [Getting red in the face.] I reject that.

CLOSE
[Shrinking down inside her raincoat.] I'm sorry. I only
meant . . .

IVORY
[Looking over the top of her head.] I reject that totally.

She said she needed a month to think about our offer, but meanwhile terms were gone into and some provisional dates were set aside. We left for Cannes with *Heat and Dust*. What we didn't know was that her agent, Clifford Stevens, was in negotiations for her over *The Natural*, starring opposite Robert Redford, and for a lot of money.

Meanwhile, Vanessa Redgrave came back into our lives. As Glenn Close debated in New York, Ismail, who can't stand indecisiveness in any form and feared we would lose more time if she ended up saying no, sent *The Bostonians* screenplay again to Vanessa, whose career seemed to have stalled because of the continued fallout over her PLO and anti-Zionist stands. She read it and came right back: she wanted the part very much. Ismail cautioned her that Glenn Close had also been offered the part and was hesitating; she hadn't definitely turned it down.

Now Clifford Stevens had a brainstorm. Why couldn't his client play *both* parts, and commute between Boston and Buffalo, New York, where *The Natural* was to be shot? She would be needed in Buffalo for only ten days; if we agreed to this, she would play Olive Chancellor. Used to these kinds of arrangements in India, we said we would try to work it out. Glenn Close still had many reservations about who and what Olive Chancellor was—she wanted to read the revised script before she *really* committed herself—but she said she'd go to London for costume fittings. Vanessa, somewhat irritated by now, waited to see what would happen, while the production managers of the two films tried to work out a schedule. Such situations are a nightmare for low-budget films. A single episode of an airport's being fogged in would cost us thousands of dollars. The more comfortably financed film would be able to absorb losses like that without difficulty.

Glenn, back in New York from the fittings for *The Bostonians*, now read the new script. It did nothing to allay her fears and if anything intensified them. So I, from Boston, set up a meeting between her and Ruth Jhabvala. On that same day, Clifford Stevens escalated his demands for more shooting days for his client on *The Natural*, saying that it was "*vital* for Glenn to work in that film." The ten days became fifteen, and that might not be the end of it. If we wanted Glenn, he told Ismail over the telephone from New York, the bottom line was that we would have to release her not only when she wanted to go to Buffalo, but as *often* as she wanted to go. At this, a furious Ismail, acting in the imperial style of the Hollywood czars of yore, gave orders from London to an underling to fire the leading lady and, rapidly passing on to more important matters, set about replacing her with Vanessa Redgrave.

While all these telephone calls were being made, Glenn Close was making progress in Ruth Prawer Jhabvala's Manhattan apartment on an understanding of Olive's character. Every obstacle had been overcome and actress and screenwriter had passed on to fictitious projections of Olive's future: how that tragically disappointed lady, once she had climbed down from the lectern in the music hall, would catch some slow, wasting disease and soon die, etc. Glenn Close made her way to her agent's office, and in the midst of reporting that her problems with the script had been settled, the telephone rang. This was the MIP underling (if one may call, for the purposes of this tale, the dignified production manager Ted Morley an underling). He was calling from *The Bostonians* company in Cambridge, Massachusetts. The unexpected news was related. I knew nothing of this drama; while it was going on I was in an airplane. When I reached La Guardia, Ruth Jhabvala told me what had taken place. That evening in London, Vanessa went to Cosprop, the London costumiers, for fittings. When it was found possible to sew a foot or so of cloth on to the hem of dresses being made for Glenn Close, which were far along by this time, that was done and other things, which Vanessa had worn in the miniseries *Wagner*, were packed.

There is a moral in all this, I think, for agents who use too peremptory a tone with the prospective employers of their clients: it may happen that a preferred first choice for a part is suddenly available. And though Glenn Close rendezvoused successfully with Robert Redford in Buffalo, I sometimes felt her ghost hovering over our shoot. I felt—I still feel, perhaps illogically—that I owe her a film.*

IN APRIL 1982 Vanessa Redgrave was in effect fired by the Boston Symphony Orchestra without notice when a series of performances of *Oedipus Rex* at Symphony Hall in Boston and Carnegie Hall in New York were cancelled.

She had been engaged to narrate the Stravinsky work. No official reason was given for the symphony's action, but it was widely suspected that her well-publicized sympathies for the PLO made her unacceptable to the symphony's Jewish trustees and donors. There had been unsubstantiated rumors of threats of uproar and violence by the Jewish Defense League if she were allowed to perform, and the symphony management was thought to have panicked, justifying their action to themselves on the grounds of public safety. News of all this—or just some bad rumors—had a sort of domino effect in New York and she lost a Broadway part because of the cancellations. For fourteen months after that she did no work.

She decided to sue the symphony, alleging that she had been denied her civil rights under a new and still untested Massachusetts statute, and asked for damages. Her going to court was no small thing. As it developed, she was taking on the Boston establishment. At first only she took her suit seriously, and it was dismissed as having merely a nuisance value. Boston's artistic community took sides and in time the Museum of Fine Arts, the Boston Athenaeum, and the Fogg Museum at Harvard all lined up behind the orchestra, declining to host benefit premieres of *The Bostonians* because the star of the film was in litigation with their "sister organization." But influential members of Boston's Jewish community were saying that the cancellation of *Oedipus Rex* had been a disgrace to the city; old friends weren't speaking to each other anymore. In this atmosphere we arrived in Boston with Vanessa to make *The Bostonians*.

---

* We cast her in 2002 in *Le Divorce*, a film made in Paris from the novel by Diane Johnson, in which she played a famous author.

Chateau-sur-Mer, Newport, Rhode Island

We stayed long enough there to have rehearsals and then the unit moved to Newport, Rhode Island, our first location. Some of us—Vanessa, Christopher Reeve, Madeleine Potter (who played Verena Tarrant), and Merchant-Ivory-Jhabvala—put up at Richmere, a turn-of-the-century Newport "cottage" that was being run as an executive retreat. Life seemed to center around the kitchen, where Vanessa did a lot of the cooking. We were doing night shooting next door at Chateau-sur-Mer, and she prepared herself every afternoon with large servings of steak tartare. This kitchen was the scene of heavy script conferences. Strengthened by years of polemical discussion and doubtless by her steak tartare, Vanessa began to bear down ideologically on *The Bostonians* and on Henry James, who was not there to defend himself, and on Ruth Jhabvala, who had imagined that all this sort of thing had already been gotten resolved.

Was not the reactionary Basil Ransome a slave-beater, Vanessa asked? Was he not deeply evil, and should he not therefore be made to seem more satanic? Had Ruth shown this clearly enough? Hadn't she made Basil much too sympathetic? Shouldn't he be shown in his true colors so that she, Olive, by contrast should shine forth—not be

Christopher Reeve, Vanessa Redgrave, me, and Jessica Tandy
on the set of *The Bostonians*

seen just as a hysterical eccentric, but as a figure of righteousness? That being the case, added Madeleine Potter, she—Verena—didn't want to be put in a bad light by loving Basil, she was only there to reform him. Since Basil was so villainous, wasn't her attraction to him suspect? There was about Madeleine Potter and Vanessa's relationship throughout the film a similarity to that of a mama bird and baby bird: the mama bird flies down with a worm; the baby bird goes cheep, cheep and opens its beak; the mama bird puts the worm in it.

It hardly needs saying that Christopher Reeve knew nothing of these discussions, but when Basil and Verena were out filming one of their rare dates together—at Harvard, or walking by the sea—it seemed to him that Verena, the character, wasn't having as much fun in his company as she should be. Why was that? Why at first did she wear a look of such concentration, frowning down at the path and kicking at stones when she should be smiling up into his face? Why did she seem so often to be on the verge of tears?

Some people said that Vanessa, too, was often on the verge of tears, because she was forced to spend so much time in enemy territory—i.e., Boston, a place that had shown itself to be hostile to her—and that the strain of being there made her tense and unhappy.

Furthermore, she was helping to prepare her case for trial, which caused her to spend a lot of time on the telephone with her New York–based lawyers, adding further to the strain. These things may have been true, but the principal impression she made on most people was that she was having a good time in Boston.

There were no threats, no pickets, none of the disruptions that were supposed to take place when she appeared in public as a performer. She was always visible and accessible, in a way Christopher Reeve could not be. She carried requests for autographs in to him, and when he'd signed, she brought them out again to be distributed and posed for photographs. She did not try to push her political views on her coworkers, as we had been told in England she might try to do. Some people said she elected herself the shop steward for the actors and extras hired for the film; others, that nobody else wanted the job and somebody had to do it. Every morning she went through *The New York Times*, *The Boston Globe*, and *The Wall Street Journal* during hair and makeup time, reading aloud articles that interested her and puffing on a cigarette. When she arrived on set, all corseted, her petticoats rustling, murmuring to the throng, the feather on her hat high above other people's heads as she passed through, she was a queen by natural rights and in everything she did or said.

Me with Madeline Potter and Vanessa Redgrave on the set of *The Bostonians*

But it seemed to me that her recent identification with the People, meaning the underprivileged and disenfranchised, had perhaps had the unconscious effect of politicizing her portrayals of members of the Privileged, so that she could make them seem the monsters her propaganda said they were. Thinking of herself for so long as a People's Revolutionary, in her playing she had effaced some of her natural noblesse oblige. In her mind perhaps she had become a Woman of the People, who never possessed that quality, and who cannot easily introduce it when called on to be a fastidious great lady thrown among the nasty proletariat—as during the scene of the Tarrants' tea party in *The Bostonians*, at which she made faces and noises to indicate ostentatious distaste.

Vanessa Redgrave filming *The Bostonians* on Martha's Vineyard

This led to our only real row, but when I tried to tone her down a bit, she refused to take my direction; for the only time in my life I left the set, saying I'd come back when she agreed to do it my way, without all that sneering. In the lunch line by accident I hit on the key word that would bring her round: I told her that her morning's work had had the unfortunate effect of making Olive seem a little common,* and after we went back she was more in character again. This

---

* The word "common," introduced to describe the manner, or behavior, of a certain kind of educated middle-class English person, kills them, I've found—stops them dead in their tracks.

episode is strange, be-
cause you could say Va-
nessa Redgrave's whole
life of idealism and gen-
erosity to others (though
not to Zionists) is a lesson in noblesse oblige,
carried sometimes to
lengths of real depriva-
tion for her and personal
sacrifice for the causes—
mostly unpopular—she
supports.

There were other
scenes like these. When
are there not, on a film
set? She could be as stiff-
necked as Olive out of a
sense that she was right
and the rest of us deeply
wrong. On a bad day this could be carried to ludicrous lengths, when
a detail—any detail: a line of dialogue, some bit of action, a prop, a
piece of costume—seemed to her to be invested with the full weight
of the entire enterprise, an absolute moral weight, so that if she did
not get her way everything would be compromised. If I had said to
her, "Vanessa, you cannot wear that dresser scarf around your neck,"
her mood might have been spoiled and the scene reduced. These ec-
centricities seemed a small price to pay for the performance I could
see she was giving. In the end we parted as friends and collaborators.
This was the second way I learned to look at her and to think about
her, in the course of the intense relationship, tinged with lunacy, that
a film shoot forges between director and star.

SHE WENT BACK to England—to a successful production at the
Haymarket Theatre of her father's adaptation of *The Aspern Papers*,

opposite Christopher Reeve and Dame Wendy Hiller; to Cannes, with *The Bostonians,* where the French seemed almost desperately grateful to see her, and ready to admire her in the film; and finally back to Boston for a PBS production, *Three Sovereigns for Sarah,* about the Salem witch trials, and to her own suit against the Boston Symphony Orchestra. Meanwhile, *The Bostonians* opened in America, where it became a popular success and, for her, a critical triumph. No one picketed outside Cinema One in New York. And not one critic commented on her English accent. I attribute people's acceptance of her as an upper-class Bostonian to a kind of holdover from Hollywood films of the 1930s and '40s, fed by television and revival house reruns. An "aristocratic" American woman always had good diction in those films, sounded distinctly Anglophile if not English. It was a speech convention; American actresses were trained to speak well then (and they got some first-class lines to deliver also): Bette Davis, of course, but also Myrna Loy and Mary Astor. We remember the cultivated mid-Atlantic accents of Olivia de Havilland and Joan Fontaine. That's how a lady talked (and anyway, there's a popular belief in the United States that a Boston Brahmin sounds like an Englishman).

When Vanessa Redgrave finally took the witness stand at her own trial in October 1984, this impression was enhanced for those of us who could remember films like *The Letter.* She was every distressed lady whose good name had been dragged in the mud, speaking, *The Boston Globe* reported, in "a clear and carrying voice." The paper also commented that she played her voice "the way Rostropovich plays the cello." Was this consummate performance to be her greatest?

The issues of the case were tangled and the positions of both sides were seen to be compromised in the course of the testimony. Vanessa Redgrave was asking for damages, but not solely for breach of contract. She held that, because she had been fired by the orchestra, she had lost much other work by having become the victim of blacklisting. She also maintained that her civil rights had been abridged. The symphony set out to demolish these arguments. They now stated that the official reason for the cancellation of her contract was that her presence was an invitation to disorder and possible violence. At the least, no music would have been played, none of her fine words spoken. In addition, members of the orchestra threatened a boycott if she appeared, though they were reminded by the symphony management that their contracts had a no-strike provision.

The trial was full of these murky reversals. Oppressed workers were also her oppressors. But the sight of the completed jury must have reassured her: other workers (of whom only two had ever attended a concert at the elitist Symphony Hall), a self-employed electrician, a furniture restorer, a clerk, a janitor, etc. When they heard testimony of the kind of money she would make from her films before she was blacklisted, their eyes grew round: $250,000, $350,000, $400,000. What she'd managed to eke out since didn't sound so bad either: more than $200,000.

There are countries where a jury might not feel much sympathy at hearing the beautiful lady on the witness stand describe how she had lost a million and had to console herself with a couple of hundred thousand. But in a country where so many people are hooked on the endearing antics of the rich shown in serials like *Dallas* and *Dynasty* and *Falcon Crest*, she would not be the subject of envy or censure. She hadn't even inherited her money, she'd made if for herself. It would only be right to try to console her, which the jury subsequently did. Her attorneys, Daniel Kornstein and Marvin Wexler, argued that what was at stake in this case was a fundamental American principle: "to keep your job even if they don't like what you stand for." Their courtroom manner was restrained,

Peter Sellars, 2011

their questioning of witnesses seemingly tentative, matching the tone of superpoliteness set by Vanessa Redgrave.

One of the principal witnesses for the plaintiff was the twenty-seven-year-old Peter Sellars, who was to have directed *Oedipus Rex*. He gave his reasons to the court for wanting her as narrator, citing, according to the *Globe*, her "fiery directness" and the appropriate timbre of her voice. "She has the ability to deliver flat unequivocal statements that build to the height of tragedy." He thought of his narrator as a dispassionate television news anchor, "bringing us bad news." When, in the hours of panic and muddle before the cancellation, it seemed to the orchestra management that there was a danger of violence, Sellars suggested that the Boston police ring the stage, but the orchestra general manager, Thomas Morris, and Seiji Ozawa, the conductor, wouldn't agree to the fittingness of that as a metaphorical comment on *Oedipus Rex*. "Society," said Morris, "was not ready for this living theater."

Ismail Merchant was also called as a witness. He was indignant that the orchestra in a pretrial motion for summary judgment had represented the shooting of *The Bostonians* as something of a small affair in an attempt to play down the evident lack of animosity to the actress in the city. He set the record straight. His star had been the toast-of-the-town, at the highly visible center, with Christopher Reeve, of a large-scale operation that went all over Boston for months without incident, dispensing smiles, autographs, *keema*, and dhal. Ismail was asked by Wexler how *Variety* had referred to the film on its release. It was "boffo" and "socko," he said. The judge and jury laughed, and the defense declined to cross-examine the too amiable and possibly volatile witness.

Vanessa Redgrave's contention that she began to lose work in the wake of the cancellation of *Oedipus Rex* was reinforced by the testimony of Theodore Mann of New York's Circle in the Square Theater, which had approached her to star in *Heartbreak House* with Rex Harrison in the fall of 1982. Mann told the court he was afraid to hire her after the Boston Symphony Orchestra cancellation because if the symphony feared disruption by people opposed to her, he also had that fear.

Ismail Merchant: Boffo! Socko!

But everything else that was submitted to try to prove that she had been blacklisted was thrown out as hearsay. The manner of Robert E. Sullivan, the defense lawyer, contrasted with Kornstein and Wexler's: brisk, aggressively self-assured, he tried to undermine the civil rights part of the case by citing an instance of her own belief in blacklisting. Had she not presented a motion for consideration by British Actors Equity urging that British actors should not perform in Israel and that British film and television projects there should be cancelled? "I would never suggest a ban on Israeli artists and films," she testified. "Never. Israeli artists are welcome to come to Britain to work, but I do say that British artists should not go there, the way we say that they should not go to South Africa."

Sullivan tried to show that far from being the victim of blacklisting, she had turned down job offers with substantial salaries because she hadn't liked the material submitted to her, to which she replied that these had not been serious offers, with financial backing. He tried to show that she had not been forthright with the orchestra, who were naïve about her history of political notoriety and had not warned them, when they offered her the job, that she hadn't worked in the States in several years and had provoked bomb threats when she recently worked in Australia.

Witnesses called for the orchestra during the two-week trial sometimes made an unfortunate impression. It had always been the assumption by people interested in the case, on both sides of the issue, that Vanessa Redgrave had been dumped because of pressure brought on the orchestra by its rich Jewish backers who couldn't stand her, and this was confirmed by the testimony of an orchestra trustee, Irving Rabb, who said he feared the loss of Jewish subscribers. He admitted phoning the orchestra's general manager and asking, according to *The Boston Globe*, "Is there any way you can get out of it and not have the performance?" The telephone logbooks of the orchestra were read into the records: "Miss Redgrave is a disgraceful person. She should perish," one caller said; another, that she was "an accessory to murder."

Seiji Ozawa, 1990

There were dozens of protest calls, many from people who identified themselves as subscribers and patrons, who said her hiring was an "affront" to the Jewish community, and that it would be a factor in their future support of the orchestra. But there were also many calls of support, the logbook showed, urging the management not to give in to pressure. The log quotes Arthur Bernstein, a subscriber and contributor, who also identified himself as founder of the Massachusetts chapter of the Jewish Defense League, as saying, "You will have nothing but bloodshed and violence." (On the witness stand, he denied saying this, and claimed that he had merely promised to picket.) The artistic administrator, William Bernell, telephoned Vanessa in England to tell her about these calls and letters, and to ask her if she feared disruptions. She told him it was her belief audiences would prevail over hecklers. Supposing she was shot at? She was sure the Boston police would apprehend her killer, she said by way of reassurance.

It was Seiji Ozawa's suggestion that Redgrave withdraw from the program. In testimony it came out that, like most of the jurors, he had never heard of the actress; his wife told him (approvingly) who she was when the furor began. "I disagree that politics and music must live together," he stated during the trial. "Music must remain neutral, in order to stay alive as an art." Kornstein asked Ozawa for his opinion of the philosophical and political context of *Fidelio*, an opera Ozawa had conducted ten times. Ozawa replied that he and many people thought its libretto was "stupid." He told the courtroom the opera had a "happy ending" because "the good man comes to save people from the bad king." He told Kornstein, "Don't waste time talking about *Fidelio*, it has nothing to do with this case."

Sometimes the trial seemed to degenerate into a wrangle between some prosperous, willful, and dynamic Asian gentlemen over how best to serve old Boston's civic interests. And sometimes it seemed that Vanessa herself, whose long-necked profile in the witness box suggested the wavy-haired figurehead of a ship, personified Truth riding triumphant above the fray.

The jury, in a commonsense if split decision, found in her favor. The Boston Symphony Orchestra had not cancelled the concert for causes and because of circumstances beyond its reasonable control, but had bowed to community pressure. The jurors did not agree that she had been denied her civil liberties or that she had lost her job because the orchestra disagreed with political views she had publicly expressed. She was awarded $100,000 in damages, plus the $27,000 contract fee. Both sides claimed victory. Vanessa, leaving for Moscow to play Peter the Great's sister in an NBC miniseries, sent a message to the Boston Symphony: "Not for the Management but for the musicians I had hoped to work with. My case was not brought against them. In fact, my defense is theirs, for it means that their jobs, too, can be secure." This merges uncannily with her impassioned statement on the stage at the music hall at the end of *The Bostonians* and, like it, might have been set to martial music:

> I say we will be harsh as truth. As uncompromising as justice. On this subject, we will not think or speak or write with moderation. We will not excuse—we will not equivocate—we will not retreat a single inch. And we will be heard!

One could say that this trial, widely reported by the American news media, was her finest hour, if one concedes that an actress can have hours finer than those spent in front of a camera or on a stage. No one will deny that her fight was well worth making, or that the stand she took was anything but admirable, with larger implications than a mere breach of contract. Whether she won or lost, it would cost her dearly in legal fees, in valuable time, and in energy. The case might be a future irritant. Still, she fought it, often in a cuckoo world with the memory of voices crying, "She must perish!" Had she lived in Massachusetts three hundred years earlier, she might well have been branded a witch—or at the very least, an extreme troublemaker—and been hanged on the village common.

Bruce Chatwin

Bruce Chatwin in the eastern Oregon desert, 1972

Letter to Nicholas Shakespeare

Dear Nicholas,*

You asked me in Claverack if I'd ever had an affair with Bruce Chatwin. I told you it hadn't been anything as grand as that. That was deliberately misleading; I was trying to be discreet. In fact, our relationship at first was mostly a sexual one, lasting three years during which time we were often apart. I was either in India or the United States, and he would be in Europe, or maybe somewhere off in Africa. Both of us were ready to travel long distances so we could meet up and have sex. To me—and I'm sure to him—an "affair" implied unwanted turbulent emotions: the opposite of the easygoing relationship we actually had. Neither of us had any illusions about a "love affair."

Bruce—according to Howard Hodgkin, who told Cary Welch, who then told me, whereupon I acted on it—was evidently smitten by me when we first met at Howard and Julia Hodgkin's house in Bath in 1969. And I recall my first impression of Bruce, standing somewhat dramatically with his back against a wall just as the sun was setting, staring at me with a sort of smoldering look, saying nothing—an uncharacteristic silence for him. He struck me as being like a beautiful, soft child who's not quite real. Later, after we'd talked a bit, he gave me his telephone number. Finding him attractive and the things he said funny, I called him up when I was in London on my way to India. We had dinner in some smart restaurant he chose. He chattered away amusingly, telling me, when I ordered an artichoke, that it would make me fart, etc. He asked me back to the house in Kynance Mews he sometimes shared with Oliver Hoare, where we sat on a little divan with spindly legs and soon began to kiss. His flies were swelling and I ran my fingers over them, whereupon we went upstairs to bed. I followed him up a ladder hoping I wouldn't fart and stayed the night with him. In the interest of England's literary history let me supply the information—if others

---

* Most of the quoted material in this piece is from Bruce Chatwin's letters to his wife, Elizabeth, and to me (*Under the Sun: The Letters of Bruce Chatwin*, edited by Elizabeth Chatwin and Nicholas Shakespeare [New York: Viking 2011]), and from my letters to Nicholas Shakespeare, Chatwin's biographer (*Bruce Chatwin: A Biography* by Nicholas Shakespeare [New York: Nan A. Talese/Doubleday, 1999]).

haven't already—that he was always good and virile. He had an uncut, rosy, schoolboy-looking ready cock that seemed to match his high-colored, fair schoolboy's face. When I said that I'd always supposed the Anglo-Saxon ruling classes were routinely circumcised, he shrugged. He did not identify with the British ruling classes. In fact, he told me, he despised them. His hands were schoolboyish, too, with short fingers and ragged, blunt nails. Not having conventionally "fine" hands as an asset, he probably never thought much about them and put them out of his mind. His feet were equally uncared for.

Kynance Mews

Me on the set of *Bombay Talkie* (1970). Of all my sets,
the giant typewriter was my favorite.

I knew I'd found a very funny and delightfully sexy new friend. I left for Bombay after the night at Kynance Mews. We kept in touch over the next months by letters while I made my film *Bombay Talkie*. The ones I got from him were as vivid as his conversations, full of allusions (that often I didn't get) to his life in England: his likes and dislikes, personal and aesthetic, expressed in language that seemed to me, as I read it, to be destined someday for the printed page. A sample:

"I spend the weeks in Oxford now heavily disguised as a skittish undergraduate, and, I confess, celebrating my thirtieth birthday with a skittish affair. Merton College, jasmine tea, shades of Max Beerbohm, red lacquer, ecclesiastic drag, mystical excesses of the Early Church Fathers combined with the intellectual mentality of Ronald Firbank. You get the picture?" In these letters he also laid out shared ideas for films he hoped I might like to make with him. These seemed very far-fetched, not at all the kind of thing I could imagine myself doing. When I got back from India after finishing my film, we met up in London. And sometime later that year while there, or by letter, he invited me to join him in the South of France in the summer of 1971.

Kynance Mews, London

He was always an eager, affectionate, smiling lover. We touched each other immediately once we were alone, without preliminaries, not even a kiss, our hands going straight to our flies. When both of us were satisfied, he would leap up vigorously to pee, making some joke. I'm sure a big part of the sexual magnetism most people felt coming from him was the zigzagging movement of his mind, stuffed full like his grandmother's cabinet of curiosities he'd told me about, and leavened by his nothing-is-sacred humor. He was a handsome young man, he wanted to sleep with me, and once he had, he wanted to again. Who asks for more? He was also my first Englishman, so I had more curiosity about him than if he'd been a handsome American. And maybe I was his first American; I never asked. But curiosity was certainly a very strong part of my desire for him from our first night at Kynance Mews.

The week I spent with him in Haute Provence in the summer of 1971 was the most enjoyable time of our friendship. He gave me my orders: letters and telegrams full of details about getting there, etc. He sent me a telegram saying "DO COME BUT QUICK STOP HIRE CAR MARSEILLES," followed by a letter: ". . . I do badly want to see you—for lots of reasons. Apart from the obvious one, I want to ask your advice . . ." Once there, we had a good time driving around to the little hilltop towns to meet his friends, including Stephen Spender, whom I met as he mucked about in the motor of his car, his fingers covered with black oil. Bruce took me to Menerbes, hoping to spot Dora Maar

Oppedette, Alpes-de-Haute-Provence, France

trudging up the hill to the house given her by Picasso, but no luck. We wandered up and down naked like everybody else at the nude beach at St. Tropez, then afterward drove back in the night to Oppedette to the stifling little house Bruce had rented on a bleak, bare hilltop. We slept side by side on mattresses laid on the cement floor of the baking, charmless place. We fooled around a lot, mostly in the morning before getting up. But the thought of his wife, Elizabeth, driving across France to join him, as she said she would, and walking in on us some morning, made him nervous.

The Nomadic Alternative

I was relieved to learn that he didn't want my advice about his book. I have to say that whenever Bruce, all wound up, spoke of his nomads—as he often did—my eyes glazed over. This book, which his London publisher, Jonathan Cape, felt unable to publish as it stood when first submitted by Bruce, had by now become a burden to him. I would see his moods bounce back and forth between exhilaration and gloom as he wrestled with his manuscript. Then he would abruptly change course and pitch an idea about the film he was thinking about, a campy-sounding farce set in the art world, involving a Matisse paint-

Ismail with the dancer Helen on the set of *Bombay Talkie*

ing and a grotesque Miami collector named Norman Scott Lauderdale. I heard him out politely, never imagining he was serious. I would
go out and relax in a big chair in the sun, but soon he'd emerge and
I'd see him walking about in the distance, not working. And this was
pretty much the pattern of our days in Oppedette. We never cooked
anything and always ate out. Was it at one of our delicious Provençal
meals where I first heard about the weird scrap of dinosaur skin his
grandmother possessed, which later was featured in his first published
book, *In Patagonia*? Or did I hear about it the next summer when he
turned up at my house in Oregon? In my imagination I fixed on it, and
can still see it in my mind's eye, withered and scaly.

In letters, and later after meeting me again, Bruce would spin out
for me one of his fantastic ideas that he had for a "fil-um" we could
make together. He always said, and wrote, "fil-um," two syllables, in
which perhaps there was just a hint of contempt and condescension.
I was amazed by his lack of seriousness about my profession. It was
hard for me, having worked on four films, including *Shakespeare Wallah*, written by our disciplined screenwriter Ruth Jhabvala, to feign
enthusiasm for Bruce's cinematic concoctions. Could it have been,
as with so many educated, upper-middle-class English people I met,
that he looked down on the antics of show-biz types—actors and
actresses, producers of plays and films, even film directors? Did we
have for him anything more than gossip value? He never took Ismail seriously (or any Indian), or recognized their worth, so Ismail
was indifferent to Bruce, detested him even. Ismail himself claimed
nomad blood, boasting that he was descended from the nomadic
warriors who invaded North India, so Bruce might have felt some
of that spirit in Ismail, and even admired it. Bruce sometimes must
have looked at me with disappointment after pitching his latest idea
for a fil-um as I sat there like a stone, unsmiling. He must have
felt I was a very poor friend indeed, without imagination, and that
he was wasting himself on me. If I had wanted to film something
Bruce wrote, it would perhaps have been *On the Black Hill*, his moving novel published much later, about two aged brothers who lived
on a farm in Wales, and who had slept together in the same bed all
their lives.

Reluctantly, I had to leave Oppedette to join some American friends in Tangiers, with Bruce asking if he might not go with me, but then saying, half sadly, "I know myself too well. Once in Morocco, the footsteps lead to another horizon. I am a bum and I do not believe in work of any kind."

Whenever we saw each other in England, our meetings were apt to be hurried. Bruce moved out of Kynance Mews and took a tiny flat on Sloane Avenue he described as being in a building "that was a famous call-girl warren before and after the war, and the whores are still there, mainly Hungarians, who drop their handbags in the lift and ask you 'Zahling, plis . . .' to pick them up."

One day he called me at my hotel, sounding excited, telling me to come over right away, that he had something to show me. I got in a taxi, hoping there would be time for us to have sex. But instead of unzipping his pants when I arrived, what he had to show me was a very fine little Indian drawing from Kotah, in Rajasthan, which he offered to sell to me. The drawing was of a maddened elephant in *must*, or heat. I liked it and should have said okay, but didn't. He wanted too much money for it. I was used to buying things like that for far less from Indian dealers in Delhi and Jaipur.

The Chatwins' rare Inca feathered cloak, which he and Elizabeth had bought with their wedding money and which they were always about to put up for sale, hung over the little Sloane Avenue fireplace. She must on that day have been in the country at Holwell Farm, the house they owned, but on that day there was no time for sex. Bruce's usual receptive mood whenever we found ourselves alone had been replaced by the rather spiky manner of a Sotheby's expert. Indian drawings were not really his area of expertise. In fact, he was always putting Indian art down, as well as India. Cary Welch had given him the drawing, but Bruce now needed money. He always needed money. He told me that he and Elizabeth were supposed to live on a yearly stipend of five thousand American dollars that they received from her family in New York. In the 1960s, in rural England where they chose to live, that amount was just enough perhaps, but it could not pay for his travels, nor for all the champagne they drank while entertaining.

Holwell Farm

Bruce invited me to Holwell Farm in Ozleworth, Gloucestershire, for a weekend. As soon as I got off the train he took me to see his friend Sally, the former Duchess of Westminster, who was laid up at home in her dowager's cottage with a broken leg caused by a fall from a horse. A festive afternoon tea/cocktails was going on around her bed as she held court, and Bruce's jokes added to the merriment. This exalted Englishwoman would normally have been addressed as "Your Grace," but on that day everyone, except the servants, called her Sally. She was the illegitimate half sister of the writer J. R. Ackerley, who wrote a favorite book of mine, *Hindoo Holiday.* Her Grace was one of the "fun" people Bruce came to know as his special fame grew, who later included figures—stars—like Jacqueline Onassis, Salman Rushdie, and Robert Mapplethorpe.

Bruce and Elizabeth's house at Ozleworth was in a particularly dim and damp part of Gloucestershire, and he often said that he couldn't wait to escape from it, fine as it was, comfortable as it was. The place represented an England opposite in all ways to what he craved outside it: hot sun, blue skies, rugged terrain, beckoning, unknown distances and beckoning, unknown people. He would come down from London to perch at Holwell for a few days but then, he said, he counted the minutes until he could leave. Elizabeth was content there, where she had a lot of animals to look after. She was the only reason he came.

Though he lived like a bachelor in London, everyone understood he was married. Elizabeth was there in the background most of the time and sometimes she came forward and was important to him, but they were not the usual kind of couple. He never referred to her contemptuously—at least not to me. He spoke of her like a friend—his best friend—but like another boy, or man. She wasn't a weight around his neck that would stop him from having fun; she wasn't that kind of wife. When he came down to Holwell, she took good care of him, entertained his friends, cooked delicious meals, ordered the wine, saw to his shirts and clean underwear, then left him alone to work.

On another of my visits to Holwell Farm, two friends of mine from the West Coast of the United States were also there, Bruce and

Holwell Farm in the Cotswold valley of Ozleworth Bottom,
near Wotton-under-Edge, Gloucestershire

Loretta Anawalt. They were planning a car trip to Greece with their
two boys and needed a car. I'll call Bruce Anawalt "my Bruce" from
here on, as he figures in this story later. Bruce Chatwin had agreed,
through me, to sell the Anawalts his car, and a price had been settled.
While my Bruce, whom I had known since our college days at the
University of Oregon, was kneeling outside in the dirt in a drizzle
planting bulbs at the front of the Holwell house, which was handsome and dignified, his wife, Loretta, said she felt like we were all
living "in a wet head of lettuce."

The owner of the house and I walked inside by ourselves. This
walk took place in a long, upstairs room with highly polished floorboards. During our stroll, Bruce informed me that he had given up
homosexuality, and that he didn't have "those feelings anymore."
I remember sitting with him on a bench while I listened to these
discouraging words, resigning myself, as I admired the dark, glossy
floorboards. What did the English people who once had lived in this
house do in this room? I wondered. Walk up and down in it? Exercise
when it was too cold and wet to go out of doors? But Elizabeth, being an American, knew all about central heating and provided it, like

every other of her comforts in their house. I didn't want to stir, even as I was hearing Bruce out. Well, I thought, the end of a lot of fun—fun not always so easy to come by.

I needn't have despaired. We met a few months later at the Cannes Film Festival, where Ismail and I had been invited to show our new

Ismail and me in a Paris bar before traveling on to Cannes, 1972

film *Savages*. I asked Bruce to join us, and as I was loosening his belt buckle the first time we were alone, it was as if he had never spoken those disappointing words in the house with the polished floorboards.

At Cannes I wanted him to know George Swift Trow, one of the screenwriters of *Savages*. Trow was a very witty, very smart *New Yorker* writer about Bruce's age. He and Michael O'Donoghue, his coscenarist on our film, were also attending the festival. In my naiveté I'd imagined George and Bruce would take to each other, appreciate one another's mind and styles. Everyone agreed that both were "brilliant conversationalists," etc. But they eyed each other coldly upon meeting and barely ever spoke again during our parties and meals at the Villa d'Andon in Grasse, where Merchant Ivory put up the week *Savages* premiered.

In January of that same year, Bruce had taken off for Africa in order to shoot a documentary in the market at Barmou, in Niger. He described it in a letter to Elizabeth as being "the most aesthetic market I've ever seen—Tureg, Bororo Peuls and Hausas, camels, cattle that might have come from Egyptian tomb paintings." He wrote of the Bororo Peuls as being "the most beautiful people in the world who wander alone in the savannah with long-horned white cattle and have some rather startling habits like a complete sex-reversal at certain seasons of the year." It was fiercely hot in Africa and he was not used to lugging the heavy film equipment around, nor even all that sure about how to operate it, but he persevered. He wrote in his journal:

> Day of the market. Day of the film. Devoid of all human interest. Fingers tired from working the infernal machine, which didn't break down as I feared. Exhausted return to *campement* where became embroiled in discussion, black racist farrago. Insulted right and left. Five bottles of beer presented to me unwillingly had the effect (when mixed with the sour milk of the market) of turning my stomach into a volcano.

Bruce arrived back in England in March but wrote to me in high spirits: "I have a mustache. I am thinner. I am crazy about Africa and the Africans. Am about to send a letter to an Africa [sic] boy, who has just written 'I am happy I have saved the money to write to you.'" He went to work editing his film, excited, too, he told me, by the concept of trade "as a language which prevents people from cutting each other's throats." But he was uncomfortable in England, finding it "prissy" after Africa. "England is now little England," he wrote me, "with vengeance, the world of boutiques and bitchery and little else."

He felt he was "mouldering as usual in the country" and asked me how I planned to spend my summer. I told him to come visit me at Lake of the Woods in southern Oregon, where I had a cabin.

At George Montgomery's

Bruce arrived in New York in July 1972, where I met him and rented a car to drive us to New Hampshire to stay a couple of days with a friend of mine, the poet George Montgomery. Bruce had no interest in seeing, or being in, New York City. It would be a ghastly place he said, unbearable. What would he do there?

George Montgomery, a few years older than I, was the head of exhibitions at New York's Asia Society, with whom I had been connected during the making of my documentary *The Delhi Way*. He also wrote poetry and made wonderful black-and-white photographs. He lived mostly in the city, but owned a beautiful, chaste eighteenth-century Center Chimney Cape, as such houses are referred to, deep in the New England woods. Its unpainted, weathered clapboards were a silvery gray, its classical Greek Revival doorway opened out onto a large, flat stone. Orange daylilies bloomed around it. This was their season. I thought this utterly refined house, devoid of electricity and indoor plumbing, and furnished with glowing old country furniture, might intrigue and soothe Bruce. He would see that I knew Americans who lived simply yet elegantly, far away from the razzmatazz of characters like his Norman Scott Lauderdale.

George Montgomery, after serving as an ensign in the navy during the Second World War, went back to Harvard, where his studies had been interrupted by the war. But returning to college affected him badly; he suffered a nervous breakdown and dropped out. When he recovered, he sought readmission to the university. The acting dean of men then, McGeorge Bundy, later the National Security Adviser to Presidents Kennedy and Johnson, informed George that Harvard had no place at that time for a "shattered vessel" like him, so he withdrew his application and sought to make his life in New York City, where his poetry was eventually published in both English and Spanish. I was a little afraid of George, who was good-looking, quiet, but sharp and articulate, whenever we met at Asia House. I was afraid of displeasing him because of my brashly eager, young filmmaker manner. Or worse, by my bright-eyed enthusiasm for kinds of suddenly fashionable art that he thought little of. But after a time, the austere George became my good friend. His partner was the dancer and choreographer Dan Wagoner. They moved in New York's modern dance circles, and lived together in a floor-through loft above the famed choreographer and dancer Paul Taylor on Broadway, opposite Grace Church, where they could all look across the street to its pleasing early Gothic Revival façade.

George turned over the largest, best-furnished room in his house to us when we arrived in New Hampshire after our long drive. We slept on old, rope-strung beds. Cool night breezes came through the open windows. George, making noises in his kitchen the next morning, woke us up. Bruce, wearing only an unbuttoned shirt, was moving about our room appraising George's fine, old stuff. As he came up to me in bed I put my hand through the tails of his shirt, onto his naked front, and took hold of him, pulling him closer to reaffirm my affection and desire, last displayed in Cannes. When I put my hand to my nose, it reeked; he hadn't bathed since leaving London. I wanted to go further, but George, hearing us stir, called through to ask if we wanted tea. Later we all went swimming in a freezing stream. But by then I could see that Bruce was already restless, had sized up everything, including our host, and was most likely ready to move on.

George was attracted to Zen Buddhism. Without commenting on this I imagined Bruce had sized that up, too, and found it uncongenial, a kind of Eastern contemplative thought that was too lacking in action for him. George had built a Japanese teahouse, decorating it with banners in muted colors, and had set nice pieces of porcelain around, mixed with natural objects he'd picked up in the woods. The three of us sat there at dusk drinking George's tea out of little cups, brewed over a little fire in the teahouse, but the atmosphere of the place had failed to affect Bruce. If anything, it seemed to make him impatient. Was George doing a sort of quasi-meditative number? Bruce didn't want to be calmed down, he wanted to be wild now that he was in America. He hadn't come all that way to seek inaction. That would give him nothing to write about, or to build up into stories that he could dine out on back in London. For that he needed the grotesque Miami world of someone like Norman Scott Lauderdale.

As we drove down to New York the next day, I asked Bruce what he thought of George's beautiful house. Wasn't it a perfect creation? Was not George himself also a perfect and beautiful New England creation? But his praise for both was mild and qualified. I got the idea he'd seen better of both types, house and man. I wondered if Bruce had read the little card, enclosed in plastic, tacked up by George's back door. It had implored intruders to take shelter in his house if they needed to, even to take what they wanted, but not to destroy it. "My house is my only possession," the message ended. George told me that he wanted to be buried in the little overgrown family cemetery on his property.

Bruce left me in the city in order to visit his in-laws in upstate New York, and as we parted we made plans for our Oregon rendezvous later in the month.

Pullman

I don't remember why we chose to meet in Pullman, Washington, before leaving for Lake of the Woods and not in a city closer by, like San Francisco. Probably because I wanted to see my Bruce and his wife, Loretta, as I did unfailingly every summer from 1967 on, when he and I first, in a sort of *Brokeback Mountain*–like episode complete with pup tent, went camping together in the woods of northern Washington. As far as we knew we had been unseen by anybody with binoculars, unlike the couple in that film. It would have been easy for Chatwin to get to Pullman by air from the East Coast. Or he could have taken a train to nearby Spokane. For sure he would have gone mad on such a long and uneventful train trip and insulted the mostly ancient passengers, who were too timid to fly over the Rocky Mountains, and been kicked off the train for his rudeness.

Bruce Chatwin knew nothing of my closeness with Bruce Anawalt. I never talked to him about that. But the two Bruces, each formidable in his own way, and both together with me under a smaller roof than the one at Holwell Farm, produced tension—in me, anyway. That may account somewhat for Chatwin's eccentric behavior while staying with the Anawalts. He couldn't be the subject there of my undivided attention—or theirs. Surely he picked up on the intimacy between my Bruce and me and had sensed my Bruce's importance to me. He wouldn't have been much surprised were he to have viewed pictures I'd taken of my old college friend's memorable dick on another camping trip, this time to Muskrat Lake, just before Chatwin's arrival in Pullman. The images existed on rolls of partly exposed film I took at that time, showing Chatwin in his explorer's mode, tramping with me through the Oregon desert in hiking boots, shorts, and a smart-looking Argyle pullover. These rolls were not to be developed and printed, Argyle sweater, erections, and all, for twenty-five years, when Nicholas Shakespeare's biography of Chatwin—by then dead—was published.

Bruce Anawalt at Muskrat Lake, 1972

What did Bruce Chatwin make of the world where he'd landed when he first sat down to dinner with the Anawalts in their Pullman dining room? Their friends were mostly connected with Washington State University, where my Bruce taught Shakespeare and English literature. Loretta was Greek American, from a large first-generation family in Detroit: high-spirited, well-read, imaginative (she wrote), and open. Her nature contrasted with her husband's and projected a Mediterranean warmth and exuberance. His was cooler, with a streak of puritanism his looser friends teased him about. Yet my Bruce had little use for any kind of established religion and had talked me out of mine when we were still in college. At the end of most evening meals my Bruce would take up his guitar so that he and Loretta could entertain their guests with duets of country-and-western songs. All this may have seemed like a new kind of nomadic anthropology to Bruce Chatwin. For him, a new tribe of natives performing rituals along his trail: middle-class, well-off, hearty American academics, often coming from one of the big, empty, adjoining western states. These natives were welcoming and curious about the handsome, rosy-cheeked, young Englishman. In his loud, commanding voice, with his strange glamour, he tried, during the days we stayed, to contribute to the Anawalts' parties, mostly by referring to faraway people and faraway lives that his listeners could never know: a lame duchess, an African slave trader, a Sotheby's auctioneer in London selling a famous Picasso picture.

But at other times he seemed grim, unreachable—had cut himself off from all of us, and was making no effort to be his usual life of the party. I felt sometimes, as in New Hampshire at George Montgomery's, that he was judging everything and everybody, and that nothing ever measured up. He was showing an unpleasant side I'd never witnessed before. I began to feel he was behaving like a spoiled stuck-up shit in front of my oldest friends. There was an episode with a vibrator. In those days, electric vibrators were standard jokey props at parties of American forty-somethings. I never saw one being applied to any guest, but at one of these faculty get-togethers when Bruce Chatwin was in Pullman, my Bruce, or Loretta, or maybe both, went up to him with the whirring device, holding it out menacingly. He was sitting on a sofa with his bare legs pulled up under him. As the vibrator came nearer he screeched and kicked out violently with his feet. People laughed, but they thought he was being a bad sport.

And there was a trip to Moscow that Loretta described to Nicholas Shakespeare. Moscow, a small town and the home of the University of Idaho, was just over the state line from Washington:

> We got on the highway and Bruce Chatwin said he wanted to get out and walk. "But it's eight miles!" we told him. It was a hot day. The three of us watched open-mouthed in astonishment as Bruce, wearing shorts and huge hiking boots, strode into the wheat fields and headed toward the Union Pacific railroad track. He was escaping us, just getting away, getting free of what was haunting him, impelled onto the tracks. I tell you, the man was spooked. He hadn't assembled himself from where he'd been, like his atoms were scattered.

I TRACKED THE figure of my friend thrashing in the most self-willed way through the wheat and over the irrigation ditches. I felt this relentless pushing of himself to do this, some act of physical defiance, was unattractive. I felt sorry for him. I felt he was doing something wrong.

The two Bruces were very different kinds of men—almost exact opposites, including the color of their hair: one dark, one light. Bruce Anawalt was the manly western man—western in the sense of the American west, where I grew up. Taciturn, except when using his colorful cusswords. The other Bruce was the romantic English boy writer, blond and lustrous, spouting epigrams nonstop. My Bruce was an athlete, who happened to be a Shakespeare scholar and who happened to sing cowboy songs as well. He was a careful, accomplished builder, and served as the university ombudsman. His manner with people was almost always one of judicious self-containment. To both women and men he was sexually magnetic, like Bruce Chatwin, and like Chatwin his affairs with men were kept well hidden. Bruce Anawalt's energies were directed toward positive results; he had to have something to do—like planting the bulbs in the rain at Ozleworth. In Greece on a remote island where Loretta's family originated, he felt as if he didn't exist, not knowing the language and having nothing to do. He was dubious of Chatwin's talent for plucking fun almost from the air as he dazzled everyone in the room with his fanciful flights of speech. When one failed, he tried out another at once: Anawalt was not an artist, like Chatwin. He wouldn't create lasting works of modern English literature as Bruce Chatwin eventually did. When the two men parted later as we set out for Lake of the Woods, it was Bruce Chatwin's turn to be judged and measured up. I think—I know—that when Chatwin began publishing his string of books, and as his name and all the praise kept appearing in the press, my Bruce had no curiosity about them and read none. Perhaps Loretta did. But then I'm almost as remiss as Bruce Anawalt was. When *In Patagonia* was published, causing great excitement, I didn't rush to buy it. I remember thinking, I've heard those stories already. I know all about Bruce's dinosaur skin. It was not a piece of dinosaur skin, in fact, but a scrap from a Mylodon, a giant prehistoric sloth, according to Nicholas Shakespeare. Its remains had been dug up in Patagonia, and a bit of the skin with the hair still on it had been sent to Isobel Chatwin, Bruce's grandmother, as a wedding present by a cousin in Argentina. His grandmother kept it in a sort of *Wunderkammer* where as a child Bruce endlessly played with it and other romantic oddities, arranging and rearranging them on the shelves. Shakespeare proposes that this cabinet of curiosities belonging to his grandparents formed the basis of many of Bruce's imaginative impulses as a writer.

On our way to Lake of the Woods, Chatwin and I checked in to a motel in a small town in eastern Oregon and were finally able to lock our door. With two beds nearby, for some reason we found ourselves undressing on the floor, which was covered by a piece of dirty-looking black carpet. I must have pulled off Bruce's pants. I can see his bare legs and feet on the black rug as I recall our first real embrace since his arrival out west. But we didn't go any further. I remember how we pushed each other away good-naturedly and got into the separate beds.

Off Dead Indian Road

In a letter to Shakespeare later on I wrote:

> The next night in my cabin at Lake of the Woods, where we stayed in separate bedrooms, I found myself making excuses to turn in early, etc. Suddenly just like that, without explanation—and rare for me—I lost my desire for Bruce. After two or three days of this I felt bad; he wasn't being standoffish and cold, *I* was. Alone with me once again, he became his lighthearted, old, funny self. I thought he must be feeling puzzled or hurt, so one morning I got into bed with him. He seemed surprised to see me lifting his bedcovers and was appreciative and welcoming. He went into the bathroom to clean himself up. It was good, but it never happened again. That side of our friendship was over.
>
> I think Bruce loved to have men caress and fondle him (in private). I think he found sex very self-affirmative; that kind of gratification was as natural and easy as eating. He seemed—to me anyway—to be without hang-ups, or guilt. But now when I study the photograph I took of him in the Oregon desert, his image springs out at me and suggests there was a man there I might not have known as well as I thought. He must have had a more dangerous, more self-destructive kind of sex drive than I guessed. I can't help thinking of the trip he told me about that he made to Russia in order to run down some modern paintings for Sotheby's, and how, once Bruce was inside this secret collection, its keeper, big and brawny, proceeded to lock the door. Not to keep the KGB out, Bruce said laughing, but in order to passionately throw him down on the floor, where he raped the daylights out of him. Did you know of this episode? Did he ever write of it, or speak of it? A true story or a heavily fantasized one, embellished for dining out? But why should it not be true? I think he must have experienced, and not just fantasized about, such encounters in his nomad lands. His readiness, his eagerness

in a primmer Western society, to have someone open his
flies, must have had more violent developments in the much
wilder, far-off Oriental places he trudged through—not
looking very different from the rosy schoolboy in the photograph I sent you. He must have been a sexual magnet in those
lands, he must have seemed easy prey: in fact, a male version
of those romantic nineteenth-century European ladies who
were captured by sheikhs and kept in a harem for a thousand
and one nights. Is this possibility part of his image and legend? Its attraction for so many?

WITHIN A WEEK of our arrival at the lake, a crisis blew up at the
cabin of my oldest and closest Klamath Falls friends, Charlotte and
Ed Fey. He decided to leave her and announced this over the phone
from his San Francisco office. He was to have arrived from the City
on his vacation in time for dinner with his family on a Saturday night,
but didn't show up. Worried, and remembering how her brother had
been killed in a car wreck going a hundred miles an hour on his way
to the lake from the Bay Area, Charlotte called Ed, who told her he
was not coming. What happened next Charlotte described to me:
"He told me, very quietly, that he would not be coming to the lake—
ever. I broke down and started bawling." She came to find me because
she didn't want her kids to see her. I was "entertaining" Bruce, as she
called it, whom she didn't like, and she pulled me outside. At once
I told her she had to go to San Francisco and confront Ed. I told
her I would drive her to the Medford airport, which I did. When
Charlotte tried to call her husband back in his office to say she was
coming, he wouldn't take her call. I then telephoned him. Ed told me
he had to get out before it was too late—otherwise, one day he would
wake up and the coffin lid would be going down onto his face, etc.

Charlotte had to tell her four teenaged kids what was happening,
why she was so suddenly leaving for San Francisco. They just broke
up, she told me, and ran away into the woods. I put her on her plane,
but Ed refused to see her and she flew back that night. The next few
days I was running back and forth between the two cabins trying to

take care of Charlotte, and trying to take care of my guest. When I stayed too long with Charlotte, Bruce would come to find me. He would walk into her house without knocking and demand in his loud voice, "Where is Jim?" Charlotte told me later that he was the only person I'd ever invited to the lake that she couldn't stand.

Bruce was unmoved by Charlotte's anguish. Privately, he said to me that probably Ed Fey—whom he had never met—had dropped his wife because he had a boyfriend in San Francisco. I couldn't talk him out of this theory, and luckily he never proposed it to Charlotte. His instinct was wrong, although today when a twenty-three-year-old marriage breaks up unexpectedly, it quite often is the case that either the husband or the wife has found a same-sex lover.

On hot days at the lake we swam, but we couldn't lie and sunbathe on my old dock, which had gotten bashed up by the winter's ice, and lay tipped on its side against the trees along the shore. Most days Bruce tried to work on the wretched nomad book, sitting at the dining table with all his things laid out, thick reference books and earlier drafts (he told me he would never again attempt a book that had to be researched; it was too much trouble). But mostly he liked exploring on his own, thrashing up the pungent-smelling mountainside in his big boots and coming back sweaty and dusty hours later. One night he told me that he had taken off all his clothes and hiked naked for hours, the sun on his chest, and that he had wound wildflowers around his cock. Had he, was this true? Or did he make it up? Making little wreaths for his cock would normally, for me, who always loved to make things and to dress up, have been the kind of handiwork I might have gotten into and excelled at: helping Bruce make them, then adjusting them, just so—I can see myself doing that, Bruce standing naked in front of me in my cabin, as I made necessary improvements here and there, just like ones made by his Savile Row tailors in London. At that time of the year at the lake there are two colors of wildflowers, white and yellow. Laced together, they would have complemented the all-over rosy hue of that blond skin. I would think, looking at the final effect, a good, traditional English cock, all ready for Maypole dancing, just as Bruce's tailor might have thought, or even said to him, smoothing his hands over them, "A good young set of English shoulders." This work might have reignited my desire for him, as thinking about it does when I write down these new thoughts so many years after he's gone. My old affection for him, and for those days alone together with him in my cabin return: at night we might not have disappeared into separate rooms, closing our doors on each other.

Nevertheless, our two weeks at Lake of the Woods in late summer passed pleasantly enough, Bruce making me laugh with his outrageous stories about people he knew in London, which were like little comic performances, perfectly timed, with funny voices, needing only a spotlight and maybe a drummer. I ministered as well as I could to Charlotte before she gathered her kids together and headed south.

When Bruce and I left Lake of the Woods, we drove via the coast highway to San Francisco, where I said goodbye, turning over the keys of my cabin to him. He intended to return to it after a few days in the City, which he dismissed as being "so unlike anything else in the United States, it doesn't really bear thinking about. It's utterly light-weight and sugary with no sense of purpose or depth." He drove back to the cabin, where he planned to resume working on his book. I couldn't imagine him being there all alone. By that time the nights— and maybe the days—would be getting colder; he would endlessly have to stoke fires in the two fireplaces, chop kindling, there being no central heat or insulation. There would be periodic electric failures. Only the most basic staples could be bought at the lake's lodge store, which would soon be closing for the season. After that he would have to drive miles to buy food. He wrote Elizabeth from there: "The book is coming on well. I know what I'm doing instead of flailing around in a disorganized way with marvelous material and no sense of direction." On September 14 he wrote Elizabeth, addressing her as "Dear Harrubureth," saying he intended to stay until October, when "a great hunk" would be done. "I am writing fast, and then hitching the things up for the finer points of style later." He wrote to her about how he "wandered along trails STARK NAKED for miles and miles, without coming across a soul but deer and birds and that made me happy."

I imagine him meeting up one day with a U.S. forest ranger, or the lake caretaker, Charlie Van, as he strode naked through the

Winema National Forest surrounding Lake of the Woods. Van would have told Bruce to put his pants on.

A Star

Bruce Chatwin must have seemed, to my friends and acquaintances around the lake who saw him, like an updated Oscar Wilde figure on his far-western American travels nearly a century before; a creature who dropped from the late summer sky and was seen walking in the woods with a little garland of wildflowers around his pecker, replacing Wilde's lilies, and who addressed them in the same kind of braying entitled English voice, as he flung open their cabin doors to demand "Where's Jim?"

On our way to San Francisco, Bruce and I stopped in Grants Pass to see another college friend of mine, Rod Calvert. When we were still in college, it had been agreed by my other Bruce and me that Rod would become, if he worked at it, the Writer. But that had not happened, even though Rod comported himself as the years passed as if it had. He affected the pose of a literary man, or his idea of one: a kind of gravity and superior listening style of thoughtful consideration of what any of us said; one that always implied that if he wanted to, he could say much more. He never managed to publish any of his poetry, and after a while we gave up believing he ever would. In his house in Grants Pass he posted large words like "MATISSE" on the walls because he liked their sound. That was as far as he got with a presentation of words in an artistic manner. I think Rod's pretensions of the would-be writer, or poet, were apparent at once to Bruce Chatwin and gave him an uncomfortable feeling. Physically the two men even resembled each other. Trim and blond, and with a ruddy complexion like Chatwin's: the failure of Rod's hopes had not yet disheveled him too much. We made our excuses that we had a long day of driving ahead and left, but I felt that Bruce had been shaken.

But Bruce Chatwin would not similarly fail, and would in two or three years convince himself and many, many others that he was, or had become at last, the Writer through the kind of hard work, discipline, and imagination that my friend Rod entirely lacked. There would be literary prizes, rapturous press reviews, celebrity, and plenty of money flowing in to him and Elizabeth because of his efforts. During this period of his life we met from time to time in New York, where I was mostly living and working in the mid- and late 1970s. He would spin his ever funny stories over our dinners: of special interest to me at one of these was the fact that he had been able to interview Indira Gandhi. The prime minister would not have been, I imagine, one of Bruce's favorite fun people, but *she* most probably wanted to meet *him*, like everyone else who counted. His bestseller *In Patagonia* had been called one of the twentieth century's greatest travel books. He was now a star and was meeting everyone he'd ever wanted to know. He had become a sort of legend about young talent and beauty and ended up being romantically interred in an unmarked grave at the Greek Orthodox monastery on Mount Athos after his premature death in 1989.

When Bruce at last accepted the fact that he would not get better, and would probably die soon, he asked Elizabeth to send a copy of his final book to two of the "fun" friends from his former life. That book was *The Songlines*; the two recipients were myself and Jacqueline Onassis, who, I'm certain, was as touched by his gift as I was.

Mount Athos, Halkidiki, Greece

Lillian Ross, Continued

Lillian Ross and Erik Ross, 2011

This last entry completes the journal* of "the film that never was," and perhaps the nearly fifty-year-old saga of my friendship with Lillian Ross. When Ismail died suddenly in May 2005, I received a letter from her conveying her sympathy, and I called her up after a silent period of ten years or so. We'd last been in contact when she was putting together her sad book about her long affair with William Shawn, and she asked permission to use a photograph I had taken at her adopted son Erik's "ceremony" in 1966. So after Ismail's death we started to see each other again. This was usually

---

* I kept a couple of journals during the period of the "film that never was," from 1965 until the early '70s, when we gave up the idea of making *Vertical and Horizontal* into a film.

for dinner, and always with Erik. These meals took place in Upper East Side restaurants near her apartment (though one was at Wes Anderson's downtown loft), and were never easy affairs. Erik sat listening silently and rarely said anything. He was pleasant, but remote, and usually wore a dark suit or jacket and tie. By then he was forty. He was there to help his mother, who was becoming more and more lame. She had to be helped up and down any stairs, and to and from East Eighty-Fifth Street, where she still lived—and, for all I knew, where Erik still lived. Once I arrived early for our date and watched them greet each other from across Madison Avenue. Erik moved toward her like a swift, tall, knight in armor, and she hurried, with cautious steps, a smiling and eager babushkalike figure, until they embraced and went into the restaurant, where I joined them.

At these meals—they were expensive; Lillian always liked good restaurants—our conversation was somewhat halting and I chose my topics carefully, like the society hostess in my film *Savages*, moving it away from dangerous areas, and keeping it mostly to films I'd seen and plays I liked. But she didn't like *any* plays it seemed and I didn't

The '21' Club, 21 West Fifty-Second Street, New York

ask her about any of my films that she may have seen during the ten years of her silence. (These would have been *Jefferson in Paris, Surviving Picasso, A Soldier's Daughter Never Cries, The Golden Bowl,* and *Le Divorce.*) She saw *The White Countess* when it came out after Ismail's death in 2005, and praised it wholeheartedly. I think she never saw any of Ismail's films. I feel she would have liked those, too, particularly *The Courtesans of Bombay, In Custody,* and *The Mystic Masseur.* She would have appreciated Ismail's approach and the characters, who were sometimes a projection of himself: the poet Nur, played by Shashi Kapoor; the singing and dancing ladies of *Courtesans* and their raffish and desperate lives; and above all *The Mystic Masseur* and its hero, constantly reinventing himself, like Ismail.

Jason Schwartzman, Adrien Brody, and Owen Wilson in
The Darjeeling Limited (2007)

When Wes Anderson's *Darjeeling Limited* came out at the New York Film Festival in 2007, I attended the party afterward at '21' and met Lillian for the last time. This was one of those big noisy film festival parties at which, if you are alone, you wander around looking for somebody to talk to. Not finding Wes, I found Lillian with Erik in an upstairs back room, where she was holding court amid a group of young people. She wore an extraordinary evening cloak of satin squares in different pale colors sewn together rather like a patchwork quilt. It must have been a designer's gift or loan and would have cost a small fortune. I was glad to see her and she told me to sit down. And quite soon she delivered her opinion (negative) of *Darjeeling Limited*. She said that no doubt one would have to be "cool" to enjoy it, somehow managing simultaneously to congratulate her little party, yet still insult them. Then she asked me if I considered myself "cool." I thought about this for a moment and answered "Sure." There was no comment and soon after that I left her and Erik and went in search of Wes to tell him how much I'd liked his movie. He had arrived late for his own party and after I found him I thought I would go home and made my way out. At the door on Fifty-Second Street I saw Lillian being helped up the stairs in her great satin patchwork quilt by Erik. I hung back. I did not want to speak to her again that night and I waited inside until she was safely out and in her car. Since then I haven't heard from her but I see from time to time that she still is writing pieces for "Talk of the Town."

During this brief resumption of our friendship after Ismail's death and while I was at work on *The White Countess* in China and then *The City of Your Final Destination* in Argentina, I sent Lillian a DVD of *A Soldier's Daughter Never Cries*, thinking (stupidly) that its themes of adoption as well as the wonderful performance of Kris Kristofferson would interest her. She never acknowledged receiving the film. There could be many reasons for this. It had been decided decades before by Lillian and William Shawn that James Jones was some sort of crude poseur of the Great American Novelist—an exhibitionist and no doubt "corrupted" by fame, money, alcohol. So why would a novel by his daughter Kaylie, on which my film was based, describing their family life in Paris and the United States, be anything of worth? But then there might have been another and a stronger reason Lillian ignored my present: she had pretty much claimed the subject of adoption for herself as a writer—even, one could say, the subject of modern childhood, and though she never exerted herself anymore to take up these themes, they nevertheless were hers exclusively and she alone had the right—almost a moral right—to explore them, if she cared to. The more I thought about her silence, the more sure I was of her main reason and I even thought of challenging her some-time with the question: Would no one else in the country, who has been adopted, have any right to take up such subject matter? And should such a writer or director come to her first to ask her for her permission? I remembered, too, her disapproval of Dick Robbins, our longtime composer, directing a film about five-year-old children at the Mannes College of Music, where he taught piano, and of them learning to play the cello and so forth in our film called *Sweet Sounds*. She made us feel that this was a kind of theft to her, a kind of seizing sacred subject matter that by right was hers alone.

And Erik? What of his life? Is there a secret (or open?) girlfriend, any secret boyfriend? If so, neither was ever present or alluded to in these last years of our friendship. What work, after his expensive education at the Dalton School, St. Paul's, and Harvard, does he do? Is he on Facebook? Who is he now?

And what about *Vertical and Horizontal* itself, Lillian's only novel? Should we have tried so hard to make it into a film and was it likely to have been successful as a Merchant Ivory film? My feeling now is that only a Woody Allen could have pulled it off. I didn't know those kinds of New York people, Ismail even less. I understood them much less than E. M. Forster's Edwardians, or Henry James's Victorians, or the British and the Indians of the Raj. To Lillian her characters were second nature, part of herself, projections of herself. As they would have been to Woody Allen. He would have easily assembled an all-star cast and would have lightened the tone, perhaps even made the hateful Dr. Blauberman somehow momentarily human and touching, if not endearing. Allen would have transformed Lillian's seeming loathing of her privileged Upper East Side Jews into his Upper West Side comedy. I could never have done that; I wouldn't have remotely known how at that stage of my career to do that. She was right when she expressed so often that we didn't really understand *Vertical and Horizontal*. We worked damn hard trying to, especially Ismail, who did not deserve to fail. Perhaps it was a doomed project from the very beginning, though no more anti-Semitic, to the dim-witted studio executives at Paramount who felt uneasy about it when we submitted it, than *Shakespeare Wallah* was anti-Indian, to the dim-witted and uneasy newspaper critics in Calcutta and New Delhi.

Stephen Tennant

Stephen Tennant as Prince Charming,
photographed by Cecil Beaton in 1927

Henry Herbert wanted to make a film about English eccentrics, but could not get the money for this from television. He decided to do a filmed interview with Stephen Tennant before it was too late, nevertheless, as a sort of pilot. He and his wife, Claire, with Penelope Betjeman,* took Ismail and me to meet Tennant after Sunday lunch at Wilton, their house in Wiltshire. Penelope had last seen him in 1936—or thereabouts; she remembered him as being "a sweet little pansy."

---

* Penelope Betjeman was the wife of the poet laureate of England, John Betjeman, with lifelong ties to British notables of the 1930s and '40s Raj: the superdominating memsahib of all time. She was the model for Lady Gee in our film *Hullabaloo over Georgie and Bonnie's Pictures,* played by Peggy Ashcroft. She was also a tireless mountain climber in the exotic lands bordering on India.

Peggy Ashcroft, a towering figure of the English stage,
is dwarfed by a giant in the attic of the Umaid Bhawan Palace at Jodhpur,
where she played Lady G., based upon the real-life character of
Penelope Betjeman in *Hullabaloo over*
Georgie and Bonnie's Pictures (1977)

It was by no means certain he would see us. According to Henry, Tennant spent most of his life in his bed, and the people who came to see him were often turned away by the couple who answered the door and looked after him: a Mr. and Mrs. Skull. We turned up at tea-time. He lived in Wilsford Manor, an Elizabethan house of the Wiltshire

Checkerboard sort (all nineteenth century, according to the experts on that kind of thing). The approach was well kept, the front door newly painted white. Mr. Skull* let us in; Mr. Tennant was waiting for us on the landing, we were told, and we went through the front hall and up the stairs. The interior of the house bore no relation to its severe exterior. Everything was swagged in satin, upholstered and padded and tucked, leopard-skin rugs and soft lights in little shades, like a powder room—in fact, the whole place was a bit like an old-fashioned Beverly Hills restaurant. The big hewn beams across the stairs had been gilded. There was a heavy, closed-in scent of powder and old makeup. Seashells were laid about everywhere, on tabletops and spread over the shiny floors in the corners where no one would walk.

We went up more stairs and found our host propped up on a satin couch of white and gold, smiling to greet us, and apologizing for not getting up, waving his hands to beckon us to him. Tennant must have been about seventy-five; he was heavy and short of breath. His face was undefined, his mouth crooked. He had dyed his hair red and wore it long—but "wear" suggests a careful arrangement. Actually, it was hanging loose and he patted strands and locks up on the back of his head, from which they soon trailed down again. He was wearing an oddly cut suit and an aquamarine waistcoat. Instead of a pocket handkerchief, he'd put a tie in his breast pocket, which hung out back side forward. On his feet there were huge bedroom slippers with fluffy fleece cuffs. Henry congratulated Tennant on these.

In the United States, an old man like this, lying in a dirty satin bower, with its cheap crystal chandeliers and gilt chairs, would not likely be an aristocrat, with a stepfather called Lord Grey, who had been ambassador to Washington; he would be a small-town boy from the lower middle class, with a hunger for pretty things.

He remembered Penelope, recalling how she had come to that house decades ago, what rooms there she had gone into then, who she had come with. He called her "darling"—he called Henry

---

* Apart from their perhaps unfortunate surname, there was nothing about Mr. Skull, or his wife, Mrs. Skull, to suggest the sinister retainers of an Agatha Christie thriller. Both must have been in their late fifties, and were sensible, hardworking, efficient keepers of the domestic affairs of their eccentric employer.

A page from Stephen Tennant's illustrated diary

"darling"—and made him sit next to him on the sofa. Henry had warned us that Tennant, once he got going on any subject, was impossible to turn off; so now Henry rather directed the conversation, and got Tennant onto Willa Cather, whom he had known. He held forth on Cather's writing at length, on her personality and manner and appearance. Tennant spoke beautifully, and what he said was definitely worth hearing. He had said it

all before, a thousand times, so it was a polished performance, every word chosen carefully, his selected memories brought out on display.

Wilsford Manor interior, photographed by Cecil Beaton in 1938

Not one of his guests had apparently ever read Willa Cather, except for me (scarcely). Henry did not know that she is considered to be one of the greatest American authors. Tennant has written an introduction to a collection of Cather's essays on writing. He told us it is possibly the thing he is proudest of having done in his whole life. He tried to give Claire a copy of Cather's novel *A Lost Lady*, but she gently declined. He gave us Cather's opinion of Henry James: "a cross between Turgenev and Jane Austen." Henry was taping all this. For the first and only time all day Penelope was quiet.

Tea was served. There were all manner of little cakes and sandwiches, but none of us could eat them, lunch at Wilton had been so huge. Very soon after that, Henry and Claire had to leave; one of their little daughters was having a birthday party and a film was to be shown. Henry asked Tennant if the rest of us could stay, and Tennant entreated us: "Oh, please! Please stay!"

Before he left, Henry took me into Tennant's extraordinary bedroom so I could have a look. There was a huge unmade bed, heaped with little cushions, and from the foot of the bed, going out in waves, were all of Tennant's treasures: his watercolors, his scrapbook, shells arranged on little pillows, Indian miniature paintings, pieces of costume jewelry lying on a square of velvet or pinned to a scrap of lace, photographs of sleek aristocratic beauties of the twenties and thirties (he had been one such himself), film stars and actors, also from the twenties and thirties. It must have been very hard for Mrs. Skull to move through all this with her trays, for Tennant passed almost all his time in bed, reading and writing stories and plays, painting the taxi drivers and sailors from memory who turned up again and again in his garish posterlike watercolors, in which he entwined sentiments about love and happiness and tears and laughter with lines from Emily Dickinson and Shakespeare.

Tennant heaved himself up from his couch at one point and hobbled painfully into the bedroom to fetch some things ("What an old crock I am!" he said) to show us. One of these was the traditional "Queer's Scrapbook," as Tennessee Williams put it; the other, a little wicker basket containing his jewelry collection, each piece wrapped in a bit of silk. Penelope and Ismail sat next to him on the sofa and were shown the jewelry, which was all fake—bracelets with assorted pendants of old gold coins and jade tiger claws. While they were doing this I went through the scrapbook. There were photographs of Tennant as a very young man, slim, nervous-looking, elegant, with slicked-down dark hair, wearing a well-cut dandy's suit, seen in profile. He had been sculpted by Jacob Epstein as a young man, and was a friend of the Sitwells; Siegfried Sassoon was the great love of his life.

There were snapshots by Cecil Beaton of all those people in their youth, most of whom Tennant had outlived. In among the personal photographs were others of prizefighters—little British boxers of the thirties stuck next to Garbo. It all seemed terribly personal to me; I felt as if I were trespassing, but then a Queer's Scrapbook is supposed to be looked at in the old age of the person who pasted it up, by strangers—it is a record of loves and past happiness and youth long gone; perhaps the only proof of having once been desired. Anyway,

With 'that fox-hunting man', Sicily, 1930

Stephen Tennant (right) with Siegfried Sassoon

it all happened long ago. After the scrapbook pages, other pages had been used for paintings—for the imaginary and fantasy worlds of his sailors and taxi drivers and beautiful women in which he then mostly lived. The men were full lipped, smoking pipes; some wore yachting or perhaps officer's visored caps; the women came out of cabbage roses, and everything was lurid purples and pinks and electric blue or acid green—a bit like Bombay film posters.

At the end when we had to go, he got himself up, and, insisting that we see another room of the house, slowly led the way into an upstairs drawing room. Compared with the other rooms this was fairly empty, but the décor was the same. Silver foil had been laid over the ceiling. There was a sofa angled out into the middle of the room. He sat down on it and invited the rest of us to sit beside him, patting the cushions in invitation. We did, and then sat there together saying nothing, staring about us, and feeling rather chilly.

We had to leave him and he gave us paintings and drawings to carry away. I sat next to him while I chose one, and he told me how honored he was by my interest. When we left, he excused himself from going down and stood at the stair railing waving as we went, "Like Juliet," he said, waving and smiling so sweetly and saying, "Goodbye, goodbye!"

HENRY THOUGHT OF Tennant as an "eccentric" and perhaps that is what he was, but more than that it seemed to me that he was an example of a type that has developed, or been carried through, to its "logical," inevitable conclusion—for "type," substitute "individual." Tennant himself was like some outlandish work of art that you cannot put anywhere, but which has its own terrible integrity.

Susan Sontag

How was it that Susan Sontag came to be in my bedroom on rue
Bonaparte? Because I had been to dinner at Diane Johnson's down
the street, where Susan, too, had been a guest. When we were arranged in a little circle in Diane's sitting room after dinner, we all
got to talking about Paris apartments: our living in them, our buying
of them, their inconveniences, their joys (big windows), and so on.

Everybody had a story. We were mostly all Americans, I remember, so some of these were horror stories. Like being locked out in the middle of the night because the outside door code had been changed and the concierge had not bothered to inform us. We got on to Ismail and my apartment, at number 21, which had once belonged to the famous interior decorator Madeleine Castaing. Susan said at once that she wanted to see it. "Can we go? Right now?" As Diane's activities as a hostess had been completed, and our brandies drunk, most of us turned out and headed up rue Bonaparte.

Once inside, Susan methodically, room by room, proceeded to examine the place, pausing now and then to take a closer look at some object of Ismail's, or to pick up a book lying on a table that had caught her eye. In the living room she spied a slim volume of poetry by Akhmatova, and she picked it up approvingly. And so we went, the others following for a while, room by room, via what the French call the *enfilade*: the dining room with its tall, white porcelain stove, then Ismail's bedroom after another drawing room filled with boxes and costumes on racks. As Mme. Castaing lay on her deathbed there, a friend had written in lipstick on the mirror above the marble mantelpiece, *Où vas tu, Bellissima?* and it was still there when we took over, but Ismail erased it. A door next to it led to her extravagant bathroom, with its stained-glass window overlooking rue Jacob, waiting to be shattered someday by a street mob's stones. This led to my bedroom, which I identified as mine a bit nervously. We paused there awhile, next to my bed, as she picked up off the nightstand my own reading, book by book, while I hovered in silence, daring to hope for her approval. We passed into the kitchen, to which she gave a cursory glance: Ismail's magnificent stove, the de rigueur shining, mostly unused, copper-bottomed saucepans hanging on the walls, and Mme. Castaing's black-painted china cabinet, now stacked to the ceiling full of Merchant Ivory's very inferior dinner plates and common wineglasses.

I thought, as she and I stood by my bed so closely while she looked over my books, no doubt mentally grading each, What the hell is Susan Sontag doing in my bedroom? By now, early in the new century, she had begun to look quite aged; had become, probably because of her illness, an old woman, with her hair and its famous stripe of white tied loosely on top of her head in a shapeless mass. Satisfied fairly soon that she had seen everything she wanted to see, she took her leave after thanking me. This was to be our only encounter. I went back and picked up the Russian book thinking, Well, I must read this. How did it happen to be there at all? It was one of Ruth's books, of course: one that she had left behind after a visit to us in Paris.

Another one of Diane Johnson's dinner guests that evening was David Sedaris, whom I had never met, and had no idea what he did. No one informed me, but he kept an account of this dinner party in his journals called *Theft by Finding*, from 1977 to 2002. He wrote on January 3, 2002: "I'd always imagined Susan Sontag as delicate, almost brittle, but seated beside her at the dinner table, I noticed that her wrists were easily as thick as her ankles. She was tall and bulky, her trademark skunked hair now dyed a solid black . . . I was prepared for the worst,

but aside from a few displays of obvious boredom, Susan Sontag was if not warm, then at least well-behaved. She said she couldn't possibly eat cheese off her dinner plate, but that was her only show of fussiness."

Sedaris then got on to Ismail and me: "James and Ismail are making a movie of *Le Divorce* and they start shooting in early March. Ismail was seated on my right and was just as gracious as he could be. After dessert he took us up the street and gave us a tour of his grand apartment. He made everyone feel special and interesting, while James Ivory was a bit more uncomfortable, meaning that I tried my best to keep my mouth shut."

When Ismail and I moved into Madeleine Castaing's apartment in the winter of 1994, it was still furnished with her possessions.

However, as we needed somewhere to live during the sound editing of *Jefferson in Paris*, we had bought the apartment even though the Castaing heirs hadn't yet had time to clear it out. So we unpacked in the rooms where the ancient decorator had lived her last years (and, we were told, had died). In appearance the apartment resembled a film set in its sense of unreality, of fantasy, of its inhabitant's whimsical tastes and choice of magpie objects. We were used to camping sometimes on our own film sets and walking carefully at night around the prop man's arrangement of battered objects placed just so. Among the props of Mme. Castaing were seven paintings by Soutine (said to have been her lover), mostly dark and indistinct, and to my eye unattractive, smudged-looking things.

When we moved in, I had never heard of Madeleine Castaing. I was not up on the legendary French decorators of the last century. I didn't know that this celebrated inventor of costly French funk had passionate feelings for dust and for Victorian upholstered furniture that was spilling its guts. In the first of several rooms in the classical *enfilade* of her Parisian *hôtel particulier* on rue Bonaparte, which also served Castaing as a showroom, there was a large round table set with pretty china, much dimmed, for some long-ago high tea that was very much Miss Havisham. Its long white cloth fell in grimy folds. In a documentary film about Madeleine Castaing's life, there is a story of how she would take the tube of a vacuum cleaner, reverse it, and, in search of "patina," spray her client's walls with dust. Maybe she had done that to the walls of the adjoining room in our apartment as well, the one with the iconic white porcelain stove of so many photographs. She had prepared these walls to be covered with some costly fabric, as the French love to do. Yards of preparatory white cotton batten had been tacked up in the traditional way, to be covered later by blue and black damask, but then she had changed her mind. Mme. Castaing decided she liked the look of the cotton alone and left it that way, just pinning up some upholsterer's finishing ribbon in order to outline the room's various openings. In time the cotton drooped from its own weight, creating a swaglike effect right around the room from the floor to the ceiling; the pockets so formed were full of years of black dust. When you touched them, your fingers emerged as if from soot.

Madeleine Castaing

Placed here and there were brilliant pieces of Russian Empire furniture, also covered in blue and black damask. By the time we moved in, the room was a triumph; no set designer could ever have imagined such a thing. Her startling creation had outlived her. Would that it could have been moved in toto, dust patina and all, and set up in the Musée Carnavelet in Paris, among the other high-style historic French twentieth-century rooms.

I suspect that if I had led Susan Sontag through our apartment when it still held Mme. Castaing's things (she wore a black chin-strap in later life to hold her bobbed wig in place, and painted large, black eyelashes on her cheeks with kohl), and not after we had redone it, she would have had much more to ponder than what I was reading as she moved through this decaying holy-of-holies.

Ruth Prawer Jhabvala

Ruth Prawer Jhabvala, 1964

When I was living in Delhi in 1959, I was told by an English friend
that the Jhabvalas—Ruth and her husband, Cyrus—were impossible to ever know, and that they rejected all attempts by the locals,
whether Indian or foreign, to socialize. They never accepted dinner
invitations and no one was ever invited to their house on Flagstaff
Road in Old Delhi. This was all nonsense, of course. The Jhabvalas
had all sorts of friends and went out all the time, but I believed it.

It was true that Ruth accepted her dinner invitations carefully, and sometimes with a certain sense of dread, but in those days she draped herself in a sari and went, where, if it was to an Indian's house, it was accepted she would sit among the wives, during which she might pick up a great deal of information useful to her. Cyrus, known as Jhab, was the life of the party and did tricks with the dinner napkins to entertain any children allowed to stay up; in those Indian circles that was nearly every child.

A young Ruth and Cyrus Jhabvala, 1951

But on New Year's Eve in 1959, I decided to break this social code of never knowing the Jhabvalas. I'd heard from someone not invited that the Jhabvalas were having a New Year's party, so, deciding to crash it—a thing I had never done in my life before—I hired a taxi to take me out to Flagstaff Road, an action that would change my life and, I could say, even my history forever. When I got there an hour or so before midnight, there were almost no lights on and I could see no preparations for a party being made. But there were sounds coming from a lighted room upstairs and I boldly let myself in and went up, as there were no signs of any servant to keep me out. The party was in the Jhabvalas' bedroom, where Ruth lay flat on the bed surrounded by laughing and talking guests with drinks in their hands. I looked at the mysterious and unknowable lady, whose stories appeared in *The New Yorker*, none of which I had ever read. She lay extended, faceup, eyes tightly closed, on pink-and-white peppermint-striped sheets. A naked lightbulb on a long wire hung down over our heads. She had had too much to drink and the room and its many faces, which now included an unknown one, mine, must have been spinning around her. Someone said to me, "Too many martinis." I was never to see Ruth in this condition again, nor did I ever see her drink a martini again. I don't remember in what way, or when, the party moved downstairs. Ruth recovered and my next memory of her that night is one of her being spun around by Charles Fabri; I don't remember ever seeing her dance again. And I don't remember her speaking to me that night, or being introduced.

Cyrus Jhabvala in Benares during filming of *The Guru* in 1969
(with Michael York in the background)

The first time we did speak was a year later, when Ismail and I approached her for the rights to her fourth novel, *The Householder,* which we hoped to film. For Ismail this was to become a famous scene, retold in press interviews and on television until it had almost a mythic importance. It began when Ismail telephoned Ruth in order to request a meeting at her Delhi home—the same house I'd entered as an uninvited guest. She pretended to be the other Mrs. Jhabvala, her mother-in-law, but she didn't fool Ismail and he was able to make a date. Jhab warned her, she told us later, that we would be like all the others who had called her up offering to buy movie rights: we would skip off after a talk or two and she would never see us again. Ismail made his pitch to her, and ended by saying that we wanted her to write the screenplay of *The Householder*. "But I've never written a screenplay," she said, to which Ismail famously replied, "Well, I've never produced a movie, and Jim has never directed one."

RUTH WROTE IN her collection of short stories *An Experience of India*, in the foreword "Myself in India," how the feelings of foreigners visiting India tend to change over time. She wrote that India often proves too strong for European nerves. By European she meant all Westerners, including Americans, and that there is a cycle we all tend to pass through:

> It goes like this: first stage, tremendous enthusiasm—everything Indian is marvelous; second stage, everything Indian not so marvelous; third stage, everything Indian abominable. For some people it ends there, for others the cycle renews itself and goes on. I have been through it so many times that now

Ruth and me with her daughters, Renana, Ava,
and Firoza, at Juhu, Bombay, 1964

> I think of myself as strapped to a wheel that goes round and round and sometimes I'm up and sometimes I'm down. When I meet other Europeans, I can usually tell after a few moments' conversation at what stage of the cycle they happen to be.

She knew when she met me that I was still at the first stage of the cycle, and she watched me pass through the others as Ismail and I began to work in India making our films. But I was never strapped to the wheel, because at the end of each film I returned to my life in New York, taking Ismail with me. However, she could never leave India like that. She was happily married to a successful Indian architect, and she and he had three small daughters in school, so she was forced always to turn on the wheel. And there she was forced to experience the fact, exhibited whenever she left her house, that from birth to death a great many Indians never for one day get enough to eat, among other horrors, such as people dying of starvation in the streets she was passing through. She came to feel that "it was not possible to live one's life the way one was supposed to, and used to," and that it was as if she was living on the back of an animal, and that sometimes the animal moved, under her feet. She wrote that she had a nice house, and that she did her best, whenever she could, to live in an "agreeable" way:

> I shut all my windows, let down the blinds, I turn on the air-conditioner; I read a lot of books, with a special preference for the great masters of the novel . . . All the time I know myself to be on the back of this great animal of poverty and backwardness.

In 1987 she and her husband bought an apartment in the same building in Manhattan that Ismail and I lived in. This would be the third great move of her life. First, from Cologne in Nazi Germany to London, where she grew up and where she met her husband, who was studying architecture there. Then, in 1951, to Delhi, where she and Jhab raised their family. And then, at last, to New York City, where she came to feel she belonged, and where she said often she'd be destined to end up, and on whose occupants she now trained her lens. Her daughters were grown and had begun lives of their own outside India. She never said so to me, but I know—even though strapped to the wheel for all those years—that India had been the greatest adventure of her life, just as it has been for me. After moving to New York she wrote three novels—*Poet and Dancer* (1993),

Ruth in the palace at Deeg, before the filming of *The Guru*. Here she is "turning on the wheel," in which her feelings about India were still relatively benign. That's why she's wearing a sari. In a few years she would never put on a sari—it identified her with India, but she felt she had to break away, try to get off that wheel. Which ultimately she did, by leaving it and moving to the United States.

Shards of Memory (1995), as well as *Three Continents*, which was published the year she arrived, a novel she developed from a screenplay she and I had been working on before she left Delhi for good and took up life on East Fifty-Second Street. There were three more collections of her short stories published; her final story in *The New Yorker* was "The Judge's Will" in 2013, which appeared shortly after her death that year.

In Henry James's novel *The Europeans*, Felix Young, a visiting European cousin in the house of a staid New Englander, tells his uncle, Mr. Wentworth, that it is no bad thing for a young man "to go to school" to a clever, older woman. Ruth Jhabvala was only a year older than I was, but that is the role—as a clever woman—she assumed, apart from that of my screenwriter, in my own life. And from 1961, when we officially met, for the rest of my life—and hers—this was indeed the role she played: that of a preceptor. I was her prize pupil. Energized by Ismail and civilized by Ruth. In no way did she decide what films we would make, but sometimes she made suggestions: *The Europeans* and *The Golden Bowl* by her favorite author, Henry James, and *Howards End* by E. M. Forster, another favorite. But our film of *Maurice*, by that same author, she called "sub-Forster" and the film itself "sub-Ivory," an unfair dismissal I never forgave her for.

And I was not always and immediately or automatically happy with every new screenplay she wrote. I remember one morning coming down to the Jhabvalas' apartment on the seventh floor from mine on the twelfth in a rage, holding one of these in front of me and throwing it on the floor and stomping on it as they sat at the breakfast table with Ismail. They all laughed, and I had to pick the pages up off the floor and take my place at the table.

RUTH NEVER LIFTED a finger, except to her typewriter. Her servants did everything: an *ayah* to supervise in the nursery; a cook, who happily could serve up delicious English meals, including Raj-like puddings for dessert—or, if that was called for, Indian curries full of chilies, with rice and *daal*. Every morning she met with Abdul, the cook, to decide on the day's menus. There were also gardeners, a sweeper to clean the bathrooms, a *chokidar*, or gatekeeper, and a chauffeur. All the practical matters of running a house were part of an age-old memsahib's routine, and Ruth was thankful it existed. Consequently she learned no household skills and rather reveled in the notion that she was totally impractical in such matters and

The clever woman I went to school to

should never have to bother with any of them. It was accepted that she had no practical knowledge of any kind on any subject, and she was happy to have that reputation. Nor was she at all interested in reading books that explained most natural phenomena. Those were not human things; they had nothing to do with human thinking or emotion. They just were.

She was, however, very interested in what one might call the "superhuman." In the thought of saints from East and West, who, down through time, had written of their struggles to comprehend, and to enlighten themselves and others. When she died and we went through her books, there were many—dozens and dozens—by the great figures of religion and philosophy.* She had little interest in religion itself—she had long since given up Judaism. But she wanted to know how the saints of all denominations had struggled to accept their worlds spiritually and intellectually. When it came to Indian saints, she was dubious. In the only screenplay she ever wrote about one of these—the deeply revered Krishnamurti—and which was never made into a film by Warner Bros., who had commissioned the script—she did not obscure his human failings that might have displayed his shortcomings, such as that of his sexual desire for his oldest friend's wife, which the saint did act upon.

Ruth might sometimes carry an intellectual position to absurd

---

* After Ruth's death in 2013, when her apartment in our building on East Fifty-Second Street was being broken up, her books were brought to Claverack. It was a library containing many of the great fiction writers she admired, but it was also a library of relevant masters of religious and philosophic thought she most often had turned to. Here and there she marked up—always in the back—passages by page numbers in them that struck her. Some of these were: *Sheer Joy: Conversations with Thomas Aquinas on Creation Spirituality* by Matthew Fox; *The Diamond Sutra* by Mu Soeng; *Meister Eckhart: Mystic as Theologian* by Robt. K. C. Forman; *Mantramanjari: The Vedic Experience*, edited by Ruth's friend Raimundo Pannikar; *Letters from Baron Friedrich von Hügel to a Niece*; *Jewish Mystical Testimonies* by Louis Jacob; and *Kant's Religion Within the Boundaries of Mere Reason*. Strangely, her masters of fiction did not include Marcel Proust. I know she admired him, as almost every modern fiction writer does. But here is an odd thing: she did not really like France, or the French, very much. How they are—or were in recent times—displeased her, with exceptions. Apart from characters in our many French films, for which she wrote the screenplays, her own fiction is, I think, most lacking in French persons. But, paradoxically, Ruth had a number of close French friends, male and female.

lengths, which would affect even the way in which she looked at, and enjoyed, nature, about which she often wrote. In her Indian fiction there are many descriptions of vast, starry heavens. She decided, however, that there were no such heavens in the West, and in our part of America. These positions of hers were sometimes irritating to hear. One can, sometimes, see stars even above Manhattan, and certainly one can see millions of them in the night's skies over Claverack, where Ruth and Jhab lived with us for more than forty years. But she could not—or would not—accept seeing them. I once pointed out to her that the only reason she didn't see them was that she didn't know *how* to see them, how to look for them. I took her by her shoulders and made her stand, or sit still, in order to see them clustered above our heads. But no, she said, she could not see them. She had decided there were no starry skies over upstate New York. That was her position even after I adjusted her head and she was looking straight up at them.

In the Claverack house, where there were no servants beyond the cleaning women, everybody had to learn to cook. Ismail already knew. I could make soups, someone else could bake, etc., but no one expected Ruth to go into the kitchen, until one day when she an-

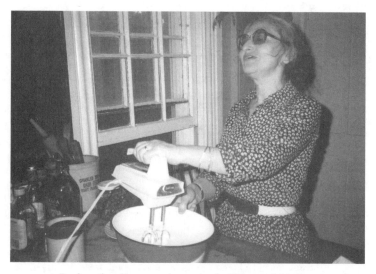

Ruth makes *blanquette de veau* in the Claverack kitchen

The Merchant Ivory collaborators in the 1990s

nounced she would make *blanquette de veau* for dinner. After we had bought the ingredients listed in Julia Child's recipe,* Ruth expelled all of us from the kitchen, saying she could not have anyone watch her cook, that she would likely make mistakes if we were there. So we stayed away until she called us back when she was ready. The dish was a complete success, but it had been an intellectual exercise that created it, based upon Ruth assembling the correct ingredients that Child decreed and exactly following every detail of the author's

---

* It's very hard to find fresh veal in an upstate supermarket.

recipe. She never made *blanquette de veau* again; she had proved her point to us, and to herself: she could do it.

What Ruth always felt for me, and for Ismail, through all our years together, was a deep tenderness. Sometimes she would become angry with us, the one or the other. And god knows we deserved her anger on many occasions. But hers was a form of superhuman acceptance, akin to that of the saints she so revered.

Ismail Merchant

Ismail Merchant, age seventeen

On Christmas Day in 1936, in Klamath Falls, in our rented house on Manzanita Street, there was a big decorated tree in the living room, with presents underneath it for me and my sister Charlotte, my mother, and my father. Almost exactly halfway around the world, in Bombay, on that same day, Ismail Noormohammed Rahman was born in that city's Pindi Bazaar, in one of the Muslim neighborhoods. He was the first, and only, son in a family of girls. He was regarded as a gift from God Almighty by his parents, who had prayed there would be no more daughters. Three more were to follow him. The six were named, in this order: Sher Banoo, Amina, Safiya, Rashida, Shaida, and Rukhsana. Six marriageable daughters could almost be regarded as a curse from on high to a family that was not rich, even if a long way from poor, as substantial dowries needed to be produced as each found a husband.

The house on Manzanita Street, Klamath Falls

Ismail became the center of his family's hopes and affections. Though coming from a conservative Muslim family, he would be—at his insistence—expensively educated by Jesuits at St. Xavier's College in Bombay. The family among themselves spoke a dialect of Sindhi—Kutchi, from Gujarat, the area they had come from—and none of them spoke English. Ismail made himself fluent in English, and then in Urdu, the literary language of North India, which he read, wrote, and spoke so beautifully that aristocratic and snobbish

Ismail in the Florence railroad station, guarding all our luggage from thieves. Already he had had a brush with them on the steps of the Santa Croce cathedral when a gypsy woman, holding her baby, distracted him and deftly withdrew six hundred English pounds from his breast pocket as he cooed over the child. It was as if each suitcase he guarded now represented a special problem he had to deal with: a financier reneging on his investment in *A Room with a View*; an agent in London, where we were headed, insisting on better terms for an actor; his marriageable sister, back in Bombay, demanding her dowry. Or, most likely, I had presented him with one of my sudden bright ideas about an expensive new location my film just had to have. It was always *my* film at such times, not his, or ours.

St. Xavier's college quadrangle, Bombay

Muslims from Hyderabad and Delhi would ask about him, "Who is that young man from Bombay who can speak such good Urdu?"

Later, living in Paris, he would have uninhibited, shouted conversations over the telephone in his French, which he really didn't know well, but he was still effective. I could never do that, after years of taking French classes and staying for long times in France; I was too vain to try, cringing at my mistakes in accent, or of blundering into some verbal thicket and getting lost. Ismail's way was always to plunge in regardless, find a way to lead, and to lead others. Handsome as a movie star, a dynamo of energy and creative ideas having mostly to do with entertainment, he soon became a master of publicity—and self-publicity. In his teens at St. Xavier's he organized variety and prize-giving programs, with full orchestras, to be held in the sacrosanct college quadrangle, and invited famous playback singers from the film studios to perform. For added publicity value, and flair, he once hired an elephant for one of these events. He shamelessly maintained that early on he had been a "freedom fighter" for Indian independence in 1947 (he would have been eleven years old then).

Middle- and upper-class Indians in the 1950s who sent their sons and daughters abroad for an advanced education usually sent them to England. Ismail chose New York University, where he studied business for an advanced degree, and in 1958, at twenty-two, he became a New Yorker and moved into an apartment on Washington Square with an Indian chum from St. Xavier's.

The city suited Ismail better than London would have; New York's spirit was more like his own. He went to work part-time in an advertising agency, McCann-Erickson, but broadened his social opportunities by hanging out with the Indian delegation at the United Nations. There he was able to entertain in a style that suited him; he didn't exactly pass himself off as a delegate, but he seemed like one, though with considerably better looks and more charm. He soon met Madhur Jaffrey, who was working as a guide. They talked about making a film together; in the years to come she would appear in six of his films, including winning best actress for her starring role in *Shakespeare Wallah* at the Berlin Film Festival in 1965.

He once told me that soon after he'd arrived in New York, he had walked into Radio City Music Hall to propose an Indian stage spectacle with musicians and dancers. As he was always selling himself in his early New York days, so was he always patriotically selling India—her arts, her traditions, her culture. It didn't much matter to him whether this took on a Hindu or Muslim form. In those days (as now), Americans couldn't keep them straight or tell the difference. Radio City turned him down, but this attempt in his early twenties was perhaps the origin of his success later in taking over Carnegie Hall when he was fifty, to present a Merchant Ivory musical spectacle with full orchestra, soloists, and simultaneous film projection, so he could show off the many film scores written by our composer Richard Robbins, his great friend.

He would soon produce his first film, *The Creation of Woman*, a dance film, professionally made with associates met during his days at McCann-Erickson. The subject was an Indian one—Hindu—and came from a myth resembling that of Eve's creation from a rib of Adam. The principal dancer and creator of the first woman was Bhaskar Roy Chowdhury, whose forte was an eerie ability to move the muscles in his back in all sorts of sinuous and snakelike ways that,

The Creation of Woman (1961)

in fact, I found faintly repellent. When this short film—it was only fourteen minutes long—was finished, Ismail, always thinking big, took it to Los Angeles and got it nominated for an Academy Award for best live action short subject. I saw *The Creation of Woman* again recently and was impressed by the sophistication of its making. I can see how it got an Oscar nomination. It had charm and humor, and a freshness people in Hollywood hadn't seen in a film about India since Jean Renoir's *The River* a decade earlier. It has nothing to do with the schools of Indian classical dancing like Bharat Natyam and Kathak, which were just beginning to be appreciated in the West. For the audience of these, Bhaskar's rippling back muscles were on the level of a nightclub act.

ISMAIL TOOK A train to Los Angeles and sent on ahead a press release that he was arriving, which was picked up by the New York newspapers: "A Real Hip Visitor from India" appeared as a headline in the *New York Herald Tribune*, above the story of his arrival, which began: "Ismail Merchant of Bombay, descendant of an ancient Indian Mogul family, will shortly depart from New York for Hollywood . . . Mr. Merchant is what we Americans greatly admire, and possibly do not expect an Indian to be: a cracker-barrel fireball, whose personality and ability epitomize all that is purposeful, vigorous, and energetic in the new India." He wrote years later about his arrival in Los Angeles, preparing himself as he got nearer and nearer for the press avalanche that would surely greet him, and for the "red carpet and flashing bulbs of dozens of newspaper photographers eager to record this historic arrival of the great Indian film producer."

But Ismail was disappointed when he got down from the train and there was no one there. To hear him tell this later on saddened me. And what saddened me more was that although he was in Los Angeles with his film, which he had been successful in getting nominated, he could get no seat at the ceremony itself and could watch it only on television. He recalled sitting somewhere at a bus stop that evening.

In order to be nominated for an Academy Award in 1961 a short film had to play with a full-length feature in a Los Angeles theater for a week. Undaunted, Ismail had found one on Wilshire Boulevard that was willing to do that, and *The Creation of Woman* was paired with a film by Ingmar Bergman at the Fine Arts Theater. That made it eligible. A significant number of Academy members saw it—enough to get it nominated, but it did not win. Ismail stayed a year in Los Angeles, visiting the studios while he worked in a men's clothing store, and being photographed as an upcoming Indian producer with leading ladies like Susan Hayward, Maureen O'Hara, and Agnes Moorehead. At that time, Isobel Lennart, a writer at MGM, changed the course of Ismail's life, as well as my own, when she told him about a novel she'd read by Ruth Jhabvala called *The Householder*. "Hollywood will never make it," she told him, "but you should." He bought

A photo op with Susan Hayward (or was it Maureen O'Hara?)

Ismail (leaning forward), a devout Muslim, introduces Agnes Moorehead,
and his friend Ernest Castaldo, to five thousand years of Hindu
spirituality. It was a ceremony of his own contrivance, held high above
Los Angeles, and another friend, obligingly marking his forehead
with a priestly tilak, helped out for authenticity's sake.

a copy, read it, then made a note in his diary that it would be his first
film in India. I never saw him write in that diary. I've never found it
and I always wondered if it existed.

Now the two roads, one beginning on Manzanita Street in
Klamath Falls, the other in Pindi Bazaar in Bombay, meet. Mutual
friends Madhur Jaffrey and her husband, Saeed, brought Ismail and
me together. The little documentary I made on Indian miniature
painting in 1959, full of intoxicating music by Ravi Shankar, and no
less intoxicating long-lashed faces, was being shown at India House
on East Sixty-Fourth Street, and I attended the screening. Saeed
Jaffrey, who spoke the narration, told Ismail to go. To this day,
whenever I pass the grand doorway and fine, wide steps of the Indian Consulate in Manhattan, I think: Why is there no plaque stating
that it was on this very spot that Ismail Merchant and James Ivory
first met? And I see us—it was that early era, now long forgotten, of
tweed sport jackets and striped silk neckties, which young gentlemen

in New York regularly wore during the day. The weather was fine; it was a May afternoon: myself on an upper step, my hand out to Ismail below, like two figures in a miniature painting. Ismail extends his strong, shapely hand, which would draw me into his life for as long as he lived, and into my Indian life more deeply than ever.

We go to get a coffee. He tells his friends later that he was surprised that a young American from Oregon knew so much about India, but he doesn't say that to me. In the coffeehouse on Madison Avenue, named the Left Bank (Ismail actually told people that there was a plaque there about us), he very soon gets onto the pay phone and uses up all his change as well as all of mine. We agree to meet in two days at my apartment on East Sixty-Second Street; maybe we will go out to a Satyajit Ray movie. The two days crawl by. But when he comes, none are playing anywhere, so we stay in and put on Nazakat and Salamat Ali, singing *ghazals*.

From then on, we were together, united in a purpose, and that purpose was to make films together. I came to feel as the years passed, and as success came, then went, then came again, a strengthening of our devotion to each other, and to our work. I came to feel that two

Ismail and Ruth show Prime Minister Nehru *The Householder* in 1963—the film that "Hollywood would never make"

Ismail in my apartment on East Sixty-Second Street, May 1961. It is
the first photograph of Ismail I ever took—and he is on the phone.

gay men, united in their commitment to each other, single-mindedly
pursuing a common goal, could end up ruling the world.

That doesn't mean that Ismail had no other partners—he was a
highly sexed man—or that I would not, but these did not last, because I was always there and he was always there. One or two of these
were very seductive, and when they were, we shared them. I was
never going to leave him because of his temporary infatuations. Nor
was I ever voluntarily going to give up our work together.

I was a bit like a powerful French matriarch, it occurred to me,
who knows her husband has mistresses, but who also knows that
she is at the center of his world, his home, his children, and if she
is clever, his very life. And, in another way, which made me laugh
when I thought about it, I recognized that this Muslim husband
would probably, in time, take a second wife, then a third, and finally

a fourth, which is all the Koran allows. I would explain my situation to my male friends, who could not understand my strange and stubborn fidelity, telling them that all this was in Ismail's blood, in his culture (however, I also witnessed his family's outrage when one of his many brothers-in-law took a second wife, saw the fury, and heard the muttered curses, Ismail's the loudest). In this way he and I went on for more than forty years, weathering everything good and bad, together.

LATER IN THE year Ismail returned to India, and I followed him there. On his way he stopped in France, where *The Creation of Woman* had been invited to the Cannes Film Festival. It was in competition as an American entry, but when he arrived to present it, he learned that its schedule had been changed and that his film had been screened the day before. In the years to come there would never again be such mishaps. He made it his business to get to know the heads of all the major film festivals, and to make them feel that premiering one of his films could elevate and enhance the festival itself.

When he arrived back in Bombay, he decided to move his family and the unmarried sisters out of Pindi Bazaar and into a place where he could entertain and put up his new friends—like myself—from America. A large four-room flat was found in a pleasant, mainly Muslim, neighborhood near Bombay's Central Station. It was a large freestanding building called Gool Villa, set in a triangular park with big trees. How often I would give that destination in the years to come to the rickety little black-and-yellow taxis attempting to make their way through the city's traffic, and always through the stifling, humid air! In time there would be a large, blue, new Oldsmobile sedan, and a sharp-looking driver named Ahmed in a crisp, white uniform. This car had been purchased as a necessary prop vehicle for our film called *The Guru* with Twentieth Century–Fox. Only a Hollywood studio like that could afford the enormous customs duty on such a car. It was to figure prominently later in the wedding celebrations of Ismail's three younger sisters.

But how Ismail hated all the calculations and frenzy of India's arranged marriages! When he heard his mother and older married sisters making them, he would rage, shouting at them, "Shaadi! Shaadi! (Wedding! Wedding!). Is that all you can think about?" and then point out that these younger sisters were too young to be marrying, and should be educated first. This raging went on over the telephone, from New York and London and Claverack, to the women in Gool Villa, until all the sisters were married—some happily, some not so. For his youngest sister, Rukhsana, he came back to give her away in style, and invited his movie-star friends from the Bombay film world. She would be the last to ride in *The Guru*'s blue Oldsmobile, which had been decorated with streams of yellow marigolds. About his own marriage he said nothing, changing the subject whenever his mother, looking as if she might break into tears, brought it up.

By the time I arrived from the United States in November 1961, and took up a new life in the midst of Ismail's family, they had moved into Gool Villa. The living room was given to the two of us for sleeping. Ismail stretched out on one of the *takhts*, me on another next to it, forming a large letter L. This big room adjoined the kitchen, where at night a servant boy slept on the floor on a mat below an array of pots and pans hung on the wall. In the middle of my first night there the boy knocked up against the pots and pans, and some fell down with a loud clatter, which woke Ismail. He sat straight up on his *takht* and shouted a curse: "*Suar-kahin-ke*," which I won't translate, and fell down again, instantly going back to sleep. I lay there in the dark, wondering. In time, I, too, would be yelled at by Ismail. Fairly soon, in fact. This was a shock. I had never been shouted at by anyone. I would soon learn about the fearful rows Indian families have, with their hysterical declarations of intended suicide, when furious female members would put a leg over the balcony railing and have to be pulled back inside, while down in the street an amused crowd would watch as if at the theater. But like Ismail's curse in the night, after a few minutes such fights would cease, and all you would hear was the ceiling fan creaking away on its long stem over your head.

Many of the people reading this book will know already of the prowess Ismail possessed as a film producer, and of his legendary abilities to raise money, so that for more than forty years we were able to carry on making our films. They might also know—if they are in the acting profession—that he was something of a skinflint when paying them was concerned. It was Hugh Grant who said of Merchant Ivory, "I did it for the curry," Ismail being a famous chef.

James Wilby and Hugh Grant in *Maurice* (1987)

MERCHANT IVORY IN time became a "triumvirate" of director, producer, and writer to the press—especially the British press, who plastered the word on us, a word detested by Ruth. However, there was from the late 1970s a fourth powerful member. That was our composer, Richard Robbins. He had taught piano at Mannes College of Music in Manhattan, and became the piano teacher of Firoza Jhabvala, the youngest Jhabvala daughter, once her parents began spending much of their time in New York. Ismail and Robbins soon formed a friendship. And, in the way Ismail had when he formed such a friendship—there were several of these, all intense, sometimes lasting years—a way must be found to make a useful place for that friend in our organization based upon any particular talent he possessed, whether that was banking, acting, or, in Robbins's case, music.

Somewhere along the way in the first months of their friendship, Robbins, who died in 2012, must have made Ismail know that he felt

Richard Robbins with Ismail,
during the 1978 filming of *The Europeans*

Merchant Ivory's music generally needed more guidance, which he could provide. His first attempt at that, in 1978 and hugely successful, was the score for our film *The Europeans*, based on an early novel by

Marie Antoinette (Charlotte de Turckheim) and
Louis XVI (Michael Lonsdale) on their way to Mass in the Hall of Mirrors
at the Château de Versailles (*Jefferson in Paris*, 1994).

A page from Richard Robbins's score for *Maurice*

Henry James. So at that time Dick became the fourth member of our team, which he continued to be until my final feature, *The City of Your Final Destination*, which was released in 2009. By then Ismail had died and Dick had become ravaged by Parkinson's disease and was unable to create a score for that film. After Dick and Ismail's intimacy waned in the early 1990s, he continued to compose our music, and, along with us, received his own Academy Award nominations for *Howards End* and *The Remains of the Day*, though he certainly deserved them as well for *A Room with a View* and *Maurice*.

In time I came to feel while making our later films, had Dick's music not been there, they would not really have been Merchant Ivory films. His compositional skills, his brilliance, and his originality in introducing all sorts of useful musical influences (for example, in *Jefferson in Paris*, when the king and queen, and the whole royal court at Versailles, are on their way to Mass in the Hall of Mirrors, they parade to a tango beat) did make an impact in viewers' minds, and in my own, as just what a Merchant Ivory movie should be. The influence of Philip Glass came to stay in 1980 with *Quartet*, so that no matter where our films were set, or when—as with *Jefferson in Paris*—our scores had a minimalist throb to them. Ruth and I felt bereft when Dick had to give up working on *The City of Your Final Destination*—he told me that after a day's work on it he spent the next day correcting his mistakes. We were saved by the young Uruguayan singer and composer Jorge Drexler, who took over, beautifully satisfying my own vague musical cravings for what a movie set in South America should be, and who was able to make Robbins happy. Dick was assured that the last Merchant Ivory film, which he lived to watch, got the score it needed.

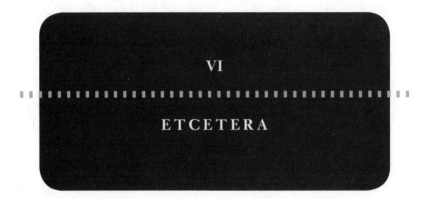

VI

ETCETERA

The Great Ball at Wilton

Wilbury House, as featured in the film *Maurice*

October 27, 1979, 4:00 to 7:00 p.m. Ismail and I leave London at a quarter to four after buying him some evening shoes—well, not evening shoes, but shoes to wear with formal dress, his formal dress being *shervani* with diamond buttons and *churidar* pajamas. He bought some black suede loafers; I tried to get him to look in Harrods for those patent leather pumps with bows on them that maharajas wore when they got *en grande tenue* in the early twentieth century to be photographed, but he said Harrods would be too crowded. We drove easily down to Wilbury Park, outside Cholderton, in Wiltshire, where we are staying, getting there about five thirty. The house is in a park all right—a huge one, stretching away: Palladian, gray stucco, modest by English country house standards, but more palatial than its American equivalent in its scale.

We ring the doorbell but no one comes. We can see people sitting inside in a drawing room at the back. Finally a young man comes out to let us in. He says, "We're all guests," and leads us back to a superb room with two great windows and immense double glass-paned doors giving onto the gardens. We introduce ourselves. One of the guests is the writer Peter Shaffer.* Others are godsons and in-laws and I don't know who of Lady St. Just,† our hostess. We pour ourselves tea and in a little while she comes in, very energetic, and brings us all to life, orders more tea, takes cakes around, rearranges the logs in the fireplace, says to one of her guests, "You look just like your mother—don't look sad, she was very pretty!" She tells us how she loved *The Europeans* and takes us around the outside of the house so we can see the garden façade. She tells us it was built in 1712, the first Palladian country house in England. It's a rectangle, with a one-story wing at each end. The Wiltshire Downs and far-off hazy trees make a beautiful vista.

She shows us to our rooms but before she does she takes us on a little tour of the downstairs, showing us a portrait of her husband in uniform. ("He won't be here tonight; for twenty years I've been telling people he has a cold or whatever; now I've given that up and just tell the truth: he suffers from depression.") She also shows us a portrait of her husband's father, the first Lord St. Just, who ran the Morgan Grenfell bank with J. P. Morgan, and the huge Chippendale

---

* Peter Shaffer (1926–2016), British playwright, best known for *Equus*, *Amadeus*, and *Lettice and Lovage*.
† Maria St. Just (1921–1994), born in Russia as Maria Britneva, the wife of Lord St. Just, a partner in the British bank Morgan, Grenfell. Her parents fled Russia in a snowstorm, carrying her to safety, wrapped in a blanket, to England, according to the romanticized version of her life. She was brilliantly witty, spoke in a deep voice, was generously openhanded and at the same time tightfisted. She was a terrible snob, speaking of her daughter's boyfriends disparagingly when she thought they were not sufficiently *bien né*, as she put it—well-born. (I understood her to be saying *bien aimée*, meaning "well-beloved," and wondered how she'd come to that judgment, and why, if true, that would be a drawback in a future son-in-law.) When we were shooting *Maurice* in her house in 1986, Hugh Grant did manage to pass muster on all counts as a possible boyfriend for her younger daughter, Natasha Grenfell. As the literary executor of the great friend of her youth, Tennessee Williams, Maria became known on both sides of the Atlantic as "Lady St. Nightmare" among aspiring producers of Williams's plays, whom she also tended brutally to reject out of hand when they didn't pass muster.

partners desk, covered by a cloth, where Grenfell and Morgan used to sit together. "We keep it covered," she says, "because we're selling it; I tried to get the Morgan Library in New York to buy it, but they don't want it."

She exclaims over everything and shows us each room she's had redecorated, or those with the original decoration still there. That picture is so and so, that is such and such; that, of course, is Tolstoy; I'm Russian, so there's some Russian things here, too. Ismail is given what she calls a *wagon-lit*, and it does look like an old-fashioned, narrow, European *wagon-lit*, with a shiny black bed and red walls; I'm taken up to the next floor to a room overlooking the great panorama. Ismail tells her to call us Ismail and Jim, and she says she will if we call her Maria. On my bed there is a felt-and-fur lap robe

Peter Shaffer, 1966

like the one at Claverack. There are many Claverack touches—lamps with cockeyed lampshades on them, fine floors all scarred up; I hope that the hot water is reliable, as it sometimes is not at our own dear Stately Acres.

8:00 TO 9:00 P.M. The evening gets off slowly, so I go downstairs and fix myself a drink. The younger generation is watching an American movie on TV; I go in and talk to Peter Shaffer—he's not doing anything just now, he tells me, he's having himself a rest, so necessary. He goes up to change and Ismail and I roast chestnuts in the fire. While we're doing this, a white-haired gentleman comes through and goes back to the State Suite, which I know is being kept for Lord and Lady Rothermere. And in a minute a squat-looking woman with frizzy hair comes in, wearing a glitzy down coat with boots. I give her a half smile, just in case: not too much, not too little. Ismail says in an undertone when she has passed through: "the maid." But the next time we see her she is drinking champagne and the elderly white-haired gentleman, who turns out to be her husband, Lord Rothermere, passes us with an immense amount of clothing on hangers and in plastic closet bags, trailing these across the marble floor. Seconds later Lady St. Just appears; she is made up, her hair done, a tiara in place, but she is in a terry-cloth bathrobe and stocking feet. She greets the Maid rapturously, says "Excuse me, my dear, I'm in *moitié coiffeur*." A tall young man goes past, saying, "I need a razor and some shaving cream," and disappears upstairs. The Maid sits next to me, and wonders where she can borrow a tiara, and a slim young man nearby tells her, "There must be lots of them around."

I go up to change. On my landing I hear loud drunken singing from somewhere. Who? Lord St. Just, going into a manic phase? When I try to put on my lights, nothing works—no lights. I find Her Ladyship walking along the corridor with the Maid and I tell her of this. It must be a fuse, she says, and shouts to her daughter to

Wilton

tell the butler (a man below in a white cable-knit sweater). So I go back downstairs to wait for the lights to go on. When they do, Ismail comes in and deals with my knot-tying dyslexia and ties my bow tie for me.

Everyone is saying Henry Herbert's ball is just a publicity trick—that it's to get publicity for Wilton, though why he would want more publicity for Wilton is hard to say.

I wonder whether the I.R.A. will blow us up at midnight. We are to be twenty at dinner tonight. I will go down now.

9:00–11:00 P.M. (written at 5:00 a.m.) There's a superb flower arrangement of autumn leaves, pink roses, and large red berries in the drawing room. It has been "thrown together" by one of the clever young in-laws or godsons, Andrew McCall, and put into a large white urn. We go in to dinner. Things are every which way; we're told to sit where we want; we serve ourselves from the buffet and start out with a very good sorrel soup. At dinner the zipper at the back of Lady St. Just's dress breaks and she has to excuse herself and go off to be sewn up; while we eat we're photographed. After dinner, there are more photographs. I'm told by my hostess to arrange everyone for

Lady Rothermere, 1991

a group photo, so I do, making them stand on the stairs. The Maid wants to stand in front, but I firmly put her on the side; the voluminous hoopskirt she has gotten into takes up all the room where Maria and her pretty daughters should be. The photographer snaps away. The Maid reminds me of the unfortunate wife of George IV—what was her name? Queen Caroline? Queen Adelaide?

Ismail and I are rather taking over. We arrange the cars, who will ride with whom, to Wilton. It's decided that I'm to go with Maria, the Maid and her husband, the Press Lord (it turns out he owns the *Daily Mail*). A chauffeur drives us. When we get in the car, the chauffeur says—"I was resting; I was having a bit of a rest," and Maria says sharply, "Resting from what?" We head for Salisbury and Wilton; Lady St. Just and the Maid shout at the chauffeur— Slow down! Drive on! Hurry up, turn to the right! Etc. The Maid sits in front in tiers of taffeta; Maria and the Press Lord sit behind, next to me, his arm around her. On the way Maria talks about Wilbury, how she's sure the Romans must have had a villa there, the position is so commanding, and there are no less than seven springs. We pass Old Sarum on the left— the Romans' ancient Salisbury. Old Sarum sounds like a smart address in Connecticut. When we finally get to Wilton, there is a long line of cars

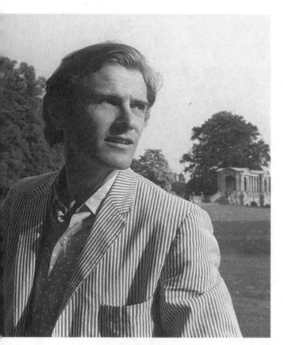

Henry Herbert,
17th Earl of Pembroke
and 14th Earl of Montgomery

heading for the gate of the courtyard and we join it. We creep along, other people going by on foot calling out to one another. Security is heavy; Prince Charles is there, and all that jewelry; Maria says Cartier is empty tonight and Garrard,[*] too. At the gate the Maid, who is named Pat,[†] shouts to the policeman, "Lord and Lady Rothermere!" and Maria shouts "Lady St. Just!" I shout, too: "Ivory!" But to themselves they moan, "Oh god. I don't have the card . . . I've left mine in my suitcase . . ." Etc. We finally get into the courtyard and leave the car, but no one knows how to enter the house. There's quite a crowd of tiaraed ladies and tuxedoed gentlemen wandering from door to door, none of which open. We all go around to the front of the house, which is floodlit.

A white marquee has been put up and we join the queue. Inside, three girls sit with the long guest list, and detectives look us over. I give one of the girls my name, she smiles, and I join the crowd in the hall. This is where the house tours normally start, but tonight there is a vast throng of splendid-looking people standing and waiting to go up the stairs. At the top I see our hosts, Henry and Claire.[‡] I wait for Ismail. I don't want to go up without him, and pretty soon I see him and we start up. It's a slow process. Photographers stand at the top. Finally we reach the Herberts, who are having a great time, and we are greeted. Henry tells us that Bap-ji[§] is already there, but not wearing any of his famous diamonds, and not looking nearly so splendid as Ismail. We pass on to the cloister and upon entering, a girl gives us champagne (this champagne never ran out; when we left hours later, it was being consumed with breakfast). We pass into the Double

---

[*] Garrard is the great London jeweler on Regent Street; its equivalent in New York would be Tiffany and Harry Winston on Fifth Avenue. We borrowed jewelry from Garrard again and again while shooting various films, which sometimes would be accompanied to the set by a guard.

[†] Her nickname was actually Bubbles.

[‡] Henry George Charles Alexander Herbert, 17th Earl of Pembroke and 14th Earl of Montgomery (1939–2003). He was on the board of directors of Merchant Ivory Productions in London and a film director in his own right. Claire Herbert (b. 1943) was Henry's beautiful countess, and is the mother of his heir, William Alexander Sidney Herbert, born in 1978 and the current Earl of Pembroke. Their house, Wilton, where the ball was taking place, is one of England's grandest and most visited stately homes. It contains the famous adjoining Double and Single Cube Rooms, hung with a tremendous series of full-length portraits by Anthony Van Dyke of assorted Herbert family members and reigning monarchs of the mid-seventeenth century. The band was playing there and everybody danced (frugs, waltzes, what have you) under the impossibly haughty stares of Henry's ancestors. Henry and Claire divorced in 1981.

[§] The Maharaja of Jodhpur, Gaj Singh II (b. 1948).

Cube Room, where the band is playing and people are dancing. It is very noisy and packed, couples energetically frugging. The very first person I see is Prince Charles, who runs past me, mopping his brow

Wedding of Claire Pelly, Countess of Pembroke, and
Henry Herbert, 17th Earl of Pembroke (1966)

and looking desperate. He is alone and that strikes me as unusual; I assume he'd move around everywhere with a sort of retinue. And in fact, every time I see him he looks like he's escaping from something or someone, darting past people, head ducked, alone.

Ismail, Maria, and I decide to circulate—we make the rounds, going first across the dance floor, where we see Lindy Dufferin* and

---

* Serena Belinda Rosemary Hamilton-Temple-Blackwood, Marchioness of Dufferin and Ava (b. 1941). A member of the fabled and complicated Guinness family by birth

exchange kisses with her, into the Single Cube Room, and out again into the cloister and along its four sides, where, at the point we'd originally entered, we find Bap-ji and his maharini, Hemlata Rajye, who, outside India it seems, doesn't do anything so gauche as to wear her *pulla* over her head.* Lots of hee-hee, ha-ha talk with them about the Good Old Days (!) in Jodhpur.

I begin to feel this party is something extraordinary, has some special meaning for everybody and is not just a big hype. Everybody is so excited, so animated, there is a sort of electricity in the atmosphere, not like any party I'd ever been to. Was it the flocking of an endangered species? Partly. Was it a sort of showing of the colors? Was it a defiant throwing off of austerity, even poverty, and dullness, after the collapse of the swinging old London of the '60s had plunged these people into dreary caves again, into horrors even, when they didn't know whether they might not get shot or blown up. So why was Henry giving this party? In the car on the way to Wilton this was discussed. He'd had his fortieth birthday recently, so it was to mark that; and now he has an heir, it is to mark that, too; and they're now master and mistress of Wilton, so it is to mark all of that as well. It must have been all these things, but probably it was something more, too. But what?

I myself have no interest in society, of being in high society. Society is a subject for me, and anyway, I am outside it and above it. Yet, this party has brought out in me whatever dormant or lingering hankering after society I may have. Why, after all, had I come three thousand miles? What was I doing, thrilled to be on a guest list at a private party with the Prince of Wales? And what was Ismail doing there? For merit, and because we are "interesting"? This party isn't

---

and marriage, she became a good friend of ours and agreed to interview the very prickly Rajmata of Jaipur for *Autobiography of a Princess,* our 1975 film about Royal India. She herself now presides over Clandeboys, a two-thousand-acre estate in Northern Ireland. On being invited there by her for the weekend about this time—the time of the "Troubles"—I stupidly declined, fearing I might be shot. Ismail and I had earlier been entertained by another marquess in Northern Ireland who *was* shot to death afterward, so I wasn't taking chances.

* Royal Indian ladies, while in public in India, would lift the edge of their saris (or *pulla*) to modestly cover their heads—an aristocratic gesture and perhaps a salute to their tradition of remaining in *purdah* away from outsiders' eyes. Other well-off Indian women tended to ignore this style.

just some ordinary big party; as parties go it is a kind that used to be reported on in *Life* and *Time* magazines, that socialites congregated at, often given by some tin or copper millionaire from Bolivia, where movie stars rubbed elbows with European nobility, and if you didn't get invited you pretended to be out of town, or actually left. Well, Henry's party was that sort of a big affair obviously, and Ismail and I are probably not the only ones who were asking themselves, Why this party? Not that Ismail would ask a question like that, anyway . . .

[As I write this next morning, I hear him down the corridor, saying to our no doubt very sleepy hostess—"But your guests have come!" People have been invited to lunch, and I'm still in bed and he's probably barefoot and in a *lungi*.]

Well, having reached the Apex of Society, what is now left for me? (Not quite the Apex of the Apex: we weren't put up at Wilton and did not dine with Prince Charles as Bap-ji and his maharani did;* Maria told Ismail that Prince Charles had been pursued by young women, and later on during the party, I did really see him

Double Cube Room, Wilton

---

* When Ismail was introduced to Prince Charles, he at once asked him if he had seen our new film, *The Europeans*, then playing very successfully at the Curzon Theater in London. When the prince told him that he hadn't yet, Ismail is supposed to have pulled the show times out of his pocket. It sounds likely, but that may be a joke of Maria St. Just's, told to tease him later.

being pursued by various girls.) Just what is left for me? Only rude, colonial hoedowns, I guess, provincial gatherings of pretentious upstarts. (That's what French courtiers felt about English parties they attended in the eighteenth century.)

Anyway, back to the party. I went with Maria to sit on that great bench in the Double Cube Room in order to watch the dancing and listen to her tell me bits of gossip about the other guests, our acquaintance having gotten to that stage. Sample bits of gossip:

> "That's W. He's mad! To think he's going to inherit Longleat! Boring, dirty, hippie dropout!"*

> (Of Princess Michael of Kent) "She was living with someone I know, then Prince Michael fell for her and she made him go through a Catholic wedding service, so he lost his right to the throne!"

> (Of a beautiful, delicate, black-haired girl in a lace collar with whom Sheridan Dufferin† was dancing vigorously) "She's the lover of that girl who's staying with us," etc. etc. etc.

Ismail came to sit with us and as Maria wanted to waltz and since I don't know how to waltz, I made him take her off and he spun her around the room quite expertly. Bap-ji and Maharani Hemlata Rajye appeared and sat down with me, and when one of Henry's young daughters‡ came up, Bap-ji asked her sweetly to dance and he took

---

* The "hippie dropout" was Alexander Thynn, who became Viscount Weymouth and then Marquess of Bath. I liked him fine when he showed us through his house, Longleat, on a location scout for *The Golden Bowl*. I stole the color of his upstairs walls for my big front bedroom at Claverack—a vivid, paleish acid green that I had never seen anywhere before. But of all the things I saw at Longleat, the one that fascinated me most was the fine white linen shirt King Charles I had worn when he was beheaded, displayed in a glass case in the entrance hall (after the king's Lady Rothermere blood had been washed out of it).

† Sheridan Hamilton-Temple-Blackwood, 5th Marquess of Dufferin and Ava (1938–1988), was Lindy Dufferin's husband.

‡ The Herberts had three charming daughters, all with Jane Austen names: Sophia, Emma, and Flora.

The 1964 wedding of Sheridan and
Lindy (Guinness) Hamilton-Temple-Blackwood,
the Marquess and Marchioness of Dufferin and Ava

her off, holding her at arm's length as older men do when they dance
with little girls who don't always know the steps and who keep looking down at their feet.

Ismail and I sat with Lindy Dufferin for a while. Her tiara* seemed

---

* The Dufferin Tiara was commissioned in the 1860s for the wife of the 1st Marquess
of Dufferin and Ava, and has subsequently been worn by marchionesses at grand
events. It is composed of large diamond shamrocks above a diamond base with pear-
shaped pearls and diamond floral clusters.

to be real; the stones flashed and I wondered if it was the tiara which Sheridan's ancestress wore as vicereine of India.

We all went to eat a breakfast of bacon and eggs and to swill more of Henry's champagne.*

WE WENT HOME and drank cocoa. There was much indignant talk of the behavior of the Rothermere chauffeur, who, when Maria went into the kitchen, got up and offered her his hand to shake (she says she did not take it, of course, and Peter Shaffer says the chauffeur, who later on had offered to help her when her zipper broke, must learn that his hands were for three things only: gripping a steering wheel, using a jack, or picking up a suitcase). There was lots of talk of servants and they reckoned there had been one

The Classical Temple at Wilbury

---

* Lady Rothermere (aka the Maid/Pat/Bubbles) sat beside me at breakfast and told me of her marital problems: Lord Rothermere has this Korean mistress whom he sneaks off to see, and when she complains about this, he says, "We'll make mincemeat of you if you cause any trouble." "No one's going to make mincemeat out of me!" she said, pulling herself up, all the spangles in her hair quivering, her taffeta-covered bosom heaving. "I'm not taking any shit like that!"

thousand nannies at Wilbury over the period the two girls, Katya and Natasha, were being brought up, if you reckoned on there sometimes being two at a time. Now most of the staff was made up of New Zealanders, but even they could be troublesome. Shaffer thought the servants should pay for the privilege of working in such a wonderful place.

All this began to pall a bit by early afternoon on Sunday. Ismail and I decided to go back to London as soon as we'd had lunch. Everybody talked so loudly, and I noticed that as each person left the lunch table there followed a discussion of them by the younger set, and not always in the kindest way. So after taking a walk around Wilbury Park to see the classical temple, etc., we left.

Me and Maria St. Just, dressed for her part of
Mrs. Vyse in *A Room with a View* (1985)

The party itself, because of the beauty of Wilton, existed on another and better level than most such events would—almost was lifted into the realms of art. We thought at one time that we might use Wilton for a big party scene we had planned for our film *A Lovely World*, so in a funny way it was as if I'd been there before, or done this before: the floodlit façade, the packed staircase, the pounding music in the Double Cube Room. But that film, set in London's swinging '60s, was never made.

I see now on reading this that as I've depicted her sometimes, Lady St. Just might come off as something of a titled monster, that an actress hired to play her might complain that the part was "unsympathetic." I suppose that's because the malicious things she said are often very funny and stick in my mind more than the kind ones; for instance, she was always worrying, and always ready to defend Lord and Lady Rothermere (who were fighting all night) to each other, always trying to "ease the situation."

The Ismail Merchant Collection

Front cover of catalogue for Christie's auction
of the Merchant Collection, London, 2009

When I first met Ismail Merchant in 1961, he had not become a collector of any of the kinds of objects being offered in this sale of his belongings. He would have claimed, "Oh, I'm a collector of people!" He surely was that, an avid collector of people who felt warmly about him and would become the enthusiastic supporters of his films and other projects. He never forgot a name or face, never failed to write down a telephone number, and later, when he began to buy works of art, this served him as well as it did in the financing and promotion of our movies.

I supposed he picked up the collecting virus from me. When that happened, he plunged into the market without hesitation, as with everything else he did. He was never a timid buyer. There are people who form collections, but when faced with a onetime opportunity to buy a truly great piece for just that little bit (or even a great deal) more, they pull back and buy a second or third choice because it is cheaper, while the great piece vanishes. That was never Ismail's way. The covers of auction house catalogues seemed especially to beckon to him; several of the lots here first came to his notice on the full-color covers advertising earlier auctions. Or he would wander along Bond Street on his way to his office in Soho, and find himself in an auction energetically bidding for something that had just caught his eye (but he had been too busy to examine): a Chinese vase, a kilim, a sideboard, a large oil painting of Rhett Butler embracing Scarlett O'Hara,

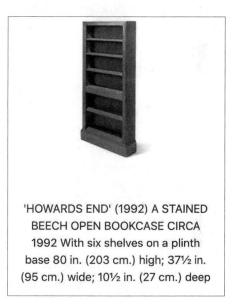

'HOWARDS END' (1992) A STAINED BEECH OPEN BOOKCASE CIRCA 1992 With six shelves on a plinth base 80 in. (203 cm.) high; 37½ in. (95 cm.) wide; 10½ in. (27 cm.) deep

This was the rather heavy bookcase that in *Howards End* falls over symbolically onto Leonard Bast and kills him. The bookcase, full of books, had to be rigged with pulleys and whatnot and manned by several grips so that its fall wouldn't injure the actor, Samuel West.

with Tara in the background. Once we were making a film in New York called *Jane Austen in Manhattan*. We took our cameraman, Ernest Vincze, into the back of the main salesroom of Parke-Bernet, where a sale of carpets was going on, in order for him to assess the lighting requirements for a scene we had arranged to shoot there in a few days. While the cameraman checked the light with his meter, I saw with dismay—ours was a very low-budget film—that Ismail had raised his hand and was bidding insistently for a striking Russian rug with a mad floral design run amok. He kept waving his hand in the air until he had gotten it—he had no paddle—after which one of the courtly African American gentlemen who worked there, wearing a formal black suit, came up with a little pad for Ismail to sign his name on. Fortunately, the rug is not included in this sale; it is under my feet as I write these notes.

Ismail really began as a collector in Bombay while we were planning and then making our first feature film, *The Householder*, in 1961. Deep in one of the Muslim quarters was an old furniture market, Chor Bazaar (Thieves Market). On first going there I was surprised to see a lot of early furniture. It was not the heavily carved early Victorian kind you see so much of in India, but classic revival in style—distant cousins of the furniture you find in plantation homes in the American South, and like that, made of rosewood, and solid, not veneered. I liked this very much. Ismail would bargain for me with the shopkeeper, while in the back, workmen could be seen busily scraping the original finish off the oldest and best pieces with knives, stripping them down to the raw wood. This was years before the present trade in old (and reproduction) nineteenth-century Indian furniture got going, years, too, when prices in Chor Bazaar were very low.

In among all this furniture and, like it, dusty from the road alongside, all sorts of old export china were displayed: plates and platters, bowls and teapots, in the patterns once popular in India and Persia. Overhead hung glass chandeliers in red and green, with quantities of prisms and tall shades for candles. To send such things to America then was next to impossible. Ismail soon began buying porcelain and silver. Much of this had originally come from the mansions of rich Parsis, which were being pulled down in order to build apartment towers on Malabar Hill, at a time in India when only foreigners treasured Victorian things. When we came home with big hallmarked George IV serving spoons and showed them to his mother and grown-up sisters, they looked at him unbelievingly: "Why is Baba bringing home these old British things?"

There are civilizations like the Egyptian, the Greek and Roman, and the Chinese, that preferred to sit upright on chairs. There are others, equally ancient, that preferred to curl up on cushions piled on carpets and mats spread on the floor. India is one of these, so is Persia and, in its own way, Japan. So when Ismail began to furnish his quarters in India with uncomfortable, straight-backed chairs, his family did not much support his new enthusiasm. They preferred their low *takht*, a platform covered with sheets and piled with white bolsters on which one can nap, sleep, take tea, make love, fight, do business, and talk comfortably on a cell phone. As it turned out, the antique chairs were for the few foreigners who couldn't bring themselves to sprawl on a *takht*. Ismail himself was always the most at home there.

When Merchant Ivory began spending more time in England in the early 1980s, Portobello Road Market replaced the Chor Bazaar as a place to shop. It was there Ismail started buying antique Kashmir shawls, which by then were virtually unobtainable in India. The violent climate and every kind of insect bred of that had destroyed almost everything long ago.

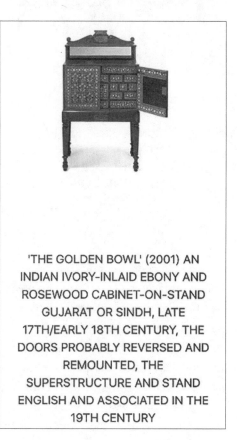

'THE GOLDEN BOWL' (2001) AN INDIAN IVORY-INLAID EBONY AND ROSEWOOD CABINET-ON-STAND GUJARAT OR SINDH, LATE 17TH/EARLY 18TH CENTURY, THE DOORS PROBABLY REVERSED AND REMOUNTED, THE SUPERSTRUCTURE AND STAND ENGLISH AND ASSOCIATED IN THE 19TH CENTURY

But for a couple of centuries English families with ties to India had carefully put things away, and now they were coming out of storage and into the stalls of the Portobello market. In time Ismail also began to buy shawls at auction in London, not to wear, but just to have, or on occasion to present to some great maestro of Indian classical music, for instance, who might wear this gift while playing in concert. Ismail always claimed to be descended from Pathan raiders. Whether that was true or not, his acquisitions were all highly portable: valuables that could be gathered up in minutes—carpets and costly shawls and tent hangings, silver, rugs, miniatures, jewelry of course. He could not pass a jeweler anywhere in the world without pausing to look into the window closely. He did not buy it for himself—he wore no jewelry except a watch—but to dispense to the many women in his family and sometimes to friends. He made an exception for the jeweled buttons, set with diamonds or emeralds, that he wore on his *shervanis* at film festivals, and that, too often, he forgot to remove when he sent such to the cleaners. Or

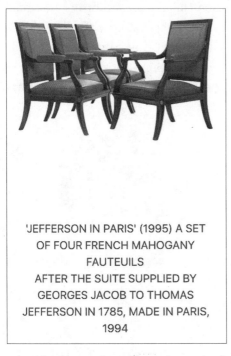

'JEFFERSON IN PARIS' (1995) A SET OF FOUR FRENCH MAHOGANY FAUTEUILS
AFTER THE SUITE SUPPLIED BY GEORGES JACOB TO THOMAS JEFFERSON IN 1785, MADE IN PARIS, 1994

when he forgot them in a suitcase in the back of a taxi, so that they had to be replaced the next time he went to a city like Jaipur.

Over the more than forty years of our association, Ismail's various collections grew. Often he did not tell me that he had bought something: it would just appear one day. When he did tell me, he rarely mentioned the price. If I asked, he would make it sound as if it had been nothing at all, or on other occasions he would inflate it ten times. So I was rather astonished when recently, with the help of Christie's experts, the contents of the London and Paris apartments were all tallied up. And unworthily, I looked more closely at certain objects, about which I had shown little curiosity until then, wondering. He had paid all that for such and such? (Then why did he yell at me for paying whatever I had to pay in order to get something *I* wanted?) We look at things in our homes for years without really seeing them, I think, without taking the time to imagine what it was our partners or our parents saw in these long familiar objects, which often possess unnoticed qualities and style. It was sometimes that way with me, I'm sorry to say, I who have always prided myself on how deeply and, I thought, intuitively, I appraised the valued possessions of this world, both mine and others'. But the range of my taste had often been narrow; I had sometimes judged Ismail's acquisitions dimly, too hurriedly. And as a fellow collector I had not encouraged him to express his enthusiasms, explain his choices, exult in the particular beauties that had attracted him and caused him to shell out quite

From the Christie's catalogue: "An Indian polychrome wood figure of Garuda, eighteenth century. Shown in the style of a European cherub, with raised wings and wearing dhoti, a snake headdress and jewelry, on original stand."

a lot of money sometimes. An example of this is the eighteenth-century figure of Garuda. One day it turned up in Orchard Court in London a bit like an orphaned child, I suppose. I scarcely looked at it. That is because I've never much liked Indian sculpture depicting deities that are half human, half animal. But over time the touching, the very human, the very vulnerable expression on the creature's face slowly revealed itself to me, along with the sturdy, muscular, and charming pose of the child deity's body. But by then the history of the piece had been lost along with the opportunity to congratulate Ismail on this acquisition, which I now see was unique, a precious thing. It was an object I ought not to have sold at the Christie's sale. If I could find out where it went, I would try to buy it back.

A Rajput Dinner Party

The Umaid Bhawan Palace, Jodhpur, India

In the spring of 1973, Ruth Jhabvala, Ismail Merchant, and I made a trip to Jodhpur in Rajasthan, from Delhi. We had been invited to stay with the maharaja, Gaj Singh II (nicknamed Bap-ji) and his maharani, Hemlata Jajye, in the vast, modern Jodhpur palace built in the 1930s. We had come to know him through our associate in Merchant Ivory, Anthony Korner, who had been at Cambridge with Bap-ji. The maharaja had also been our guest the year before at the Cannes Film Festival. He'd had a bad cold then, and I could hear him coughing through my bedroom wall at the Villa d'Andon.

Tony Korner and Ismail had begun to make a documentary film about the India of the hereditary princes—about Royal India, the former independent princely states, in the 1970s under siege by Prime Minister Indira Gandhi, who had recently taken away their

Ismail and me in the 1970s

The Royal Family of Jodhpur: Gaj Singh (center), flanked by
his mother the Rajmata (left) and Maharani Hemlata Rajye (right).
Perched on the sofa's arms are (left) Baijilal Shivranjani Rajye
and (right) Yuvraj Shivraj Singh.

privy purses and even their special, regal red license plates, and was trying generally to do away with *them*. Ismail and Tony, working with a small crew, were going around to cities in Rajasthan like Jaipur, Bikaner, and Jodhpur in order to interview, on film, the former rulers of these states. And they had discovered, in the basement of the Jodhpur palace, a great many old reels of 35mm film shot in the heyday of that royal state by European cameramen for Bap-ji's father, Maharaja Umaid Singh, in the 1930s.

It had been decided to use this archival footage in the documentary: splendid wedding ceremonies, religious events, great hunting parties—and the former maharaja himself, flying his own plane and doing loop-the-loops. When the new art deco palace where we were staying was finished, it replaced the medieval palace-fort on the ramparts overlooking the city. That palace had had its interests, and tourists climbed up to see it and go through its beautifully carved and painted bat-filled chambers. But it was no place for modern people to live, and Umaid Singh had moved into the new palace he'd built, with its splendid modern bathrooms, and named it Umaid Bhawan.

When we arrived from Delhi by plane, we were given comfortable guest suites in the heart of the new palace not far from that of the royal couple. We usually had cocktails and dinner with them in their own rooms. Apart from Ruth, Ismail, and myself, Bap-ji had invited one of his chums from Cambridge to stay. I don't remember his name, but I will call him Alistair. He was physically slight and very funny, and he must have had very strong nerves, which would be needed as it turned out. Another member of our party in the evenings after work was Tutu—Bap-ji's younger half brother, the illegitimate son of Umaid Singh's mistress, a movie actress named Zubeida. Tutu was being raised, almost as her own son, by the Dowager Maharani Krishna Kumari, the widow of Umaid Singh, who had been killed along with his mistress as he did loop-the-loops in his plane with her. Tutu was a presentable young semi-prince, good-looking and very fair, with light hair, but having a disconcerting manner sometimes. I sat next to him at dinner, listening carefully to what he was saying as he attempted to make bright conversation at the table, but for the life of me I couldn't follow it. The other members of his family did not try to and were too busy entertaining their foreign guests and laughing at Alistair's jokes.

Before sitting down to dinner at the long table, we had been served drinks in Bap-ji's drawing room. Also present was a royal lady of some sort, whose name I have also forgotten. I will just call her the Princess. She was a relative of the Jodhpur family and had been guiding us around during our stay. She had admired a sharp Jermyn Street shirt I was wearing, so I gave it to her and she was now wearing it. The Princess was in no way one of those traditional *purdah* ladies who sat quietly as custom usually demanded, not putting herself forward in any way and contributing little more than murmured, smiling agreement to any remarks addressed to her. The Princess had been able to get away, and had visited London, Paris, and New York, where she had friends. She had many opinions, she laughed; we liked her. During our drinks the dowager maharani sat holding a gray, velvet-covered case in the shape of a woman's neck, which she had opened. It contained an elaborate diamond necklace. Some of the stones—and these were sometimes large—had come loose from their settings, and when they had, she lined them up on the table next to her chair. But some had fallen into her lap and into the folds of her sari, so she had to search for them, which she did deftly, placing them beside the others.

After dinner we all reassembled in Bap-ji's big drawing room, sitting in a circle of sofas and chairs. The Princess perched on a long, low stool in the middle, while the Rajmata went on with her diamonds, which, while we were at the dinner table, she had just left out, like the pieces of a puzzle she had been working on, to which she planned to return after eating. Then there was a sudden silence, the Princess broke off midlaugh, and all conversation ceased. Tutu, who had not come back from the dining room with us, now entered the room. He stalked in, carrying a large Rajput sword with a sharp, gleaming blade, and held it out as if he meant to use it. As he entered with his sword, all the servants left, just melted away. We were now only the Jodhpur royal family and their foreign guests. Tutu went up to the Princess, grabbed her by her long hair, and put the sword to her throat, muttering something about how she loved to entertain the English. By now it dawned on the nearsighted Ruth that this was no game of charades, as she had first thought, and that something bad was happening in the room. She leapt up and confronted Tutu, still holding the Princess in his grip, his sword still against her bare throat, shouting, "What are you doing?" and "Put that down!" Also leaping up was Bap-ji's Cambridge friend, Alistair, flailing his thin arms in the air fearlessly, and also shouting at Tutu to stop doing what he was doing at once. His tones were suddenly those of all the British officers barking sensible orders, in all those movies we've seen from the Second World War. Alistair was now a man of that officer class; it was in his blood and he knew exactly how to behave and how to take command in all dangerous situations.

The Rajmata had put her diamond necklace aside, and like her son and daughter-in-law, she ordered Tutu in sharp Hindustani to let the Princess go. But Hemlata Rajye had only one thought: Tutu might try to kill his only rival for the throne, Bap-ji. She pushed her husband away, out of the center of the room, toward a tall window, and pulling the curtains of heavy velvet in front of him, and then standing protectively, her arms crossed, shouted things like "You will have to kill me first!" It was a violent moment and a favorite line of dialogue that could have come from one of today's Bollywood films. If this polo-playing bastard son had not been so dangerous, this scene would by now have progressed to its most grotesque and comic moments. In the commotion Ismail had also leapt up, but Tutu kneed him in the groin as Ismail came forward to save the Princess. And where was I? I don't remember. Watching, obviously. Tutu now had the Princess by the neck, twisting my former shirt collar as if to strangle her. I know that during this I remember thinking, He's going to tear that shirt of mine if he keeps on doing that!

And then suddenly it was over. Tutu let loose of his sword, and as it fell from his hand, the barefoot servants silently reappeared. One of them caught the sword before it could hit the marble floor and took it out of the room. This I saw, and can see it still: the servant in his white uniform catching the sword.

Of course, the party broke up then. Tutu must have been led away raving, by Bap-ji's aide-de-camp, who had been summoned from some other part of the palace. Bap-ji, mortified by all this, apologized to us over and over. We took our leave. Perhaps it *had* all just been a game of charades, a Rajput entertainment. Tod's *Annals of Rajasthan,* a book from the previous century, describes just such entertainments. Our little party of dinner guests made its way along the dim stone corridors half expecting Tutu to accost us. We entered our rooms and bolted the doors. Alistair made jokes: "So unlike what goes on in our own, dear Buckingham Palace, I'm sure!"

When we returned to Delhi, we could not tell this story to anybody. It was one of those violent events that seem unspeakable, should not be revealed. And when we saw Bap-ji again either in India or England, none of us wanted to speak of that terrible night in his palace in Jodhpur. But we were later told a gruesome thing about Tutu. He had been immensely unpopular and was hated by the farmers around Jodhpur. It was said that he had raped a girl, and not long after that his severed feet had been brought on a silver tray to the door of Umaid Bhawan and left there.

Lake of the Woods

My dock at Lake of the Woods, with Mt. Pitt in the distance

For most of us with cabins at Lake of the Woods, our oldest and deepest memories of it are likely to be of its spectacular view—a view that might almost have been created by an artist on paper or canvas: a long lake, but narrow at the middle, so that the opposite side is clearly visible. And not too large in scale with—if one sees it from its eastern side—a perfectly shaped cone of a mountain, artistically placed, you might say, at one end. The cone used to be dotted—again artistically—with patches of bright, clean snow about its summit all summer long. It is a view like that of some iconic Japanese woodcut, starkly dramatic in color: brilliant blue sky, bright blue water of a deeper hue, a broad strip of tall, dark green pine trees along the shore across from you, dividing the composition into halves. Darker hilltops rise behind, leading the eye to the commanding, reddish-brown triangle of volcanic stone that in my lifetime has had two names—Mt. Pitt and Mt. McLoughlin.

As a bird flies, Mt. Pitt (which I prefer out of long habit) is about fifty miles from the border of what was once a mighty New World empire: New Spain, or more familiarly, California, with its own dramatic views of extinct volcanoes and bodies of water. Ours is a more easy, straightforward kind of view, one hard to forget, sticking in our early memories and appearing in our nightly dreams again and again if one is lucky enough to have first seen it as a child, and lives on the edge of that view all of one's adult life and into old age. For me, now a New Yorker, it's as straightforward as the Manhattan skyline and as unforgettable, and like it, as beautiful in all weathers and at all times of the year.

I did not always think of the lake and its view in this way. I had to leave for a while and then come back after having seen many other views; some of them world famous and on other continents. Seeing these others gave me a way of measuring ours against them: our lake views do most emphatically stack up, and with them the views as we approach, especially along Klamath Lake. But as I've said, I didn't really see these worlds at first, or take in their beauty. Though happy to be brought up to the lake as a child, where we sometimes rented a cabin in the summer for a few weeks, by the time I was an adolescent and my father had bought one of our own in 1941, I preferred to stay in Klamath Falls, where my friends and interests were.

There might have been a special reason my father wanted to own a cabin at Lake of the Woods. When he was a boy at the turn of the last century, the Ivory family lived in Norwich, New York, which was a few miles from Lake Chenango. That lake, too, had summer houses around it, some of them quite substantial, which were owned by the town's most prosperous and entrenched old families. My father—the son of Irish immigrants—as a boy delivered groceries in a horse-drawn buggy to those houses and families, and that lakeside community must have represented wealth and ease, and stability. So to own a cabin at Lake of the Woods, in Oregon, where we had moved, and where he had become prosperous himself, forty years later, surely had a symbolic value for him. Once moved in, he began a series of improvements that continued right down to his death in 1967, and have been continued by me.

The cabin, which had been put up about the time of the First World War, was Spartan and uncomfortable when we moved in. My mother always felt cold. There was no indoor plumbing and at first no electricity. Drinking water had to be hauled long distances and there was little privacy, and of course no telephones. For budding teenagers that is hellish. When my parents had guests, it seems as if I had to sleep any old place, and on a creaky old bed that gave off a musty smell. The road from Klamath Falls was also a hell of ruts and dust, and our tires would often blow out. All you could find at the lodge store were baked beans. And my father had his projects that I was expected to labor at, like pushing wheelbarrows up the steep hill full of smooth pebbles from Merryman's Point to scatter over our paths,

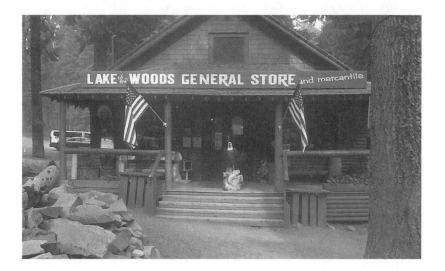

when I would rather have been in the water, or reading a book, or been in town at the Pelican Theatre.

However, the summer I turned sixteen my feelings about Lake of the Woods changed, as it dawned on me what a social asset our cabin could become for me. It was a place where I might invite my friends whose own parents didn't have a cabin at the lake. A new era opened; there were new possibilities and new friends who didn't seem to mind the creaky beds and using a privy, which for some reason we called "Egypt." Nor did the boys seem to mind being put to work by my father. They brought their sleeping bags and lay out at night on the deck, or on our dock, under the stars. In the day my friends water-skied, and smoked if my parents were away, and by my college years, sat around all day playing bridge and drinking beer. On weekends there was a dance at the lodge, the music coming from a big jukebox. Sometimes we had a big fire in the outdoor fireplace my father had built, as he led us in singing sentimental songs like "Over There" and "Danny Boy." As these years passed, the old World War I cabin acquired many, many things that had not been dreamed of when it was built: a flood of labor-saving devices like washers and dryers, soon followed by dishwashers; gas and electric stoves to replace the big, black cast-

Me at work on *The Golden Bowl* (2000) in the cabin at Lake of the Woods

In our unreliable motorboat with Ismail and our friend Anita Peabody, 1963

iron one that we had to keep feeding wood into; then microwaves, television sets, and hi-fi speakers. Go to the dump now and see the heaps of these thrown-away things. It had once been a pleasure and a sort of moral virtue to live simply by the lake. "Roughing it" was a means of fortifying one's self, "building character," or so the old-timers told us.

There was a kind of family ritual one followed at the seasonal openings and closings of the cabin, strictly supervised and mostly carried out by the senior male—at first my father, who followed his own clear businesslike procedure, taking necessary steps at the lakeside and about the cabin in his never deviating plan. Then it became my turn in a generational transfer of power, leading in my late thirties to actual ownership. As the senior male it was now up to me to maintain this valuable but sometimes unreliable vacation property, where many things, large and small, could go very wrong and everyone's fun (and good moods) could be spoiled for days: power failures, once we had electricity; a missing vital part in the failing motorboat; septic tank issues; and worst of all—apart from falling limbs—a missing dock that had been carried far away and broken up by the winter's ice.

But I kept coming back to the last of my childhood homes. By my twenties "going to the lake" had become a way of life, a fixed annual excursion made sometime between the Fourth of July and Labor Day, when I could count on the weather being good. Everyone I knew and worked with accepted that I would make this trip out to Oregon. I hardly missed a year (and when I did during the 1960s, it was because I was making a film somewhere in some far-off place like India). But almost always I managed somehow to get there, bringing my work with me if necessary. I would fly thousands of miles in order to be met at the Medford airport. I remember flying once from Paris nonstop to San Francisco, where I would take a United flight north, and looking straight down from the window of my Air France jet as we flew over the lake nearly thirty-five thousand feet below—a bright blue bead, with Mt. Pitt beside it. There were summers when no one met me at the Medford airport and then I would rent a car and drive up alone. I would be waiting to see the first glimmer of the lake's sun-shot waters from my car windows, excited as a child, through the trees along the old Dead

Indian Road, where my sister and I, in the backseat of the family car, used to fight over who had seen the lake first. And when I would get to the cabin at the end of my long, long trip, I didn't unload the car as my father would always have done, but would run straight down to our dock to see the dreamed-of view, and Mt. Pitt against the glowing western sky.

Solid Ivory

Virginia O'Brien in *Hullabaloo* (1940)

When I was a teenager in Oregon in the early 1940s, there was an actress-singer named Virginia O'Brien who was featured in MGM musicals. She was slim, dark-haired, pretty, with very pale skin. She would do a little turn, almost always singing a song, standing motionless, with an expressionless face and singing in an expressionless tone. I can still hear her. "In a little Spanish town 'twas on a night like *this.*" I remember her in *The Harvey Girls* with Judy Garland and in several other MGM musicals like *Ziegfield Follies* and *Lady Be Good.* She was an early minimalist, I guess, and it seemed amazing that she could have had such a vogue appearing in raucous, high-energy MGM musicals. She was the opposite of all that. I always waited for her to come on; it was probably the high point in the movie for me. Does anyone else remember her these days, or recall her fondly? Does she now have a cult following?

Then, when I was about sixteen, very skinny and pale like her, I developed a little comedy routine of my own called "Solid Ivory." This I performed at the Friday high school assemblies in the Klamath Union High School auditorium (usually held before a big football game). And, similarly, the audience would wait for me to appear at the side of the stage as a sort of frivolous interruption of the proceedings, then glide across and disappear. Dressed in a baggy sweater and holding a large, bright pink paper mum in my hand, I crossed in front of my teachers and schoolmates with a completely deadpan face to much laughter. From time to time I would turn my head just like a robot and stare out at the audience. Solid Ivory became a feature of these assemblies for a couple of years, like Virginia O'Brien's solos in MGM movies. I never altered my routine; there was something of the alien from outer space, and also something perhaps a bit androgynous, in this act. In my last appearance I seemed to glide in a determined sort of way toward the band, or maybe it was the football players—so that they scattered. This was Solid Ivory's swan song; perhaps I felt I'd gone too far, or—more likely—that I was becoming too "sophisticated" and even too grand, in the high school social scene, to do such a silly thing anymore. In that year I also gave up acting in school plays. I did write a gossip column for the high school newspaper, and my dispatches always began, "Solid Ivory knows . . . Solid Ivory hears . . . Solid Ivory says . . ." When a new faculty adviser was appointed to oversee the paper, I was fired, and the gossip column, considered to be unnecessary, was killed.

The roar of applause for Solid Ivory was the last I was to hear coming specifically my way until, decades later, I would stand up to bow at film festivals, to acknowledge the applause of my audience, but on these occasions smiling—though no doubt, if the ovation was a long one, my expression became as fixed as Virginia O'Brien's had been.

Me, dressed as an Anglo-Indian gentleman,
complete with hookah, Claverack, 2010

Acknowledgments

The following chapters originally appeared, in different form, in other publications:

"Venice" originally appeared in *Inside Venice: A Private View of the City's Most Beautiful Interiors*, by Toto Bergamo Rossi (Rizzoli, 2016).

"What I Do" originally appeared in *Directing*, edited by Mike Goodridge (Rotovision, 2002).

The first section of "Maestro" originally appeared in *The New Yorker*, July 22, 1967.

"Raquel Welch" originally appeared as "Raquel Welch: Star vs. Actress," in *Close-Ups: The Movie Star Book*, edited by Danny Peary (Workman Publishing, 1978).

"Vanessa Redgrave" originally appeared as "The Trouble with Olive," in *Sight and Sound*, spring 1985.

"The Ismail Merchant Collection" originally appeared in *The Ismail Merchant Collection* (Christie's, 2009).

"Lake of the Woods" originally appeared in *Cabin Cruising: A Lakeside History: Lake of the Woods, Oregon*, by Bill Dodge (Lake of the Woods Recreational Association, 2018).

"Solid Ivory" originally appeared in *James Ivory in Conversation: How Merchant Ivory Makes Its Movies*, by Robert Emmet Long (University of California Press, 2005).

Illustration Credits

page vii: (*top*) Photograph by John Swope, from the collection of James Ivory; (*middle*) photograph by James Ivory; (*bottom*) from the collection of James Ivory

page 2: From the collection of James Ivory

page 3: Cinematreasures.org / Creative Commons, CC BY 3.0

page 5: Fox Film Corporation / Photofest

page 7: From the collection of James Ivory

page 8: From the collection of James Ivory

page 9: From the collection of James Ivory

page 11: From the collection of James Ivory

page 12: From the collection of James Ivory

page 13: Photograph by James Ivory

page 14: Photograph by James Ivory

page 15: From the collection of James Ivory

page 17: From the collection of James Ivory

page 19: Photograph courtesy of the Sisters of Charity of Nazareth (https://scnfamily.org)

page 21: Photograph by Derrick Santini. *The Remains of the Day* © 1993, Columbia Pictures Industries, Inc. All Rights Reserved. Courtesy of Columbia Pictures

page 23: Larry Turner Photography (https://www.larryturnerphotography.com)

page 24: From the collection of James Ivory

page 26: From the collection of James Ivory

page 27: From the collection of James Ivory

page 28: From the collection of James Ivory

page 30: From the collection of James Ivory

page 31: From the collection of James Ivory

page 34: Pacific Novelty Co. / Collection of Peter Cameron

page 37: From the collection of James Ivory

page 39: From the collection of James Ivory

page 43: Woolworth's dime store lunch counter, Duluth. Fred J. Roleff / Minnesota Historical Society, Saint Paul, MN

page 45: The Lion Match Company / Collection of Peter Cameron

page 50: Photograph by Kennell Ellis, from the collection of James Ivory

page 51: Photograph by Seth David Rubin, used with permission

page 52: Bono's historic orange. Photograph by Uzma Gamal, Wikimedia Commons

page 55: (*top*) From the collection of James Ivory; (*bottom*) Schwabacher-Frey Company / Collection of Peter Cameron

page 56: Vintage postcard, Palace Hotel Ballroom, 1920, Lothers & Young Studios, public domain, from the collection of Peter Cameron

page 61: Photograph from *El Rodeo* yearbook, Klamath Union High School

page 63: Photograph by Kennell Ellis, from the collection of James Ivory

page 64: Vintage postcard, high school, Klamath Falls, Oregon, author unknown, public domain, from the collection of Peter Cameron

page 65: From the collection of James Ivory

page 67: Photographs by Kennell Ellis, from the collection of James Ivory

page 70: Photograph by James Ivory

page 72: Photograph courtesy of the San Francisco History Center, San Francisco Public Library

page 77: *Strength and Health* magazine, Wikimedia Commons

page 80: Photograph by Declan Haun, from the collection of James Ivory

page 85: Emerson, Ralph Waldo, et al. *Journals of Ralph Waldo Emerson* (United Kingdom, Houghton Mifflin, 1909)

page 89 (*top*) Photograph by Kennell Ellis, from the collection of James Ivory; (*bottom*) photograph from *El Rodeo* yearbook, Klamath Union High School

page 90: Photograph from *El Rodeo* yearbook, Klamath Union High School

page 91: Photograph by Kennell Ellis, from the collection of James Ivory

page 99: From the collection of Peter Cameron

page 100: Photograph by Kennell Ellis, from the collection of James Ivory page 102: Photograph by Philip W. Scher, used with permission

page 103: From the collection of James Ivory

page 104: José Limón and Betty Jones in Limón's 1949 work, *The Moor's Pavane*, n.d. Walter Strate Studio. Alvin Ailey Dance Foundation Collection, Music Division, Library of Congress (041.00.00)

page 107: Photograph by James Ivory

page 108: From the collection of James Ivory

page 119: From the collection of James Ivory

page 122: Photograph by Bill O'Neill, from the collection of James Ivory

page 123: Photograph by James Ivory

page 124: From the collection of James Ivory

page 126: Photograph by James Ivory

page 129: Photograph by James Ivory

page 130: From the collection of James Ivory

page 132: Photograph by James Ivory

page 133: Photograph by James Ivory

page 134: From the collection of James Ivory

page 135: © G.A.VE Archivio fotográfico—"su concessione del Ministero della Cultura—Gallerie dell'Accademia di Venezia"

page 136: © G.A.VE Archivio fotográfico—"su concessione del Ministero della Cultura—Gallerie dell'Accademia di Venezia"

page 138: Alen Ajan / 123RF

page 139: From the collection of James Ivory

page 141: Photographs by James Ivory

page 143: Photograph by Juan Quirno © Screen Media, used with permission

page 145: Photograph by James Ivory

page 147: Photograph by Jack English, from the collection of James Ivory

page 155: Photographs by James Ivory

page 156: Photograph by James Ivory

page 158: Photograph by Christopher Cormack. *Heat and Dust* © 1983, Luroak, Ltd. All Rights Reserved. Courtesy of Cohen Media Group / Cohen Film Collection

page 160: Photograph by James Ivory

page 161: Photograph by James Ivory

page 167: Photograph by James Ivory

page 168: From the collection of James Ivory

page 169: Photograph by James Ivory

page 171: Photograph by Sarah Quill. Cinecom Pictures / Photofest

page 172: Photograph by Seth Rubin. October Films / Photofest

page 173: Photograph by Mikki Ansin, from the collection of James Ivory

page 174: Photograph by Jack English

page 175: From the collection of James Ivory

page 176: © Nancy Rica Schiff, 2004

page 178: Unknown author, Wikimedia Commons

page 180: Oriental International Films / Alamy Stock Photo

page 181: From the collection of James Ivory

page 182: Photograph by Derrick Santini. *In Custody* © 1993, Merchant Ivory Productions, Ltd. All Rights Reserved. Courtesy of Cohen Media Group / Cohen Film Collection

page 185: Unknown author, Wikimedia Commons

page 186: Warner Bros. / Photofest

page 190: From the collection of James Ivory

page 192: Photograph by James Ivory

page 194: Sony Pictures Classics / Photofest

page 199: Photograph by Fred W. McDarrah / Getty Images

page 201: Photo courtesy of the Ray Society (https://satyajitrayworld.org/index.html)

page 202: Photograph by Picky Talarico, from the collection of James Ivory

page 203: Photograph by Van Bucher, from the collection of James Ivory

page 204: *Shakespeare Wallah* © 1965, Merchant Ivory Productions, Ltd. All Rights Reserved. Courtesy of Cohen Media Group / Cohen Film Collection

page 205: (*top*) Ronald Grant Archive / Alamy Stock Photo; (*bottom*) from the collection of James Ivory

page 209: Photograph by James Ivory

page 210: Photograph by James Ivory

page 211: Photograph by James Ivory

page 212: Photograph by Chris Terrio, from the collection of James Ivory

page 217: © Roger George Clark / National Portrait Gallery, London page 220: Unknown author, Wikimedia Commons

page 221: Photograph by Juan Quirno. *Quartet* © 1981, National Film Trustee Company, Ltd. All Rights Reserved. Courtesy of Cohen Media Group / Cohen Film Collection

page 222: (*left*) Photograph by Allan Warren, Wikimedia Commons; (*right*) Photofest

page 223: Bookplate designed by Paul Landacre, from the collection of Peter Cameron

page 224: Everett Collection / Alamy Stock Photo

page 225: Warner Bros / Photofest

page 227: kpa Publicity Stills / Alamy Stock Photo

page 228: Photograph by James Ivory

page 230: Photograph by Douglas Webb. *The Guru* © 1969, Twentieth Century Fox. All rights reserved

page 231: MGM / Photofest

page 235: *New York World-Telegram* and *Sun* Collection, Library of Congress, Public Domain

page 237: Smithsonian Institution Archives. Image # 88-8669-12

page 238: History Company, used with permission (https://www.historycompany.com)

page 239: © Mary Ellen Mark / The Mary Ellen Mark Foundation

page 241: From the collection of James Ivory

page 242: From the collection of James Ivory

page 243: (*top*) Photograph by James Ivory; (*bottom*) photograph by Douglas Webb. *The Guru* © 1969, Twentieth Century Fox. All rights reserved

page 247: Photograph by Popperfoto / Getty Images

page 249: American International Pictures (AIP) / Photofest

page 251: American International Pictures (AIP) / Photofest

page 253: American International Pictures (AIP) / Photofest

page 255: Photograph by Karen Kapoor. *The Bostonians* © 1984, Bostonians Productions Ltd. All Rights Reserved. Courtesy of Cohen Media Group / Cohen Film Collection

page 257: Photograph by Karen Kapoor. *The Bostonians* © 1984, Bostonians Productions Ltd. All Rights Reserved. Courtesy of Cohen Media Group / Cohen Film Collection

page 258: Mary Evans / Studiocanal Films Ltd. / Alamy Stock Photo page 260: Warner Brothers / Photofest

page 265: Unknown author, Wikimedia Commons

page 266: Photograph by Karen Kapoor. *The Bostonians* © 1984, Bostonians Productions Ltd. All Rights Reserved. Courtesy of Cohen Media Group / Cohen Film Collection

page 267: From the collection of James Ivory

page 268: Photograph by Karen Kapoor. *The Bostonians* © 1984, Bostonians Productions Ltd. All Rights Reserved. Courtesy of Cohen Media Group / Cohen Film Collection.

page 269: Photograph by Karen Kapoor. *The Bostonians* © 1984, Bostonians Productions Ltd. All Rights Reserved. Courtesy of Cohen Media Group / Cohen Film Collection

page 271: Antandrus at English Wikipedia, Wikimedia Commons

page 273: Photograph by Aubrey Hart / *Evening Standard* / Hulton Archive / Getty Images

page 274: Photofest

page 277: Photograph by James Ivory

page 279: From the collection of James Ivory

page 280: The Royal Borough of Kensington & Chelsea

page 281: Public domain (https://www.luberonweb.com)

page 282: From the collection of James Ivory

page 286: Photograph by Brian and Jackie Cross, 2013, used with permission (http://brianandjackiecross.blogspot.com)

page 287: Photograph by Stephen K. Scher, used with permission

page 292: Photograph by James Ivory

page 301: Photograph by Koprinco Laskof, released under the Pixabay License

page 302: Photograph by Patrick McMullan / Patrick McMullan / Getty Images

page 303: Photograph by David Shankbone, Wikimedia Commons

page 304: *The Darjeeling Limited* © 2007, Twentieth Century Fox. All rights reserved

page 307: Cecil Beaton Studio Archive / Sotheby's London, used with permission

page 308: © Mary Ellen Mark / The Mary Ellen Mark Foundation

page 310: (*top*) Master and Fellows of St John's College, Cambridge, used with permission; (*bottom*) published by Alfred A. Knopf, 1949

page 311: Cecil Beaton Studio Archive / Sotheby's London, used with permission page 313: Wikimedia Commons

page 315: Jesse Nemerofsky, 1995 © Globe Photos / https://www.zumapress
.com / Alamy Stock Photo

page 317: © Jean-Francois Jaussaud

page 318: © Jean-Francois Jaussaud

page 320: © Jean-Francois Jaussaud

page 321: From the collection of James Ivory

page 322: Photograph property of Cyrus and Ruth Jhabvala LLC, used with
permission

page 323: From the collection of James Ivory

page 324: From the collection of James Ivory

page 326: Photograph by James Ivory

page 328: Photograph by James Ivory

page 330: From the collection of James Ivory

page 331: Photographer unknown

page 333: From the collection of James Ivory

page 334: Photograph by James Ivory

page 335: (*top*) From the collection of James Ivory; (*bottom*) Wikimedia Commons
© Government of India, and licensed under the Government Open
Data License—India (GODL)

page 337: *The Creation of Woman*. All Rights Reserved. Courtesy of Cohen Media
Group / Cohen Film Collection

page 339: From the collection of James Ivory

page 340: From the collection of James Ivory

page 341: USIS photographer, American Embassy, New Delhi, India, 1963

page 342: Photograph by James Ivory

page 345: Photograph by John Gardey. *Maurice* © 1987, Merchant Ivory
Productions, Ltd. All Rights Reserved. Courtesy of Cohen Media
Group / Cohen Film Collection

page 346: (*top*) From the collection of James Ivory; (*bottom*) photograph by Seth
Rubin. Buena Vista Pictures / Photofest.

page 347: Estate of Richard Robbins

page 351: Photograph by Natascha Grenfell. *Maurice* © 1987 Merchant Ivory
Productions, Ltd. All Rights Reserved. Courtesy of Cohen Media
Group / Cohen Film Collection

page 353: AP Newsfeatures, Wikimedia Commons

page 354: Photograph by Gerd Eichmann, Creative Commons Attribution-Share Alike 4.0 International / Wikimedia Commons

page 355: Photograph by Richard Young / Shutterstock

page 356: National Portrait Gallery © Cecil Beaton Studio Archive / Sotheby's London, used with permission

page 358: ANL / Shutterstock

page 360: Chronicle / Alamy Stock Photo

page 362: Photograph by Ken Mason © *Daily Telegraph*, 1964

page 363: Photo by Peregrine-Bryant Architects (peregrine-bryant.co.uk), used with permission

page 364: From the collection of James Ivory

page 366: From the collection of James Ivory

page 367: Private Collection Photo © Christie's Images / Bridgeman Images

page 369: Private Collection Photo © Christie's Images / Bridgeman Images

page 370: Private Collection Photo © Christie's Images / Bridgeman Images

page 371: Private Collection Photo © Christie's Images / Bridgeman Images

page 373: Photograph by John Swope, from the collection of James Ivory

page 374: (*top*) From the collection of James Ivory; (*bottom*) photograph by Tripal Singh Chauhan, Creative Commons Attribution-Share Alike 4.0 International / Wikimedia Commons

page 379: Photograph by James Ivory

page 381: Photograph by Michael Meyer, used with permission

page 382: Larry Turner Photography (https://www.larryturnerphotography.com)

page 383: From the collection of James Ivory

page 384: Photograph by James Ivory

page 386: Virginia O'Brien in *Panama Hattie* (1942). Photograph courtesy of Robert Strom, Internet Archive / Community Images

page 388: Photograph © Craig J. Barber, from the collection of James Ivory

Images from the films *Shakespeare Wallah, Quartet, Heat and Dust, The Bostonians, Maurice, Howards End, In Custody,* and *The Creation of Woman* are all courtesy of Cohen Media Group, who are currently restoring the Merchant Ivory library of films.

James Ivory wishes to acknowledge the following still photographers and the films they worked on: Van Bucher (*The Delhi Way*), Douglas Webb (*The Guru*), Morgan Reynard (*The Wild Party*), Peter Abrams (*Roseland*), Mary Ellen Mark

(*Hullabaloo over Georgie and Bonnie's Pictures*), Christopher Cormack (*The Europeans* and *Heat and Dust*), Juan Quirno (*Quartet* and *The City of Your Final Destination*), Karen Kapoor (*The Bostonians*), Sara Quill (*A Room with a View*), John Gardey (*Maurice*), Natascha Grenfell (*Maurice*), Mikki Ansin (*Mr. and Mrs. Bridge*), Derrick Santini (*Howards End*, *The Remains of the Day*, *In Custody*), Arnaud Borrel (*Jefferson in Paris*), and Seth Rubin (*Jefferson in Paris*, *A Soldier's Daughter Never Cries*).